COMPLETE
COMMUNICATIONS MANUAL
FOR COACHES AND
ATHLETIC DIRECTORS

COMPLETE COMMUNICATIONS MANUAL FOR COACHES AND ATHLETIC DIRECTORS

P. Susan Mamchak
Steven R. Mamchak

PARKER PUBLISHING COMPANY
West Nyack, New York 10995

Library of Congress Cataloging-in-Publication Data

Mamchak, P. Susan
    Complete communications manual for coaches and athletic directors
    P. Susan Mamchak, Steven R. Mamchak.
      p.   cm.
ISBN 0-13-159229-7
    1. Coaching (Athletics)   I. Mamchak, Steven R.   II. Title.
    GV711.M34 1988
   796′.07′7—dc19   88-19521
                                                    CIP

ISBN 0-13-159229-7

PARKER PUBLISHING COMPANY
West Nyack, NY 10994

A Simon & Schuster Company

On the World Wide Web at http://www.phdirect.com

Printed in the United States of America

Acknowledgment and Dedication

We could not have done it alone. A book of this nature requires the support and contributions of many people. Throughout the planning, compiling, reviewing, editing, and writing stages, we have been privileged to have had the unfailing aid of some of the finest professionals it has ever been our honor to know. They have given freely of their time, their expertise, and their material in order to make this book as complete as possible for their fellow sports professionals. We, therefore, gratefully acknowledge the following people and dedicate this book to them.

C. A. Baugh, Principal, Tomiyasu Elementary School, Las Vegas, Nevada

Elmer Blasco, Publisher, *The Athletic Journal*, Evanston, Illinois

Phil Braun, Athletic Director, Middletown Township, New Jersey

Donald D. Burger, Athletic Director, Bonanza High School, Las Vegas, Nevada

Tim Cechin, Communications Manager, Rawlings Sporting Goods Company, St. Louis, Missouri

Rick Dell, Coach, Trenton State College, Trenton, New Jersey

William Eckman and the Estate of the late Dr. Carol A. Eckman, LaPlata, Maryland

Tom Erbig, Coach, Middletown Township, New Jersey

Lynne D. Foosener, Public Information Officer, Clark County, Nevada

Roy Fujimoto, Executive Secretary of Athletics, Big Island Interscholastic Federation, Hilo, Hawaii

Mike Galos, Coach, Middletown Township, New Jersey

Sharon Goodrich, Keystone Life Insurance Company, Dallas, Texas

Michael Hayden, Assistant Principal and Athletic Director, Parkersburg High School, Parkersburg, West Virginia

Rob Heidt, Coach, Middletown Township, New Jersey

Gary Hindley, Head Coach, Los Angeles Lazers of the National Indoor Soccer League, West Covina, California

J. R. Johnson, Assistant Principal for Athletics, Muskogee High School, Muskogee, Oklahoma

Bruce Keith, Athletic Director, Sheridan High School, Sheridan, Wyoming

Beth Knutson, Administrator, Secondary Education, Anchorage School District, Anchorage, Alaska

Mary Ann Nagy, Director, Parks and Recreation Department, Red Bank, New Jersey

Chris Patterson, Wilson Sporting Goods Company, River Grove, Illinois

Jack Mannion, Athletic Director, Chaperral High School, Las Vegas, Nevada

Carol Marturano, Librarian, Sports Medicine Library, Olympic Training Center, Colorado Springs, Colorado

Mike McCray, Coach, Middletown Township, New Jersey

Dr. Bruce Miller, District Athletic Director, Clark County, Nevada

Dr. Kiyoto Mizuba, Superintendent, Hawaii School District, Hilo, Hawaii

Bill Moore, Coach, Middletown Township, New Jersey

Rhonda Rosenbaum, The Keds Corporation, a Division of Stride-Rite Corporation, Cambridge, Massachusetts

Dr. Brad Rothermel, Athletic Director, University of Nevada at Las Vegas, Las Vegas, Nevada

Andy Russo, Coach and Athletic Instructor, Red Bank Regional High School, Red Bank, New Jersey

Mike Scantlen, Athletic Director, Hillsdale High School, Muskogee, Oklahoma

Tim Schum, Editor, National Soccer Coaches' Association of America's *Soccer Journal,* State University of New York at Binghamton, Binghamton, New York

Dr. Guy Sconzo, Superintendent of Schools, Middletown Township, New Jersey

Mark Sessa, Coach, Middletown Township, New Jersey

E. R. Shovlain, Superintendent of Schools, School District #2, Sheridan, Wyoming

Robert Stranger, Athletic Director, Red Bank Regional High School, Red Bank, New Jersey

John Tigert, Athletic Director, Carlsbad Junior High School, Carlsbad, New Mexico

Byron Toone, Athletic Director, Pocatello High School, Pocatello, Idaho

William L. Wall, Executive Director, Amateur Basketball Association, USA, Colorado Springs, Colorado

...and...

Jan Black, Keith Austin George, Ingrid Pedersen, Tom Power, Mary Beth Roesser, Rhoda, Sandy, and Jackie Shick.

How This Book Will Help Coaches and Athletic Directors

Let's see if we can agree on a basic assumption. We contend that the chief duty and responsibility of the coach and the athletic director is to act as an educator. Surely, there can be no real argument with this statement. As coaches and athletic directors, our primary task is to instruct and train the youth who come within our jurisdiction. We must help them develop physically and mentally. We must increase their knowledge of the sport while, at the same time, seeing to it that they acquire the skills and physical conditioning necessary to effective participation. We know this to be true, because we *live* it, each and every day of our professional lives.

Certainly, this is a responsibility that may not be taken lightly, and, at times, can be overwhelming.

And, if we all share a common purpose, then we all share a common enemy in this process. That enemy, simply put, is *lack of time.*

There is just so much to do! On a daily basis, we face a deluge of meetings, phone calls, conferences, and, perhaps worst of all, *paperwork.* Indeed, the paperwork we face each day can often leave little time for other, more productive activities. We have reports to file, letters to write, budgets to prepare, memos to dictate, guidelines to formulate, and a host of other communications to be developed and composed, all of which rob us of that most precious commodity—*time.*

Yet, as we are all aware, we must —*WE MUST*—find some way to manage that paperwork, or, very quickly, that paperwork will end up *managing us.*

If you feel this way, you are not alone, for coaches and athletic directors across the nation have expressed the same pressing need to tame the "paper tiger" before it devours us, our time, our energies. Yes, we all share in the same problem, and, thankfully, we all share in its *solution* as well.

Across our great nation, innovative coaches and athletic directors, meeting a growing need, have put in hours and hours of time and hard work to develop the forms, memos, policies, reports, bulletins, guidelines, and other written materials that meet their needs and the needs of *all* coaches and athletic directors throughout our land; written materials on a wide variety of coaching and sports-related topics that comprise the basic framework of today's sports scene; materials that are intrinsic to good coaching *and* good administration.

Thankfully, these coaches, athletic directors, sports administrators, and other sports professionals are willing to share their efforts with other members of their profession. From the Atlantic coast to the shores of Hawaii, from the Mexican border to the natural grandeur of Alaska, these people have been most generous in sending us those written forms, guides, policies, procedures, letters, and other materials that have served them so well in solving their paperwork problems, and which will help *all of us* in the effective performance of our written work as well.

Because we all share common problems in coaching and sports-related activities, the materials in this book wait to serve our needs. With the change of a name or date, they can be adapted to meet our direct needs. Or, they can be used exactly as they are in order to help facilitate budget preparation, disciplinary codes, scouting reports, evaluation systems, and a host of other sports-related activities, all of which can be made easier for us thanks to this generous sharing of knowledge. This is, after all, what true educators do, and being an educator is what coaching is all about.

Within the pages of this book, you will find *highly effective* forms, letters, guides, and memos for handling such topics as BUDGETS, PUBLIC RELATIONS AND THE PRESS, AWARDS, INVENTORY, ETHICS, and much, much more.

Here is material that strikes at the very heart of our day-to-day functioning as coaches and athletic directors. Here are topics such as INSPIRATIONALS, ACADEMIC REVIEW, CUTTING, JOB DESCRIPTIONS, ELIGIBILITY, and VISITING SCHOOLS.

This is also material that allows for the effective and quick handling of our most troubling situation, such as, ACCIDENT, INJURY, INSURANCE, MEDICAL, VIOLATIONS, RECRUITING, TRANSFER OF ELIGIBILITY, TOURNAMENT, POLICIES AND PROCEDURES, RULES AND REGULATIONS, TRANSPORTATION, TRAVEL, AND TRIPS, and so much more.

The encompassing nature of the materials in this book is unparalleled. Meticulously gathered from front-line coaches, athletic directors, sports administrators, and sports professionals across the country, these are usable written materials that have worked for others, are working now, and will work for you.

All in all, we cannot help but feel that this is a book that will serve the needs of the busy and involved coach, athletic director, and sports professional by providing practical and usable models of written materials which may be easily adapted or used as is to fill pressing, individual needs.

We think you will agree that *Complete Communications Manual for Coaches and Athletic Directors* is a book you will want to use in order to save time, make your day-to-day operation as a coach easier and more efficient, and manage that load of paperwork, in turn leaving you free to be the innovative educator that coaching so vitally needs. We know that this book will find a favored place on your desk, ready to use in preseason, in postseason, and throughout every season of your professional career.

P. Susan Mamchak
Steven R. Mamchak

Contents

How This Book Will Help Coaches
and Athletic Directors v

A

ABSENCE *1*

  absentee warning form...*1*

  player absence record form...*1*

ACADEMIC PERFORMANCE
REVIEW *2*

  athletic academic progress
report...*2*

  review of performance...*3*

ACCEPTANCE *3*

  of a coaching contract...*3*

  of an athletic director...*4*

ACCIDENT REPORT FORM *4*

  example of...*4*

ACTIVITIES *6*

  out-of-school activity form...*6*

  prermission slip...*7*

  philosophy of...*7*

  request form...*7*

AMATEUR STANDING *7*

  policy on...*7*

  rules and regulations for...*8*

ANNOUNCEMENTS *9*

  beginning of a season (two
examples)...*9*

  tournament...*11*

ANNOUNCERS' FORMS *11*

  baseball...*11*

  basketball...*12*

  football...*13*

  track and field...*14*

  wrestling...*15*

ASSISTANT COACH *16*

  job description...*16*

  qualifications...*17*

ATHLETE *18*

  contract for...*18*

  evaluation form for (two
examples)...*20*

  letters to (two examples)...*23*

  of the year...*25*

ATHLETIC *26*

  information sheet...*26*

  principles...*28*

ATHLETIC DEPARTMENT *28*

  evaluation form for (two
examples)...*28*

ATHLETIC DIRECTOR *36*

  checklist for...*36*

  job description...*37*

  organization for...*38*

  record keeping by...*38*

ATHLETIC INJURY REPORT *39*

ATHLETIC INVENTORY INFORMATION *39*

ATHLETIC SCHEDULES *39*

ATHLETIC TRAVEL *39*

AWARDS *39*

criteria for (in all sports)...*39*
Hall of Fame...*44*
information sheet on...*45*
varsity letter award (sample)...*46*
varsity letter requirements...*47*

B

BASEBALL *48*

announcer's form...*48*
award criteria for...*48*
schedule (sample)...*48*
season record form...*49*

BASKETBALL *50*

announcer's form...*50*
award criteria...*50*
game checklist...*50*
performance sheet for...*51*
season record form...*52*
team roster...*52*
tournament...*52*

BEHAVIOR POLICY *52*

citizenship rating form...*53*

BID SURVEY *54*

form for (sample page)...*54*

BOOSTER/PEP CLUBS *55*

information sheet...*55*

BOWLING *56*

awards...*56*

BUDGET *56*

allocation request form...*56*
athletic budget forms (two examples)...*56*

BULLETINS *58*

sample athletic information bulletin...*59*

BUS *60*

pick-up schedule form...*60*
trip information form...*60*
trip permit...*60*

C

CASH FUND *61*

ledger form...*61*

CERTIFICATES *61*

CHECK REQUISITION FORM *61*

CHEERLEADERS *61*

tryout form for...*61*

COACHES *64*

application for...*64*
associations...*65*
checklist for (two examples)...*66*
contract for...*67*
"creed"...*67*
evalution of...*68*
volunteer...*68*

COACHING STAFF *69*

information sheet on...*69*
roster and credentials of...*71*

salary criteria of (two examples)...*72*

CODE *74*

of ethics (two examples)...*74*

COMPETITION AGREEMENTS *75*

CONSENT FORMS *75*

CONSTITUTION *75*

of a conference (an exerpt)...*76*

CONTEST *78*

cancellation of a...*78*

number of...*79*

CONTRACTS *79*

for a coach...*79*

for an athlete...*80*

for officials...*80*

for participants (two examples)...*80*

CROSS COUNTRY *82*

awards criteria...*82*

meet...*82*

CROWD CONTROL *82*

CUSTODIAL ACTION REQUEST *82*

D

DANCE, REQUEST FOR *83*

DISTRICT ATHLETIC PROGRAM *83*

chain of command structure...*83*

DUAL AND TRIANGULAR MEETS *83*

E

ECKMAN SYSTEM *84*

ELIGIBILITY *84*

academic progress report (two examples)...*84*

academic requirements for...*85*

certificate of (two examples)...*86*

list (two examples)...*87*

policy on...*90*

END-OF-SEASON CHECKLIST *90*

sample form...*90*

ENTRY BLANKS *90*

EQUIPMENT *90*

check-out forms (two examples)...*90*

form for lost equipment (two examples)...*92*

inventory forms (two examples)...*92*

notice...*95*

return form for...*95*

EVALUATION *96*

of athletes...*96*

of coaches...*96*

of coaches (by the Eckman System)...*98*

seasonal report on coach...*101*

EVENTS CARD *101*

EVENTS VOUCHER *102*

EXAMINATIONS *102*

health...*102*

state standard physical form

for...*104*

EXPENSES *105*

   and income sheet (sport specific)...*106*
   travel form for...*107*
   trip sheet for...*107*

F

FACILITY *108*

   bulletin on locker use...*108*
   maintenance checklist for...*108*
   usage permit...*109*
   usage, request for...*110*
   usage schedule...*111*

FIELD TRIP *111*

FINANCIAL REPORTS *111*

FLIERS *111*

   request for distribution of...*112*
   sample of...*112*

FOOTBALL *112*

   announcer's form...*112*
   equipment checklist form...*113*
   game checklist...*114*
   information sheet...*115*
   safety in...*116*
   schedule guidelines...*116*
   season record form...*117*

FUND RAISING *118*

   opportunity for, sign-up sheet...*118*
   report of fund raising (example)...*119*
   solicitation activity report...*120*

G

GAME CHECKLIST FOR AN ATHLETIC DIRECTOR *121*

GAME CLOTHING *121*

GAME REPORT *121*

   form for (two examples)...*121*

GOLF *122*

   season record form...*122*

GYMNASTICS *123*

   entry form for...*123*
   meet (general information sheet)...*123*
   policy on...*125*

H

HALL OF FAME *126*

HANDBOOK *126*

   suggested outline form for...*126*
   table of contents of (partial sample)...*127*

HEAD COACH *128*

   job description (two examples)...*128*

HEALTH CERTIFICATE *132*

HEALTH EXAMINATION FORM *132*

HEAT CHART *132*

HIGH SCHOOL ATHLETIC CODE *132*

HOME GAME ACTIVITY *133*

   home game activity checklist...*133*

HONORS, ATHLETIC *133*

I

INCOME/EXPENSE SHEET *134*

INJURY *134*

permission to treat a minor...*134*
policy on (two examples)...*135*
referral form for...*137*

INSPIRATIONALS *137*

Think Like a Winner...*137*
What We Expect...*138*
What You Receive...*138*
You Can Do It...*139*

INSURANCE *139*

notice to parents on...*139*
policy statement to parents...*140*

INTEREST SURVEY *141*

sample of...*141*

INTERSCHOLASTIC CONTESTS *141*

INTERVIEW *141*

checklist for (two forms)...*141*

INTRAMURAL PROGRAM *142*

suggested activities in...*142*

INVENTORY *143*

athletic inventory form (two examples...*143*
ticket seller's inventory sheet... *143*

J

JOB DESCRIPTION *144*

assistant coach...*144*
athletic director...*144*
head coach...*144*

JUNIOR HIGH SCHOOL *144*

eligibility list...*144*

K

KEYS *145*

bulletin on...*145*

L

LETTER AWARD, VARSITY *146*

LETTER OF RECOMMENDATION *146*

sample of...*146*

LETTER ON/TO: *147*

an official's conduct...*147*
athletes...*147*
parents...*148*

LIABILITY, LEGAL *148*

release form...*149*

LOCKER ROOM USAGE BULLETIN *151*

LOCKERS, CLEANING OF *151*

notice for...*151*
loss of eligibility...*151*

LOST EQUIPMENT *151*

M

MAINTENANCE *152*

facility checklist...*152*
requisition form (custodial)...*152*

MEDICAL *152*

consent form...*152*
report form (two examples)...*153*

MEETS *155*

assignments for swimming...*156*

cross country, record form for...156

diving, notice of...157

dual and triangular (types and schedules)...157

entry forms for...158

MEMOS 159

agenda...159

athletic requirements...160

meeting summary...161

multiple activities...161

sports banquet...162

N

NATIONAL INTERSCHOLASTIC ATHLETIC ADMINISTRATORS ASSOCIATION (NIAAA) 163

general information on...163

NATIONAL OPERATING COMMITTEE ON STANDARDS FOR ATHLETIC EQUIPMENT (NOCSAE) 165

questions and answers concerning (bulletin on)...165

NUMBER OF STUDENTS PER COACHING STAFF 167

notice on...167

O

OFFICIALS 168

conduct of, improper...168

contract for...169

report on...170

use of movies to check calls of (notice on)...170

ORDERING 170

rulebooks...171

scheduling of...172

P

PARENTS 173

letters...173

release form...173

PARTICIPATION 173

athletic contests, contract for...174

PEP CLUBS 175

PERMISSIONS 175

parental (four examples)...175

PERMITS 179

for activities...179

to participate...180

PERSONNEL 181

PHILOSOPHY 181

activities checklist...181

athletic department (two examples)...182

PHYSICALS 183

POLICIES AND PROCEDURES 183

activities...183

attendance...187

budgets...187

competition agreements (three examples)...187

crowd control (bulletin on)...189

eligibility...189

financial report, notice on...190

fund-raising agreement...191

injury...191

insurance...191

loss of eligibility notice...192

participation...192

practice bulletin...193
recruiting guidelines...194
rules and regulations...194
scouting notice...194
student managers...194

PRACTICE 195

time of, guidelines for...195

PROPERTY DAMAGE 196

report form...196

PUBLIC RELATIONS AND THE PRESS 196

policy on (two examples)...196
press releases (three examples)...197

PURCHASE ORDER 199

purchase order receiving ticket...199

R

RECOMMENDATION, LETTERS OF 200

RECRUITING 200

REQUESTS AND REQUISITIONS 200

budget form for...201
for a check...202
for activities...203
for athletic participation from parents...204
for custodial action...205
for distribution of fliers...206
for equipment...206
form for general use...207
for program information...208
for transportation...208

ROSTERS 209

form...209

RULES AND REGULATIONS (BULLETINS) 210

concerning equipment and uniforms...210
concerning trips...210
for athletes...210
for athletics...211

S

SAFETY 213

heat/humidity chart...213
helmet...214
how to kill a player...215
treatment administered, form for recording...216

SCHEDULES 217

bus pick-up...217
change of athletic schedule (two examples)...217
sample schedule...219
season...220
sports programs...220

SCHOLAR ATHLETE 221

memo on (two examples)...221

SCOUTING 223

baseball (two examples)...223
basketball (two examples)...225
football (two examples)...228

SCRIMMAGE 230

schedule of...230

SEASON 230

length of...230
record form...231

report...*231*

SOCCER *233*

schedule ...*233*

season record form...*234*

team rules...*234*

SOFTBALL *236*

season record form...*236*

team rules...*236*

STUDENT MANAGERS *236*

information for (two examples)...*236*

SWIMMING *237*

schedule...*237*

season record form...*237*

T

TELEPHONE *238*

telephone call record slip...*238*

THEFT *239*

memo on...*239*

TICKETS *239*

inventory sheet...*239*

report sheet...*240*

TOURNAMENT *240*

announcement of...*240*

basketball (sample)...*241*

double elimination, round robin, or single elimination...*242*

entry form for (sample)...*243*

information on...*244*

TRACK AND FIELD *245*

announcer's form...*245*

equipment checklist...*245*

event card (sample)...*246*

TRANSPORTATION, TRAVEL, AND TRIPS *247*

advance itinerary guidelines...*247*

expense claim...*248*

financial report on...*248*

out-of-district, checklist for...*249*

permit for (two examples)...*250*

requests for (two examples)...*252*

U

UNIFORMS *255*

care of...*255*

cleaning of...*257*

material composition sheet...*259*

measurement chart...*260*

ordering and fitting...*261*

V

VISITING SCHOOLS *264*

information for...*264*

welcome to...*265*

VOUCHER *266*

for an athletic event...*266*

W

WAIVER *267*

transfer of eligibility waiver...*267*

WRESTLING *269*

match record form...*269*

COMPLETE
COMMUNICATIONS MANUAL
FOR COACHES AND
ATHLETIC DIRECTORS

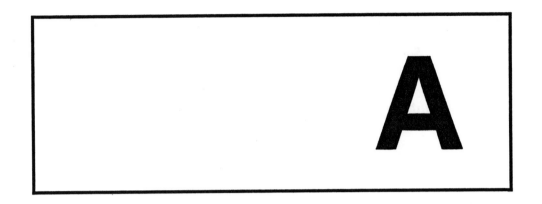

ABSENCE

See Also: ELIGIBILITY; POLICIES AND PROCEDURES

absentee warning form...

TO: _____

DATE: _____

This is to advise you that you have been absent without permission from _____ practice on the following date(s): _____

Continued absence from practice will result in your reassessment as a member of our team. If you have any problems with this, please see me at once.

COACH: _____

player absence record form...

NAME	POSITION	PRACTICES	GAMES

ACADEMIC PERFORMANCE REVIEW

See Also: AWARDS; CODE; ELIGIBILITY; EVALUATION; POLICIES AND PROCEDURES; SCHOLAR ATHLETE

athletic academic progress report...

WAIAKEA HIGH ATHLETICS

To: All teachers
From: M. Otani, Athletic Director
Subject: Athletic Academic Progress Report

Each student athlete will be required to submit to his coach this academic progress report. Please indicate the letter grade in the appropriate space. For borderline grades, please indicate the lower grade. Note any comments on the back of this form.

- -

NAME: _____ GRADE: _____ DATE: _____

SPORT: _____ COACH: _____ DUE DATE: _____

SUBJECTS	INSTRUCTOR	ELEC/REQ	GRADE TO DATE	SIGNATURE
A.				
B.				
C.				
D.				
E.				
F.				

review of performance...

STUDENT'S NAME	PERFORMANCE REVIEW CARLSBAD MUNICIPAL SCHOOLS	DATE
GRADE		TEACHER
SUBJECT	School Phone Number	CONFERENCE PERIOD

_____

_____

_____

_____

_____

ACCEPTANCE

See Also: COACHES CONTRACTS; INTERVIEW

of a coaching contract...

Dear Coach Harris,

Enclosed you will find a signed copy of my contract as head coach of the Rock Township High School football team for the coming school year. I thank you for the faith and trust you have placed in me by offering this contract, and I am signing it in full expectation of justifying your hopes.

From our interview, it was evident that you are not only knowledgeable and experienced in sports, but that you have the best interests of the student athletes foremost in your concern. It was evident to me that we could work together in a positive manner for the good of all the players and the ultimate benefit of the school.

I look forward to the challenges as I look forward to working with you throughout the coming year.

Sincerely,

of an athletic director ...

Dear Mr. Walton,

It gives me great pleasure to inform you that the committee has unanimously voted to offer you the position of Director of Athletics for Rock Township.

Upon review of your credentials and references and coupled with the personal interview, it became evident that the student athletes of Rock Township would greatly benefit from your expertise, your insight, and your philosophy of athletics.

We look forward to having you as our new Athletic Director, and may we collectively wish that this is but the beginning of a long and promising relationship for us all.

Yours sincerely,

ACCIDENT REPORT FORM

See Also: EXAMINATIONS; INJURY; LIABILITY, LEGAL; MEDICAL; SAFETY

example of ...

STATE OF HAWAII DEPARTMENT OF EDUCATION Office of Business Services P.O. Box 2360 Honolulu, Hawaii 96804	**STUDENT ACCIDENT REPORT** Form No. 411

School_____ School Code #_____ Accident Report #_____

Report Filled Out By_____ Position_____ Date of Report___/___/___
                                                          Month Day Year

A. STUDENT INVOLVED

Name_____
     (Last)   (First)   (Initial)

Grade____Age____Sex____Reg.____Spe'l____

Accident Date___/___/___Time_____AM____PM____
           Month Day Year

E. PART OF BODY INJURED

☐ Abdomen ☐ Eye ☐ Knee
☐ Ankle ☐ Face ☐ Leg
☐ Arm ☐ Finger ☐ Teeth
☐ Back ☐ Foot ☐ Wrist
☐ Chest ☐ Hand ☐ Other (Specify)
☐ Elbow ☐ Head _____

B. LOCATION OF ACCIDENT

☐ Agriculture Field   ☐ Playground
☐ Athletic Field   ☐ Shop
☐ Cafeteria   ☐ Stairs/Steps
☐ Classroom   ☐ Swimming Pool
☐ Gymnasium   ☐ Walkway, Outdoor
☐ Hallway   ☐ Other (Specify)
☐ Parking Area   _____

F. IMMEDIATE ACTION TAKEN

☐ First Aid   By _____
☐ Send to Health Aide By _____
☐ Sent Home   By _____
☐ Sent to Doctor   By _____
   Doctor's Name   _____
☐ Sent to Hospital   By _____
   Hospital's Name   _____
   By What Means   _____

C. ACTIVITY INVOLVED IN ACCIDENT

☐ Agriculture Field   ☐ Playground
☐ Athletics   ☐ Play/Free Time
☐ Classroom   ☐ Transportation/Trip
☐ Physical Education   ☐ Other (Specify)
                       _____

G. PERSON NOTIFIED

☐ Parent   ☐ Guardian   ☐ Friend
Name of Person Notified _____
By Whom Notified _____
By What Means _____
If so, how long after injury _____

D. APPARENT NATURE OF INJURY

☐ Abrasion   ☐ Poisoning
☐ Bruise/Bump   ☐ Puncture
☐ Burn   ☐ Shock (Electrical)
☐ Cut/Laceration   ☐ Sprain
☐ Dislocation   ☐ Sting
☐ Fracture   ☐ Other (Specify)
☐ Head Injury   _____

H. WITNESS TO ACCIDENT
(Additional witnesses may be attached)
   Name _____ ☐ Staff
                             ☐ Student
   Name _____ ☐ Staff
                             ☐ Student

   First Staff Person at Scene of Accident
   _____

I. DESCRIPTION OF ACCIDENT
(How did accident happen? What was student doing? Additional information may be attached.)
_____
_____
_____
_____
_____

_____   _____
            Principal's/VP's Signature   Date

ACTIVITIES

See Also: SPECIFIC TOPIC(S)

out-of-school activity form...

COURT SOCCER

WHEN:	Sunday Night 6:00 p.m.–8:00 p.m.
DATE:	Feb. 5th and 26th; March 4th, 11th, 18th, and 25th
WHERE:	Garry Howat's located off Harmony Road
COST:	Eight dollars ($8.00) per 2-hour session
TOTAL COST:	$12.00 per player (by Dec. 19th)
CLOTHES:	Usual Soccer Attire—Jersey, Shorts, Sneakers
NOTE:	NO BLACK SOLES ON SNEAKERS COME DRESSED TO PLAY (no locker facilities)
RULES:	Use AMF–Voit Court Soccer Rules (bring copy)

–no food or drink allowed (stay in court area)

–arrange for a prompt ride home

–a "Release of Responsibility Form" must be signed and returned before you may participate.

–report any injury to me immediately

CUT OFF THE ATTACHED "RELEASE OF RESPONSIBILITY FORM" AND RETURN WITH YOUR PAYMENT OF $12.00.

- -

I understand that Court Soccer is not sponsored by the school, and release Mr. Sessa from responsibility in the event of loss or injury.

Player's Name _____

Parent's Signature _____

Date _____

permission slip...

> See: PERMISSIONS

philosophy of...

> See: PHILOSOPHY

request form...

> See: REQUESTS AND REQUISITIONS

AMATEUR STANDING

> See Also: ATHLETE

policy on...

Amateur Standing

The student shall be considered an amateur who has, since entering ninth grade, never used and is not now using his/her knowledge of athletics or skill for material gain as a participant in athletic contests.

1. The penalty for accepting material rewards in excess of expenses, and as herein provided, shall be permanent disqualification.
2. The amateur standing rule applies to NIAA sanctioned athletic activities.

rules and regulations for ...

AMATEUR STANDING

Coaches should constantly be aware of current rules governing amateur standing. Students should at all times be advised concerning the relationship between such standing and various types of competition and the rewards thereof. The National Federation of State High School Associations, Federation Place, Box 98, Elgin, Illinois 60120, publishes annually a *Handbook* which covers the subject in detail. The following excerpt is taken from the 1979 issue:

> An amateur student athlete is one who engages in athletics for physical, mental, social and educational benefits he/she derives therefrom, and to whom athletics is an avocation and not a source of financial reward. In order to maintain his/her amateur standing, he/she may NOT:
>
> —accept merchandise of more than $100 in value;
> —accept cash awards;
> —enter competition under a false name;
> —accept payment of excessive expense allowances. To provide only for actual and necessary expenses for the athletic trip;
> —sign or have ever signed a contract to play professional athletics (whether for money consideration or not); play or have ever played in any professional team in any sport; receive or have ever received, directly or indirectly, a salary or any other form of financial assistance (including scholarships or educational grants-in-aid from a professional sports organization or any of his/her expenses for reporting to or visiting a professional team.
>
> Instructing, supervising or officiating in any organized youth sports program recreation, playground or camp activities will not jeopardize amateur standing.
>
> High school and junior high school athletes are warned against professionalism in any sport. An athlete should never accept excessive expense money or participate on a professional team. Under the circumstances, he/she may render himself/herself ineligible for high school athletics and/ or future participation. (College or Amateur).
>
> The student athlete may play Summer baseball as an amateur on any team not under the jurisdiction of professional baseball.

ANNOUNCEMENTS

See Also: BULLETINS; FLIERS; MEMOS; VISITING SCHOOLS

beginning of a season (two examples)...

MIDDLETOWN H.S. SOUTH SOCCER
SPRING MEETING

Immediate paperwork –Signed Permission Slip
                 –Self-addressed, stamped envelope
                 –Team Rules

Parents' Meeting–Thursday, June 7th, at 7:30 p.m. at High School South

Pre-season –Summer games (phone list)
          –Brookdale 7-a-side League
          –Soccer camp   <u>STRETCH OUT FIRST!</u>
          –Court soccer
          –Weight lifting
          –Sprinting

First practice–Monday, August 20th, at 8:30 am at Nut Swamp

NOTE: The following responsibilities must be met before you may participate.

    a) PHYSICAL
        1) Free Physicals are Monday, August 13th, at 8:30 am at High School South.
        2) Private Physicals must be dated after August 1st. Use the Private Doctor Physical
           Form.* This is *at your own expense.*

    b) EMERGENCY CARD*

    c) HEALTH HISTORY FORM*

    d) INSURANCE WAIVER*

    *All forms will be sent in the mail.

Priorities–Vacations, employment, etc. should end by the 1st practice. Be available to partici-
        pate every day, rain or shine, until after the state tournament.

Schoolwork–Always do the best you can in school. You must realize, however, that if you need
        to miss practice for extra help, you may lose your chance to play.

Cuts–The team should be chosen by September 1st.

* * * * *

THOMPSON NINTH GRADE SOFTBALL

Name _____

    In addition to other team responsibilities, a team member has an obligation to her team to faithfully attend practices and games throughout the entire season. In order to avoid problems in this area the following practice schedule will apply this season:

PRESEASON (3/13–4/2): Mon.–Fri. 2:45–5:15 rain or shine   Saturday 9:30–12:00

During the playing season: Mon.–Fri. 2:45–4:45 rain or shine Saturday (4/14, 5/5, 5/12) 9:30

EASTER VACATION: We have TWO scheduled games during Easter break, on 4/16 and 4/19. You will be expected to attend both games. They are scheduled for 11AM.

    Please write down ALL conflicts or commitments which would interfere with your keeping to the above schedule should you make the softball team. Please understand that THESE MUST BE TAKEN INTO CONSIDERATION WHEN THE TEAM IS CHOSEN. It is expected that no other conflicts are to come up during the season. You will be expected at every practice and game unless you are absent from school.

PLEASE LIST BELOW THINGS WHICH CANNOT BE MISSED DURING THE SOFTBALL SEASON:

- -

I have listed <u>all</u> my commitments for the upcoming season:

Signed: _____Date _____

My daughter has listed <u>all</u> her commitments for the upcoming season:

Signed: _____Date _____

Please indicate below what positions you prefer to play. This does not mean it is the position you will play; it is just to give me an idea of your preference.

Choice #1 _____Choice #2 _____

Can you pitch? _____

tournament...

See: TOURNAMENT

ANNOUNCERS' FORMS

baseball...

Welcome to _____(Home Team)_____ Baseball. Our guests are the _____

from _____ who are coached by _____

The _____(Home Team)_____ are coached by _____

1. Officials for the game are _____ behind the plate and
_____ on the bases.

2. The next game for the _____(Home School)_____ will be on __(date) at (time)__
   with _____(school)_____ at _____(place)_____

3. The next home game will be on __(date)__ at __(time)__ with __(opponent)__

4. Batteries for _____(visitors)_____ are _____ catching

   and _____ pitching.

   For _____(Home school)_____ catching _____

   and _____ pitching.

BATTING ORDER

	HOME		VISITORS
No.	Name	No.	Name
1.	_____	1.	_____
2.	_____	2.	_____
3.	_____	3.	_____
4.	_____	4.	_____
5.	_____	5.	_____
6.	_____	6.	_____
7.	_____	7.	_____
8.	_____	8.	_____
9.	_____	9.	_____

basketball...

Good evening, sport fans and welcome to basketball at _____ (Home School) _____

Our guests tonight are the _____ from _____

1. Officials for tonight's game are: _____

         and   _____

2. The next game for the _____ (Home School) _____ will be on _____ (date) at (time) _____

  with _____ (opponents) _____ at _____ (place) _____

3. The next home game for the _____ (Home School) _____ will be on _____ (date) at (time) _____

  with _____ (opponents) _____ .

STARTING LINE-UP

	VISITORS				HOME	
Pos.	No.	Name	Pos.	No.		Name
F	_____		F	_____		
F	_____		F	_____		
C	_____		C	_____		
G	_____		G	_____		
G	_____		G	_____		

COACHES _____ COACHES _____

_____   _____

OTHER ANNOUNCEMENTS:

COMING EVENTS: _____

_____

_____

_____

HALF-TIME ENTERTAINMENT: _____

_____

football...

1. Welcome to _____(Home Team)_____ football. Our guests are the _____

   from _____. Head Coach of the _____

   is _____ assisted by _____

2. The starting lineups are:

	VISITORS					HOME		
Pos.	No. Name	Cls.	Wt.	Pos.	No.	Name	Cls.	Wt.
LE	_____			LE	_____			
LT	_____			LT	_____			
LG	_____			LG	_____			
C	_____			C	_____			
RG	_____			RG	_____			
RT	_____			RT	_____			
RE	_____			RE	_____			
QB	_____			QB	_____			
B	_____			B	_____			
B	_____			B	_____			
B	_____			B	_____			

3. Coaches for the home team are _____ head coach
   and _____ assistants.

4. Season's record—Visitors _____Wins and _____ Losses.

5. Officials for tonight's game are:

   Referee _____ Umpire _____

   Head Linesman _____ Field Judge _____

   Timer _____ Announcer _____

6. Coming events announcements for home school:

   _____

   _____

   _____

track and field...

1. Welcome to _____ (name of meet)   (dual, double dual, triangular) _____

   Coaches are: for _____ (name of school) _____ _____ (name of coach) _____
   (for each team)

   Officials are: Starter _____ Clerk of Course _____

   Head Finish Judge _____ Head Timer _____

2. Give first call for all field events   15 min. before starting time.
   Tell where to report as each is called:

   | Pole vault | High jump | Shot put | Javelin | Long jump | Triple jump |

   Give second call   5 min. later

   Give third and last call   5 min. later

3. Give first call and place to report for   15 min. before starting time.
   first running event (120HH)

   Give second call   5 min. later

   Give third and last call   5 min. later

4. Give first call for each succeeding   1 min. after the last call for previous event.
   event and place to report

   Follow exact same procedure for each succeeding event

5. Give pertinent information for each track event:
   Names of runners, schools, lanes
   How race is run—in lanes or not, staggered start,
   Previous record and holder

6. Give running score after each event:

   The running score after (how many) events is: School _____ School _____

7. Periodically give the best marks in field events.

   Check on progress at high jump and pole vault and announce.

8. Give results of each event as soon as possible after receiving them.

   Results of the 120 HH—1st Place _____ of _____ Time _____
   2nd Place _____ of _____ and so on.

   In field events, give names, schools, distances, of all place winners. (Work fast.)

9. Make general announcements: Coming events

   Remind runners to return in their lanes to the finish line in the sprints and hurdles
   for identification by judges.

   Keep the track and field areas clear of participants and spectators.

10. Keep the meet moving on time by getting participants to starting areas early.

wrestling...

1. Welcome to wrestling at _____ (home school) _____

   Our guests are the _____ from _____

2. Referee for the match is _____

3. The next home match will be with _____

4. Introduce the participants (opponents first)

Visitors		SCORE		Home
	Wt.	Vis.	Home	

5. Will the audience please rise for the playing of the National Anthem.

6. At the start of each match (as rapidly as possible) announce contestants and weight.

7. Announce the winner and total team scores after each match.

ASSISTANT COACH

See Also: ATHLETIC DIRECTOR; COACH

job description...

JUNIOR AND SENIOR HIGH ASSISTANT COACH
Job Description

I. Reports to: Head Coach
II. Supervises: Athletes
III. Basic Function: To carry out the aims of the District Athletic Program and New Mexico Activities Association
IV. Primary Responsibilities:
  A. Year Around
    1. Have understanding knowledge of rules and regulations regarding his sport as presented in the NMAA Handbook and National Federation Rulebook.
    2. Keep abreast of new knowledge, innovative ideas, and techniques by attendance at clinics, workshops, and reading in his field.
    3. Assist head coach in carrying out his responsibilities.
    4. Be a member of professional organizations such as New Mexico Coaches' Association.
  B. Seasonal
    1. Before the Season
      a. Assist head coach in proper registration of all athletes.
      b. Assist head coach in making a systematic issuance of school equipment.
      c. Assist head coach in providing accurate information needed to compile eligibility lists and other reports.
    2. During the Season
      a. Assist in implementing "Athletic Standards" as outlined in Athletic Handbook and District Policy.
      b. Assume responsibility for constant care for equipment and facilities being used.
      c. Assume supervisory control over athletes and teams assigned him and to assume supervisory control over all athletes in the program when such control is needed.
      d. To be in regular attendance at practice sessions and contests.
      e. Apply discipline in a firm and positive manner.

  f. Emphasize safety precautions and be aware of best training and injury procedures.

  g. Conduct himself and his teams in an ethical manner during practice and contests.

  h. Provide head coach with information needed in making game reports and publicity releases.

  i. Instruct his players concerning rules and rule changes, new knowledge, and innovative ideas and techniques.

3. End of Season

  a. Assist in the return and inventory of school equipment.

  b. Recommend athletes for letter awards.

  c. Recommend facility maintenance and improvements.

  d. Recommend equipment to be purchased.

qualifications...

Qualifications for the Position of Assistant Coach

A. Professional preparation: employment as a teacher with coaching preparation either through experience or college preparation.

B. Background experience: possess working knowledge of all aspects of the sport.

C. Personal: demonstrated interest in and an aptitude for performing tasks listed:

1. At every opportunity urge the student body to be polite, courteous, and fair to the visiting team.

2. Always display good sportsmanship, losing or winning.

3. Maintain poise and self-control at all times, especially at the contests.

4. Teach the team to play fairly. Games should be played hard but not as "blood and thunder" or "survival of the fittest" contests.

5. Be a good host to the visiting team, coach and spectators.

6. Discipline and, if necessary, dismiss players who disregard good sportsmanship.

7. Educate the players on the sidelines to the fact that it is unsportsmanlike conduct to yell intimidating remarks at the visiting team or officials.

8. Respect the officials' judgment and interpretation of the rules. If an interpretation appeal is necessary, follow appropriate procedures.

9. Let the officials control the game and the coach control his team.

10. Publicly attempt to shake hands with the officials prior to the game and the opposing coach before and after the game.

ATHLETE

See Also: ABSENCE; AMATEUR STANDING; AWARDS; CODE; ELIGIBILITY; INTEREST SURVEY; LETTER ON/TO; SAFETY; SCHOLAR ATHLETE

contract for...

HILLDALE HIGH SCHOOL
Student Athlete's Contract

Between: _____, student, and Hilldale High School

Purpose

Participation in athletics is a privilege, not a right. The athlete must earn this privilege through dedication, desire, and discipline. Without the pursuit of those, the athlete can in no way do justice to himself or the school. The athlete must discipline himself to be a good citizen and student in order to achieve athletic excellence. The faculty of Hilldale High School believes that tradition of winning is established and maintained upon these principles. In order for a determined course of action for the pursuit of athletic achievement and the character training of young persons, the following "Athletic Policies" must be understood and agreed to between the school, the student athlete, and parents.

Attendance

All team members of each sport will attend all scheduled practices and meetings. No practices can be missed. If circumstances arise whereby the student cannot attend a practice or meeting, the coach must be notified prior to the practice or meeting missed by personal contact, phone call, or written statement from the parent or guardian. Any athlete who cuts practice, fails to appear for a game, fails to make scheduled team or individual meetings, or fails to attend school on game day or practice days may not be allowed to suit up for any game or games for a period of time to be determined by the coach and Athletic Director. Excessive absence from team practices, games or meetings may be cause for removal from sixth hour athletics. All athletes are required to attend classes regularly. Athletes delinquent in class attendance are subject to disciplinary action. Lack of attendance in classes may result in failure of class work, resulting in ineligibility in athletics.

Eligibility

To be eligible for athletics, the athlete must be in compliance with the Hilldale School Policies concerning incorrect or illegal enrollment and the rules and regulations of the Oklahoma Athletic Association. Eligibility for weekly athletic participation shall be determined by a grade-incidental sheet bi-weekly. The athlete must be passing at least three solids to be eligible for any varsity competition that week.

Sport Changes

It is recommended that all athletes participate in as many sports as they are capable. Once an athlete begins the in-season training period of a sport, he should not quit while that sport is in season. Any athlete who quits a sport to participate in another sport shall be subject to being withheld from participation until the season of the sport dropped by the athlete is over. It shall be the prerogative of the coach of the in-season sport to release the athlete to another sport. No athlete may participate in a second sport until the athlete has been cleared from the first sport by obtaining a written release. When an athlete is released, that athlete shall be free to try out for any sport of his choosing. The head coach of that sport shall have the right to determine if an athlete is skillful enough to remain on the squad.

Jobs

The athlete shall not obligate himself to a job that in any way interferes with practice time or regular competitions time.

Personal Appearance

Because an athlete is constantly in the eyes of the public, he becomes a representative of the school and is considered to be in a position of leadership. Therefore, the athlete's personal appearance not only reflects his attitudes but those whom he represents. His hygiene must be such that it is not harmful to the athlete's well-being while participating in athletic competition. Athletes will be required to abide by the following rules established by the Board of Education and Hilldale High School:

1. Hair: The athlete's hair shall be groomed in such a way as not to interfere with the athlete's performance.
2. Dress Attire: Athletes are expected to dress appropriately at all times during school hours and when attending school-sponsored activities.

Lack of adherence to the above rules may result in the athlete being held out of practice or games. Failure to comply after further notification may result in suspension from the team and/or removal from athletics.

Personal Health Practices

Due to the harmful effect upon the health of the individual, all athletes will refrain from use of: tobacco, drinking alcoholic beverages, including beer, abusive drugs of any kind, improper diet, and improper rest. Verification of drinking of alcoholic beverages or the use of abusive drugs by the athlete may result in immediate dismissal from the team.

Equipment, Fees, and Physical Examination

All athletes will be required to replace lost gear either by payment or with the equivalent of the lost article. All athletes will be required to have a signed physicians' examination on file, before competing in varsity competition. All athletes will be required to clear with their coaches on gear before entering another sport. The school or athletic department assumes no financial responsibility for injuries occurring to athletes nor for ambulance fees.

School Decorum

An athlete is expected to govern his or her conduct in accordance with the rules and regulations of the "Student Handbook" and that violation of the student's obligations under that handbook may result in removal from competitive athletics.

Lettering

The provisions or criteria to be met for earning a letter will be furnished to the athlete by the coach in that sport prior to the beginning of the season.

I understand that if I have not kept my agreement to fulfill the above obligations, I will be removed from athletics.

Date: _____

Student's signature: _____

Parent's signature: _____

evaluation form for (two examples)...

PLAYER REPORT

SAMPLE   SAMPLE

REPORT BY: _____POSITION HELD: _____

DATE: _____CLUB: _____

NAME OF PLAYER: _____

ADDRESS: _____

PHONE: _____BIRTHDATE: _____

HEIGHT: _____WEIGHT: _____AGE: _____POSITION: _____

PLEASE RATE THE PLAYER IN THE FOLLOWING CATEGORIES: (1–5) 1 poor, 5 excellent, etc.

MENTAL ATTRIBUTES	MOVEMENT		COMPETITIVENESS		CHARACTER	
	QUICKNESS	_____	DETERMINATION	_____		
LEARNS						
QUICKLY _____	AGILITY	_____	AGGRESSIVENESS	_____	COACHABLE	_____
AWARENESS _____	BALANCE	_____	TOUGHNESS	_____		_____
ANTICIPATION_____	COORDINATION	_____	STAMINA	_____		_____
	MOBILITY	_____	HUSTLE	_____		

SKILLS		TACTICS	
CONTROL	_____	ABILITY TO READ GAME	_____
CROSSING A BALL	_____	PLANS AHEAD	_____
HEADING	_____	USE OF TEAMMATES	_____
LONG PASS	_____		
RETAINING POSSESSION	_____		
SHOOTING	_____	AVERAGE	_____
SHORT PASS	_____		
TACKLING	_____		

WHAT ARE THE PLAYER'S STRONG POINTS? (OFFENSIVELY/DEFENSIVELY) _____
_____

WHAT ARE THE PLAYER'S WEAK POINTS? (OFFENSIVELY/DEFENSIVELY) _____
_____

BEST POSITION: _____
_____

* * * * *

PLAYER REPORT CARD

BY GARY HINDLEY

The periodic assessment and evaluation of players during and just after a season is an integral part of an individual's athletic progress. In the majority of cases, a coach provides immediate verbal feedback, but seldom prepares a comprehensive, written report. For this reason, a Player Report Card was developed by our coaching staff.

Each player receives a mid-season and post-season report. Both the head coach and an assistant coach (preferably the one that works closest with his functional training area) submit separate reports to the player. Short positive and/or negative comments were included and a grading system of 1-10 was used (1 being lowest and 10 being highest.)

From both a player and coach standpoint, these Soccer Report Cards were well received and proved very beneficial. They can be easily altered and adapted to the various levels and coaching situations that an individual coach might be involved in.

I. Technique	Grade	Comments
ball control	———	————————
shooting	———	————————
passing	———	————————
dribbling	———	————————
tackling	———	————————
heading	———	————————
creativeness	———	————————
throw-ins	———	————————
free kicks	———	————————
technical speed	———	————————
II. Physical		
practice work rate	———	————————
game work rate	———	————————
endurance	———	————————
strength	———	————————
speed	———	————————
quickness	———	————————
agility	———	————————
balance	———	————————
flexibility	———	————————

III. Psychological

desire   _____   _____

communication   _____   _____

attitude   _____   _____

responsibility _____   _____

cooperation   _____   _____

aggressiveness _____   _____

intelligence   _____   _____

mental preparedness _____   _____

emotionality   _____   _____

coachability   _____   _____

teamwork   _____   _____

IV. Tactical

knowledge of game   _____ _____

reading the game offense _____ _____

reading the game defense _____ _____

Offensive Principles

attacking with ball   _____ _____

creating space   _____ _____

support   _____ _____

preparing runs   _____ _____

finishing   _____ _____

Defensive Principles

immediate chase   _____ _____

goal-side position   _____ _____

pressurizing   _____ _____

containment   _____ _____

support   _____ _____

balance   _____ _____

winning the ball   _____ _____

50/50 balls   _____ _____

Gary Hindley has been the head soccer coach at Trenton State College (NJ) for the past eight seasons. He has compiled an overall 76-52-18 record while his teams have won the NJSCAC Championship four times and have been selected for seven post-season bids. Coach Hindley was selected as the N.J. College Soccer Coach of the Year in 1978. He serves on state, regional, and national committees and is a USSF licensed coach.

letters to (two examples)...

Dear Athlete,

This letter is to remind you of the responsibilities that you must meet before you may participate in soccer. All forms must be dated after August 1st.

1) Physicals are given free of charge on Monday, August 13th, at 8:30 AM, in the Nurse's office at South. Enclosed is a form which you can use if you want a private physical. Private physicals are at your own expense.
2) An emergency card has been enclosed. It must be filled out in full.
3) An insurance waiver has been enclosed. It also must be filled out in full.

All forms must be submitted at the physical, or before the first practice. The first practice will be on Monday, August 20th, at 5:30 PM, at Nut Swamp field. Be on time! You will need to bring a soccer ball and plenty of water. Everyone is required to be at all practices.

Soccer is a game of skill. This skill must be practiced and used often in order for you to be competitive in our tough conference. Only the most dedicated players will play for Middletown South. Be prepared to impress us on August 20. Don't let a day go by without doing something to make yourself the best player possible. Our season depends upon your dedication.

Sincerely,

Mr. Mark A. Sessa
Head Soccer Coach

* * * * *

Dear Parent and Football Participant:

The purpose of this letter is to welcome your son into our 19--football program. We want him to enjoy his association with other members of the team, and learn all he can from our coaches.

Our main interest for your son concerns his safety and health while he is a participant in our football program. Even though all of our football staff are professionally trained coaches and will teach your son the proper skills, there is a chance of injury while he is playing football. We sincerely hope this does not happen, but because football is a contact sport we must warn, in writing, each player and parent or guardian of the possibility of an injury while playing football.

We need each participant and parent or guardian to sign this notice that acknowledges they have read this letter and do not hold the school district liable for any accident or injury.that may occur while the undersigned participant is playing football for School District No. 25.

Sincerely,

BYRON TOONE
Director of Athletics

- -

I have read this letter and do not hold the school liable for any accident or injury that may occur while playing football.

Player: _____

Parent or Guardian: _____

Date: _____

of the year...

BONANZA BENGALS
ATHLETE OF THE YEAR AWARD

Each spring, the coaching staff will submit the names of men and women athletes for the prestigious "Bengal Athlete of the Year Award." This award will be presented at the annual Awards Night Ceremony by the Athletic Director. Although spring sports may not be completed by this time, this would be the only occasion to present this honor in front of the community. The following form will be utilized in the selection process:

Athlete of Year Nomination

Name of Athlete _____

Sports participated in while at Bonanza:

Sport	Number of Years	Coach's Signature
A.		
B.		
C.		
D.		
E.		
F.		

Add three (3) points per varsity sport for each sport. (Example: Varsity Football for two years is six (6) points.) Add two (2) points per J.V. and "B" sport for each sport.

_____ 1. Total points for participation.

_____ 2. Total points for lettering. Four (4) points each sport each year.

_____ 3. Team Captain—five (5) points per sport per year.

_____ 4. Most Valuable Player—Ten (10) points per sport per year.

_____ 5. Special recognition during a season. Example: Player of the week, most improved, etc. One (1) point each.

_____ 6. School Records —Five (5) points each.

What	When

7. <u>INDIVIDUAL HONORS</u>

———   All American—Thirty (30) points per sport per year.

———   All State—Twenty (20) points per sport per year.

———   All State Second Team—Ten (10) points per sport per year.

———   All Conference—Ten (10) points per sport per year.

———   All Conference Second Team—Five (5) points per sport per year.

———   All Division—Five (5) points per sport per year.

———   All Division Second Team—Three (3) points per sport per year.

———   Honorable Mention—Two (2) points per sport per year.

——— 8. Athletic Scholarship (Claim only those accepted) Full Ride—Ten (10) points Partial—Five (5) points

——— 9. Academic overall G.P.A. for seven consecutive semesters.

$$2.0 = 2 \text{ points}$$
$$2.1–2.5 = 3 \text{ points}$$
$$2.6–3.0 = 4 \text{ points}$$
$$3.1–3.5 = 6 \text{ points}$$
$$3.6–4.0 = 8 \text{ points}$$

——— 10. Academic Scholarship (Claim only those to be accepted and utilized.) Full Ride —Ten (10) points   Partial—Five (5) points

——— 11. Total points accumulated by athlete and verified by his coaches.

ATHLETIC

See Also: AWARDS; BULLETINS; CONTESTS; EQUIPMENT; INFORMATION; INSURANCE; INVENTORY; PARTICIPATION; PERMISSIONS; PHILOSOPHY; REQUESTS AND REQUISITIONS; RULES AND REGULATIONS; SAFETY; TOURNAMENT; UNIFORMS; SPECIFIC SPORT

Information sheet...

SPORT: _____ COACH: _____ DATE SUBMITTED: _____

WAIAKEA HIGH SCHOOL
PLAYERS INFORMATION

Name	Grade	Birth-date	Ht	Wt	Position	Uniform # Home Away		Years of Varsity Exp	Eligible

principles...

CLARK COUNTY SCHOOL DISTRICT
EIGHT CARDINAL ATHLETIC PRINCIPLES

TO BE OF MAXIMUM EFFECTIVENESS, THE ATHLETIC PROGRAM WILL:

1. Be a well-coordinated part of the secondary school curriculum.
2. Justify the use of the tax funds and school facilities because of the educational aims achieved.
3. Be based on the spirit of amateurism.
4. Be conducted by secondary school authorities.
5. Provide opportunities for many students to participate in a wide variety of sports in every sport season.
6. Foster training in conduct, game ethics, and sportsmanship for participants and spectators.
7. Include a well-balanced program of intramural sports.
8. Engender respect for local, state, and national rules and policies under which the school program is conducted.

ATHLETIC DEPARTMENT

See Also: BUDGET; COACHING STAFF; DISTRICT ATHLETIC PROGRAM; EXPENSES; HANDBOOK; INTRAMURAL PROGRAM; ORDERING; PHILOSOPHY; SCHEDULES

evaluation form for (two examples)...

EVALUATIVE CRITERIA FOR INTERSCHOLASTIC ATHLETICS
FOR MAINE HIGH SCHOOLS
SUGGESTIONS FOR USE

The evaluative checklist is comprised of a series of criteria under each major area of the interscholastic athletic program. Each criterion is a desirable goal or quality to be attained. Evaluators should read each criterion and determine the degree of attainment.

EXPLANATION OF COLUMN HEADINGS
Column headings are as follows:
0. No degree of attainment
1. Poor attainment
2. Fair attainment
3. Good attainment
4. Excellent attainment

Evaluators should apply each criterion to their interscholastic athletic program and indicate the degree of attainment by placing a mark in the appropriate column. A possible score is given for each area or emphasis. Evaluators should complete an actual score for each area and compare it to the possible score.

INTERPRETATION OF SCORING

A 0 rating indicates no degree of attainment. A rating of 1 indicates a very small degree of attainment and is unsatisfactory. A rating of 2 indicates minimal attainment and is in the border area ranging from unsatisfactory to satisfactory. A 3 indicates a satisfactory degree of attainment, while a 4 indicates a full degree of attainment.

FOLLOW-UP

At the end of the checklist, there is a heading titled A Summary of Needed Improvements. Evaluators should list improvements needed in the various areas under the appropriate heading. This will serve as a reminder list of needed improvements in the total program of interscholastic athletics at your school.

I. PHILOSOPHY AND PRINCIPLES

Possible Score __32__
Actual Score _____

	Rating Scale			
0	1	2	3	4

1. Clear statements of philosophy and principles of the athletic program exist in written form and are distributed to all concerned personnel.
2. Interscholastic athletics have as their aim the development of each student in accordance with his capacities. Opportunities are provided for all students that desire to participate.
3. Interscholastic athletic activities are harmonious with the goals of the entire educational program and are regarded by school administrators and faculty as an integral part of the total program.
4. Athletic practices detrimental to the welfare of pupils as individuals are not permitted.
5. An effort is made to cultivate the mental, social, ethical, and emotional, as well as physical, outcomes of interscholastic athletes.
6. In the determination of athletic policies and practices, the welfare of the participating students is held paramount.
7. The interscholastic athletic program supplements and complements the intramural program and the required instructional program of physical education.
8. The interscholastic athletic program contributes to a wholesome community social attitude.

II. ORGANIZATION AND ADMINISTRATION

A. Policies and Procedures

Possible Score __40__
Actual Score _____

Rating Scale				
0	1	2	3	4

1. Interscholastic athletics are administered as a division of the overall secondary education program under the administrative head of the school.
2. School athletic policies and procedures are determined by administrators, administrative heads, coaches or representative athletic board or committee in accordance with Maine Secondary Schools Principals Association regulations.
3. Athletic practice sessions cause no disruption in the daily academic program.
4. There is a written policy prepared in consultation with local medical personnel which designates the procedure to be followed in case of accidents or injuries that occur during a practice session and/or game. Such a statement covers:
   a. prevention—by wearing properly fitted protective equipment
   b. first aid treatment
   c. procedure for obtaining medical help
   d. notification of parents
   e. recording the facts regarding the accident
5. There is a written policy statement, read to the athletes and distributed to parents, which informs parents of their legal and financial responsibilities including insurance coverage regarding injuries incurred in interscholastic athletics and specific procedures to be followed.

B. Administrators

Possible Score __36__
Actual Score _____

Rating Scale				
0	1	2	3	4

1. The board of education has adopted policies and procedures for the supervision and regulation of the interscholastic athletic program.
2. The board of education is familiar with the rules and regulations of the M.S.S.P.A.
3. The school administration establishes the objectives for a sound program of interscholastic athletics.
4. The school administration makes policies relating to sportsmanship in the school and community.
5. The school administration employs a coach on the basis of teaching ability rather than coaching ability.
6. The school administration does not appoint teachers to coaching assignments if they resort to unethical practices.
7. The principal utilizes school assemblies for emphasizing sportsmanship to players, students, adults, and courtesy to guests.
8. The athletic director keeps his immediate superior informed about all aspects of the interscholastic athletic program.
9. All school personnel set good examples of sportsmanship for the public by their conduct at interscholastic athletic contests.

III. RULES AND REGULATIONS

A. Administration

Possible Score __36__
Actual Score _____

1. The school cooperates with the M.S.S.P.A. in establishing and maintaining high standards in the conduct of school athletics.
2. Interpretations regarding M.S.S.P.A. rules and regulations are referred directly to the Executive Director's office by the administrative head of the school or his designated representative.
3. Consent of the Executive Director is obtained before participating in contests with Maine teams that are not members of the M.S.S.P.A.
4. In interscholastic sports that are not recognized by the M.S.S.P.A. all participants are listed on M.S.S.P.A. eligibility blanks and all M.S.S.P.A. rules are followed.
5. Contest contracts and contracts with officials are made only on the official association contract or similar forms.
6. Specific faculty members appointed by the administrative head are present at all interscholastic athletic contests and tournaments.
7. No student is allowed to participate in interscholastic athletic competition until he has had a thorough medical examination. These examinations are required annually, seasonally, and after illness or injury.
8. Athletic facilities and equipment are safe, sanitary, and carefully maintained.
9. Specific policies are followed in granting approved awards which are symbols of participation and achievement.

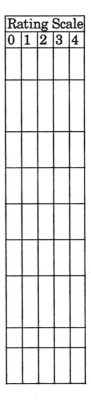

B. Contest and Eligibility Requirements

Possible Score __36__
Actual Score _____

1. Contests are conducted in accordance with rules and regulations of the M.S.S.P.A.
2. Scheduling is a cooperative effort involving the administrative head, coaches, athletic director and representative athletic board or committee.
3. Eligibility lists are sent to opponents at least three days prior to a contest.
4. Eligibility certificates are sent to the office of the Executive Director before the first contest in each of the sports.
5. Efforts are made not to schedule contests on a night preceding a day of school.
6. The school emphasizes good character, superior conduct and excellent citizenship as prerequisites for interscholastic participation.
7. Athletes are kept informed regarding loss of their eligibility if they violate association rules and regulations as applied to the participants.
8. Athletes, coaches, and administrators are aware that "weekly grades" must meet minimum scholastic requirements.
9. Eligibility of transfer students is thoroughly checked by the receiving principal before eligibility decisions are made in accordance with the Transfer Rule of the M.S.S.P.A.

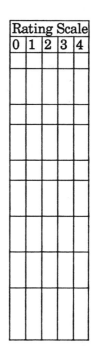

C. The Coach

Possible Score __28__
Actual Score _____

Rating Scale				
0	1	2	3	4

1. Coaches support the administration in the total educational program.
2. Coaches are exemplary in their behavior and sportsmanship.
3. Coaches accept the decisions of medical personnel when the question arises concerning whether or not to allow a student who has been ill or injured to compete.
4. Coaches do not permit their coaching assignments to infringe upon their teaching responsibilities.
5. Coaches insist that squad members be good hosts, good guests, and good citizens. The coach teaches respect for property and emphasizes that players represent the school and community.
6. Coaches accept the decisions of the officials.
7. Coaches and trainers are acquainted with first aid procedures and have first aid supplies available.

IV. FINANCE

Possible Score __20__
Actual Score _____

Rating Scale				
0	1	2	3	4

1. The board of education or a representative board or athletic committee controls the finances of the interscholastic athletic program.
2. Complete and accurate financial records are kept of all athletic monies and financial reports are filed after each contest.
3. An audit is conducted annually.
4. All sports sponsored by the school receive equal consideration in determining the interscholastic budget.
5. Standardized forms are used for budget and financial matters to facilitate a businesslike operation.

V. PUBLIC RELATIONS

Possible Score __20__
Actual Score _____

	Rating Scale				
	0	1	2	3	4

1. Administrators and coaches acquaint the student body, faculty and community with the importance of having a high degree of sportsmanship at all interscholastic athletic contests.
2. All coaches attend faculty meetings and are actively involved in school functions.
3. Communications media and community organizations are informed of the educational objectives of interscholastic athletics.
4. Personnel assigned to the athletic program take part in civic affairs, attend professional meetings, and answer correspondence promptly.
5. The responsibility for the release of information to the communications media is assigned to a designated individual.

SCORE

	Possible Score	Actual Score
I. Philosophy and Principles	32	_____
II. Organization and Administration		
A. Policies and Procedures	40	_____
B. Administrators	36	_____
III. Rules and Regulations		
A. Administration	36	_____
B. Contest and Eligibility Requirements	36	_____
C. The Coach	28	_____
IV. Finance	20	_____
V. Public Relations	20	_____

Total Possible Score   248
Total Actual Score _____

* * * * *

WAIAKEA HIGH ATHLETICS
PROGRAM ASSESSMENT

POSTSEASON

Postseason coach/athletic director conference shall be conducted. The preseason objectives will be reviewed and the Coach's Evaluation form completed. Coaches are to make an appointment to meet with the Athletic Director <u>no later than 3 weeks</u> from the conclusion of the season.

AGENDA—INDIVIDUAL COACH'S CONFERENCES (AFTER SEASON)

COACH'S NAME: _____ SPORT: _____ DATE: _____

Equipment returned.

Recommendation for awards prepared and submitted.

Season and squad summary reports to Director of Athletics.

Budget:

a. Inventory sheets complete.

b. Recommendations complete.

Staff conference with assistant coaches completed.

a. Individual conference with assistant coaches.

b. Review of season by levels completed.

Complete/Review Written Plans for the Coming Season form.

a. Review of specific objectives adopted for preseason.

 —Rate each item 5 (excellent), 4 (above avg), 3 (avg), 2 (needs improvement), 1 (unacceptable).

 —Discuss those objectives not accomplished.

Review Coach's Evaluation.

 —Establish overall rating.

Establish major objectives for next year.

WRITTEN PLANS FOR THE COMING SEASON

PRESEASON SPECIFIC OBJECTIVES	PRE-SEASON MEANS TO ASSESS ACCOMPLISHMENT	POST-SEASON RATING
Example: Improve teaching of pass blocking	Example: Allow fewer than 1 QB sack per game (avg). 50% reduction in holding penalties over last year on pass plays	(5-4-3-2-1)
1.	1.	

SPORT: _____ COACH: _____ DATE: _____

Written plans for the coming season are due prior to the start of your season.

SUMMARY OF COACH'S EVALUATION FORM

Coach:

Achieved the stated objectives this season. 5 4 3 2 1
(From preseason objectives adopted)

Coaches Evaluation. 5 4 3 2 1

Receives an overall rating (Objectives & Evaluation) 5 4 3 2 1

Signature of Evaluator: _____ Coach: _____ Date: _____
Signature indicates that the coach has read and participated in this evaluation. It does not
indicate complete agreement with all factors of the evaluation itself. Coach being evaluated
may express disagreement in writing and attach to the evaluation form. All copies of this
evaluation must have this statement of disagreement attached. Comments, positive or negative, may also be attached by the evaluator. Copy of this document will be filed in coaches folder.

ATHLETIC DIRECTOR

See Also: ATHLETIC DEPARTMENT; BID SURVEY; BUDGET; COACHING STAFF;
EVALUATION; NUMBER OF STUDENTS PER COACHING STAFF; ORDERING;
PERMITS

checklist for...

Individual Participant	Phys. Exam	Parent Permit	Ins.	Ins. Waiver	ASB Card	Eligi- bility
1.						
2.						
3.						
4.						
5.						

job description...

1. Supervision
   a. To supervise the athletic and intramural programs in consultation with the principal and/or superintendent.
   b. To recommend coaching and intramural personnel and to evaluate their performances.
   c. To act as a consultant to the administration and coaching personnel on matters pertaining to the athletic program.
   d. To hold meetings with coaches whenever necessary; to keep them informed of all matters pertaining to the athletic program.
   e. To supervise all athletic facilities; schedule practice use; to recommend maintenance and repairs.
   f. To supervise and coordinate the budget for all sports.

2. District Representative
   a. To schedule all intraschool athletic events for the district.
   b. To represent the School District in all athletic business at League and District meetings.
   c. To enforce and interpret all athletic regulations as specified by the State Activity Association, the District and the League in which membership is maintained.
   d. To prepare the district bus transportation schedule for all athletic trips and work with the supervisor of transportation in the implementation of the schedule.
   e. To assist the administration in preparation of the pass list and to administer the issuance of complimentary passes for the school district.
   f. To act as Tournament Manager for all League and District activities that are assigned to the school district.
   g. To make all necessary arrangements for all non-school facilities needed in the athletic program; for example, golf courses, swimming facilities, cross country courses, etc.

3. Duties Pertaining to Athletic Events
   a. *Release of publicity:* To release to the press and radio publicity on coming events in athletic and on all special activities in which the high schools participate.
   b. *Home activities:* To attend all home athletic events; to be responsible for over all supervision; to obtain adequate personnel to ensure smooth operation on all fronts.
   c. *Pre-game and half-time programs:* To coordinate with appropriate personnel the starting and stopping time schedules for bands, pre-game ceremonies and half-time programs.
   d. *Notifying principal:* To make recommendations to the principal regarding the conduct of each activity.
   e. *Faculty Help:* To work with the principal to determine the need and to establish a schedule of specific assignments and reporting times for all personnel involved with duties pertaining to the activity; for example, policing, ticket sales, etc.
   f. *Game program:* To assist the school in obtaining from visiting teams the information to be included in the individual game programs.

g. *Liaison:* To inform visiting teams and officials of the pertinent details of their participation—time schedule, dressing facilities, etc.

h. *Supervision of Press Box:* To supervise arrangements in the press box for the official personnel having duties there during football games, baseball games and track meets.

i. *Doctor in attendance:* To make arrangements to have a doctor present at all home football games.

j. *Printed schedules:* To develop schedule posters and pocket schedules as needed for use in publicizing all programs.

organization for an...

See: NATIONAL INTERSCHOLASTIC ATHLETIC ADMINISTRATOR'S ASSOCIATION (NIAAA)

record keeping by...

A certain number of records should be kept by the Athletic Director with the majority of the needed information being supplied regularly by the coaches. Record keeping is essentially good business practice and material thus collected can be of great value for anticipating and capitalizing on trends, for use as a valid reference source and for establishing necessary P.R. relationships with the media. Good record keeping indicates to the Administration that the athletic department is efficient and capable and a credit to the school system.

Records commonly maintained by the Athletic Director include:

1. Season report from each head coach at the end of the individual season.
   List:
   —scores of every contest held;
   —records (school, league, district, state) established by team or individual participant;
   —honor and award winners;
   —individual participation summaries;
   —honor awards (selection and award procedures);
   —recommendations for seasons to come.

2. Annual inventory—at the end of the season and prior to ordering for the next season.

3. Budget requests—from each coach; final request to administration.

4. Eligibility lists—kept up to date for all individual and team participants.

5. Letter awards.

6. Financial reports—income and expenditures.
   —gate receipts by sport.

7. Minutes of all meetings concerned with athletics, at all levels.

8. Schedules of all sports—compiled in continuing file.

9. Injury records.

ATHLETIC INJURY REPORT

See: INJURY

ATHLETIC INVENTORY INFORMATION

See: INVENTORY

ATHLETIC SCHEDULES

See: SCHEDULES

ATHLETIC TRAVEL

See: TRANSPORTATION, TRAVEL, AND TRIPS

AWARDS

See Also: EVALUATION; SCHOLAR ATHLETE

criteria for (in all sports)...

B.H.S. ATHLETIC AWARDS CRITERIA

Athletic awards are given in recognition of outstanding athletic achievement and service to the school, not as compensation of services rendered. Athletes will receive, at the coaches' recommendations, an athletic letter at the completion of his/her first varsity year in a particular sport. Chenille stars will be given to deserving athletes each year following the awarding of the first letter. A certificate is also given after the athlete has received a letter. Students not lettering will receive a certificate of participation.

Listed below are the criteria to letter for each sport. However, the head coach has the prerogative to issue or withhold a letter for extenuating circumstances such as early season injuries, value to a team without having played enough, team or district violations, etc. Coaches must provide documentation of these circumstances to the athletic administrator and athletic director. In all cases students must complete the season, as a member of the team, in order to letter.

FALL SPORTS

Football

1. Student must meet all academic eligibility and good citizenship criteria as provided for in C.C.S.D. regulations.
2. The athlete must have completed the entire season.
3. The student must attend all practices unless excused by the coach for illness or an emergency beyond the student's control.
4. Student must have suited for at least six (6) varsity games.
5. Student must have participated in the varsity games at least one-half (18 quarters) possible.
6. Student must have returned all equipment loaned to him or her by Bonanza High School in all years of participation.

Boys' and Girls' Cross Country

Our philosophy is to involve as many athletes as possible. Earning a varsity letter means the athlete has met the practice demands, racing demands and standards of good sportsmanship and coachability.

1. Earn at least ten varsity letter points in competition.
2. Regular attendance at practice.
3. Participation in cross country meets.
4. Return all equipment loaned by the coach or school.
5. Third year participant in the sport.

Letter points earned as follows:

1. One point for being in the top five Bonanza finishers (scoring team points).
2. One point for beating a scoring member of another team.
3. One point for running a personal best time in a meet.

Boys' Tennis

1. Student must meet all academic eligibility and good citizenship criteria as provided for in C.C.S.D. regulations.
2. The athlete must have completed the entire season.
3. The student must attend all practices unless excused by the coach for illness or emergency beyond the student's control.
4. Must play in at least one-half of the matches.

Girls' Tennis

1. Student must meet all academic eligibility and good citizenship criteria as provided for in C.C.S.D. regulations.
2. The athlete must have completed the entire season.
3. The student must attend all practices unless excused by the coach for illness or emergency beyond the student's control.
4. Must play in at least one-half of the matches.

Girls' Golf

1. Student must meet all academic eligibility and good citizenship criteria as provided for in C.C.S.D. regulations.
2. The athlete must have completed the entire season.
3. The student must attend all practices unless excused by the coach for illness or emergency beyond the student's control.
4. Girls will compete in matches they have qualified for.

Volleyball

1. Student must meet all academic eligibility and good citizenship criteria as provided for in C.C.S.D. regulations.
2. The athlete must have completed the entire season.
3. The student must attend all practices unless excused by the coach for illness or emergency beyond the student's control.
4. Must attend three-fourths of all practice sessions throughout the season.
5. Must attend all the games throughout the entire season.
6. Must have played in at least one-half of the games throughout the season.

WINTER SPORTS

Boys' Basketball

1. Student must meet all academic eligibility and good citizenship criteria as provided for in C.C.S.D. regulations.
2. The athlete must have completed the entire season.
3. The student must attend all practices unless excused by the coach for illness or an emergency beyond their control.
4. Athlete must play in three-fourths of all varsity quarters.
5. A senior who has played at least two years on the varsity team will automatically earn a letter.
6. All equipment must be turned in.

Girls' Basketball

1. Student must meet all academic eligibility and good citizenship criteria as provided for in C.C.S.D. regulations.
2. The athlete must have completed the entire season.
3. The student must attend all practices unless excused by the coach for illness or an emergency beyond their control.
4. Good sportsmanship should be exhibited at all times on and off the court.
5. Must be in at least 28 quarters of play of one minute or more during the regular season.

Wrestling

1. Student must meet all academic eligibility and good citizenship criteria as provided for in C.C.S.D. regulations.

2. The athlete must have completed the entire season.

3. The student must attend all practices unless excused by the coach for illness or an emergency beyond their control.

4. Score 20 or more team points on the following scale:

> 6–Pin, Forfeit, Default
> 5–Superior Decision
> 4–Major Decision
> 3–Decision
> 2–Draw
> 1–Loss by Decision
> 0–Loss by Pin

5. Place in the top four of a varsity tournament.

6. Take first place in the junior varsity zone tournament.

7. Follow all N.I.A.A. rules for athletes.

Bowling

1. Student must meet all academic eligibility and good citizenship criteria as provided for in C.C.S.D. regulations.

2. The athlete must have completed the entire season.

3. The student must attend all practices unless excused by the coach for illness or an emergency beyond their control.

4. Must bowl in a minimum of one-half of the league games plus one game or:

5. Must bowl the required number of games to bowl in championship roll offs and must participate in the championship games.

Soccer

1. Student must meet all academic eligibility and good citizenship criteria as provided for in C.C.S.D. regulations.

2. The athlete must have completed the entire season.

3. The student must attend all practices unless excused by the coach for illness or an emergency beyond their control.

4. Athlete must participate in at least three-fourths of all matches and play at least forty minutes of each eighty minute match played.

5. All equipment must be turned in.

SPRING SPORTS

Baseball

1. Student must meet all academic eligibility and good citizenship criteria as provided for in C.C.S.D. regulations.

2. The athlete must have completed the entire season.

3. The student must attend all practices unless excused by the coach for illness or an emergency beyond their control.

4. Must complete or participate in at least one-third of the total innings played by the team during the regular league season. This means that a player would need to appear in at least forty-six innings during our twenty game league season.

5. All equipment must be turned in.

Boys' Golf

1. Student must meet all academic eligibility and good citizenship criteria as provided for in C.C.S.D. regulations.

2. The athlete must have completed the entire season.

3. The student must attend all practices unless excused by the coach for illness or an emergency beyond their control.

4. Score must count in at least six dual matches.

5. Must have 97% practice attendance record.

Softball

1. Student must meet all academic eligibility and good citizenship criteria as provided for in C.C.S.D. regulations.

2. The athlete must have completed the entire season.

3. The student must attend all practices unless excused by the coach for illness or an emergency beyond their control.

4. Athletes must turn in all uniforms and equipment issued during the season.

Boys' and Girls' Track

1. Student must meet all academic eligibility and good citizenship criteria as provided for in C.C.S.D. regulations.

2. The athlete must have completed the entire season.

3. The student must attend all practices unless excused by the coach for illness or an emergency beyond their control.

4. The athlete must be in good standing with the school administration and the coaches in the track program to be eligible for an award.

5. All checked out equipment must be returned or, if lost, paid for to be eligible for an award.

6. Any athlete who enrolls in school after the season is underway, but in the opinion of his coaches that his performances would warrant an award had he been in this school all year will be eligible for an award.

7. Any athlete, who in the opinion of the track and field coaching staff, whose efforts were instrumental in the success enjoyed by the team, shall be considered for an award.

8. Any athlete can qualify for a letter award by accumulating 15 points in varsity competition.

Hall of Fame...

The High School Athletic Department maintains a Hall of Fame to honor students who have distinguished themselves in athletics either while attending high school or college. The entire coaching staff, at the end of each sports season will review the season and approve of any boys or girls who are eligible to have their pictures placed in the Hall of Fame. The following criteria will be used by the coaching staff in choosing prospective athletes for this honor:

1. Students must have fulfilled all obligations to school and squad at all times.

2. Students must be acceptable citizens and a credit to community and school.

3. Students must have met the minimum requirement of being an all-League selection.

4. Students must receive a two-thirds vote of the coaching staff. In the event that an all-League student does not receive the accepted number of votes of coaches, due to deficient citizenship, the picture will be withheld until the cause can be reviewed during the following year.

5. Pictures will not be placed in the Hall of Fame until the week just prior to graduation.

6. A student not so honored in high school, but who participates in athletics and is honored in college, will be considered and reviewed by the coaching staff for the Hall of Fame subsequent to the awarding of the college honor.

7. Team pictures will be placed in the Hall of Fame whenever a squad wins the League Championship or a higher honor. Teams which have enviable records may be placed in the Hall of Fame if they receive the unanimous vote of the coaching staff.

information sheet on ...

WAIAKEA HIGH SCHOOL
ATHLETIC DEPT.

PLAYER AWARD INFORMATION: To be submitted upon completion of season

COACH: _____ SPORT: _____ DATE SUBMITTED: _____

Name	Grade	Yrs of Var Exp	1st awd	2d awd	3d awd	4th awd	Scholar Athlete

varsity letter requirements...

General Requirements for Athletic Letters

All athletes must comply with the following to be eligible to receive an athletic letter. The criteria mentioned below are designed to insure that an honest effort is taken to upgrade the quality of the performance of the individual athlete's participation in interscholastic sports at Chaparral High School.

1. The athletes must meet the Nevada Interscholastic Activities Association and the Southern Zone Conference requirements.
2. The sport must be approved and sponsored by the Clark County School District.
3. The sport must be coached by a paid coach employed by the Clark County School District.
4. Eligibility and training rules must be observed by the coach and must take place at least four or five (5) school days per school week.
5. The organized practice sessions must be conducted and supervised by the coach for four (4) or five school days.
6. The practice session must be at least two (2) hours. Team meetings may be considered as practice time.
7. The number of interscholastic events shall not be less than eight (8). Girls may have less if approved by the conference.
8. The athlete must satisfactorily complete the season.

Specific Requirements for Athletic Awards

To comply with the requirements for earning a letter at Chaparral it is necessary for the coach of each sport to turn in a list of eligible receivers to the athletic administrator at the end of the season. This is to be accompanied with the amount of time played as required under the specific requirements. If a person is submitted for an award and has not complied with the general and specific requirements for the letter, a written explanation from the coach stating the reason for the recommendation is required. LETTERS ARE AWARDED FOR VARSITY COMPETITION ONLY!

varsity letter award (sample)...

Carlsbad Junior High School
Letter Award

This is to Certify that _____

has been awarded the School Letter in _____

for the season of _____

Principal _____   Coach _____

Broncos   **Ponies**   **Colts**   **Mustangs**

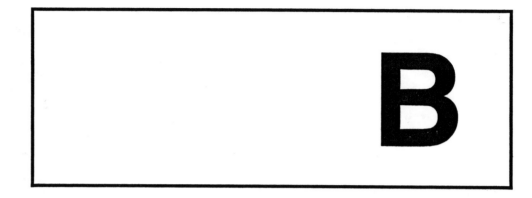

BASEBALL

See Also: EQUIPMENT; SCOUTING; SOFTBALL; UNIFORM

announcer's form for...

See: ANNOUNCERS' FORMS

award criteria for...

See: AWARDS

schedule (sample)...

CARLSBAD HIGH SCHOOL
JUNIOR VARSITY BASEBALL SCHEDULE
19XX

DATE	DAY	OPPONENT	PLACE	TIME
March 7	Thursday	Pecos Tournament	Pecos	TBA
9	Saturday	Pecos Tournament	Pecos	TBA
12	Tuesday	Hobbs	Carlsbad	3:30–5:30 p.m.
16	Saturday	Carlsbad Tournament	Carlsbad	10:00–1:00–4:00
23	Saturday	Clovis	Clovis	1:00–3:00 p.m.
30	Saturday	Eunice	Eunice	10:00–12:00
April 6	Saturday	Alamogordo	Carlsbad	1:00–3:00 p.m.
9	Tuesday	Artesia	Artesia	4:00–6:00 p.m.
13	Saturday	Hobbs	Hobbs	1:00–3:00 p.m.
20	Saturday	Clovis	Carlsbad	1:00–3:00 p.m.
27	Saturday	Roswell	Roswell	1:00–3:00 p.m.

season record form...

BASEBALL RECORD FORM
SEASON: SPRING, 19_____

PLACEMENT IN CONFERENCE: _____ PLACEMENT IN DISTRICT/DIVISION: _____

VARSITY				J.V.			
		SCORE				SCORE	
DATE	OPPONENT	HOME	OPP.	DATE	OPPONENT	HOME	OPP.

TOTALS: WIN _____ LOSE _____   TOTALS: WIN _____ LOSE _____

HONORS AND AWARDS: _____

_____

_____

COACHES: VARSITY _____

_____

J.V. _____

_____

BASKETBALL

    See Also: CONTEST; SCOUTING; SEASON; TOURNAMENT

    announcer's form for...

        See: ANNOUNCERS' FORMS

    award criteria...

        See: AWARDS

    game checklist...

GAME: _____ TIME: _____ DATE: _____

<u>VISITING TEAM:</u>
    Seating Reserved for Visitors   _____
    Visiting Team Facilities Ready   _____
    Towels and Other Amenities   _____

<u>OFFICIALS:</u>
    Room for Officials Ready   _____
    Officials Notified of Times and Places   _____
    Payment of Officials Arranged   _____

<u>MEDIA:</u>
    Game Announcer Notified   _____
    Announcers' Script Prepared   _____
    News Media Accommodations Prepared   _____
    Filming Crew Arrangements Made   _____
    Game Programs Ready for Distribution   _____

<u>AUDITORIUM:</u>
    Security Arrangements Made   _____
    Timer Notified   _____
    Scorer Notified   _____
    Any "Special Seating" Arranged   _____
    Doctor and/or Medical Personnel   _____
    Tickets and Ticket Personnel   _____
    Half-Time Program Arranged   _____
    Concessions Notified and Arranged   _____

<u>OTHER:</u>
_____

_____

_____ _____

performance sheet for...

"BASKETBALL PROFILE" STATISTICS SUMMARY

TEAM: _____ VS. _____ AT: _____ SCORE: _____ OBSERVED: _____

Player Name	Field Goals			Free Throws			Total PTS.	Rebounds			Errors			Good Plays			Fouls
	SA	SM	PCT.	SA	SM	PCT.		OFF.	DEF	TOT	Pa	VI	Fum	Ball	Rec.	Asst	
TOTALS:																	

season record form...

BASKETBALL SEASON
19_____–19_____

	VARSITY				J.V.		
		SCORE				SCORE	
DATE	OPPONENT	HOME	OPP	DATE	OPPONENT	HOME	OPP.

TOTALS: WINS _____ LOSSES _____   TOTALS: WINS _____ LOSSES _____

CONFERENCE PLACEMENT: _____   DIVISION/DISTRICT PLACEMENT: _____

HONORS: _____

_____

_____

COACHES: VARSITY _____

_____

J.V. _____

_____

team rosters...

See: ROSTERS

tournament...

See: TOURNAMENT

BEHAVIOR POLICY

See Also: CODE; ELIGIBILITY; POLICIES AND PROCEDURES

citizenship rating form...

_____ | I plan to attend the above school as a ninth grader
Last name, First

_____
School

TO ALL APPLICANTS:

1. Please read the information on the first page regarding the reasons for the selection of only highly qualified students and the process by which they are chosen. After careful consideration, sign below if you wish to pursue this office and are aware of the obligations it involves.

_____
Student's signature

2. Take this form to the teacher of each class in which you are now enrolled for his/her rating then return to your school counselor by June 1.

Teacher: Please rate characterists below
according to the scale at the right.

Scale:
1 = outstanding
2 = good
3 = average
4 = poor
5 = unacceptable

Subject	Attendance: Number of days absent	Observes rules Cooperation	Leadership	Effort	Dependability	Relationship with Peers	(For use by sponsor) TOTAL	Teacher's Signature and Comments
Social Studies								
Language Arts								
Reading/Foreign Language								
Math								
Science								
Phys. Education								
Other (Please indicate)								

GRAND TOTAL _____

TO ALL ADVISORS: Convert number of days absent to a rating of 1-5. Total for each subject.

Grand total divided by number of teachers rating = Average Citizenship Score _____

Counselor/Administrator Comment _____

_____   _____

BID SURVEY

See Also: BUDGET; EXPENSES; ORDERING; REQUESTS AND REQUISITIONS

form for (sample page)...

BID #84-85-8-4
Athletic Bid Summary

ITEM # QUANTITY DESCRIPTION	M & W	CARLSBAD SPORT SUPPLY	GARDENSWARTZ	BAUM'S
#45 6 Each Plastic Tops	$11.84/Each $71.04/Total Cliff Keen D103	$11.45/Each $68.70/Total Cliff Keen D103	NO BID	$10.71/Each $64.26/Total Betlin MCON-S25
#46 12 Each Reversible Singlets	$11.84/Each $142.08/Total Cliff Keen RS77	$11.45/Each $137.40/Total Cliff Keen RS77	NO BID	$12.98/Each $155.76/Total Betlin MWCR-90
#47 24 Pair Wrestling Knee Pads	$7.10/Pair $170.40/Total Cliff Keen K47	$7.02/Pair $168.48/Total Cliff Keen K47	NO BID	$7.72/Pair $185.28/Total Cliff Keen/K47
#48 1 ONLY Wrestling Face Guarde	$22.60/Total Cliff Keen F63	$22.87/Total As Specified	NO BID	$23.96/Total As Specified
#49 24 Pair Athletic Socks	$1.50/Pair $36.00/Total Tex-Sox C1243	$1.59/Pair $38.24/Total Twin City #TCSPK	NO BID	$1.25/Pair $30.00/Total Hole in None 2484S
#50 20 Dozen Golf Balls	NO BID	NO BID	NO BID	NO BID

BOOSTER/PEP CLUBS

See Also: BULLETINS; FUND RAISING; VISITING SCHOOLS

Information sheet...

1. Trophies will be awarded as follows:
   A. 1st-2nd-3rd and Consolation in 5th grade boys and girls and 6th grade boys and girls.
   B. An Offensive player of the tournament in each division will be awarded a medal. (5th grade boys and girls and 6th grade boys and girls.) Haskell Booster Club members will make this selection.
   C. The Defensive player of the tournament in each division will be awarded a medal. (5th grade boys and girls and 6th grade boys and girls.) Haskell Booster Club members will make this selection.
   D. A team Sportsmanship trophy will be awarded by the Haskell Booster Club.
   E. The winning coach in each division will be awarded a plaque. (5th grade boys and girls and 6th grade boys and girls.)
2. Coaches from Haskell High School and Booster Club Members will be used as officials except in the finals when registered officials will be used.
3. A hospitality room for coaches and administrators will be provided each night.
4. Basketballs will be provided.
5. Players will be introduced in the finals.
6. Two members of the Haskell High School Girls' Basketball team will be assigned to each team to provide chalk, towels, and refreshments at half-time.
7. Admission—$1.00 for Adults and Students.
8. No changes or substitutions will be allowed on the scorebooks after the first game.
9. A concession stand will be available.
10. No Tobacco or Drinks allowed in the gym area.
11. If a team is fifteen (15) minutes late, that team must forfeit the game.
12. Dressing room assignments will be posted on the master tournament bracket.
13. Coaches—please remind your players not to leave valuables in the dressing rooms.
14. Each team will be allowed five (5) minutes to warm up between games. There will be three (3) minute half times.

BOWLING

awards...

See: AWARDS

BUDGET

See Also: EXPENSES; ORDERING; POLICIES AND PROCEDURES; REQUESTS AND PROCEDURES; VOUCHER

allocation request form...

See: REQUESTS AND REQUISITIONS

athletic budget forms (two examples)...

CARLSBAD JUNIOR HIGH SCHOOL   ACCOUNT _____
ACTIVITY BUDGET 19____–19____   SPONSOR _____

GENERAL ACCOUNTS

ANTICIPATED RECEIPTS: (Itemized)

Athletic Events and Guarantees:

Concerts, Musicals and Plays:

Dances and Suppers:

Sales: (Concessions, yearbooks, etc.)

Student Dues:

TOTAL ANTICIPATED RECEIPTS _____

– –

ESTIMATE EXPENDITURES: (Itemized)

Athletic Apparel and Supplies:

Athletic Medical Expenses:

Athletic Officials:

Awards:

Dues and Fees:

Productions, Suppers, and Dances:

Supplies and Printing:

Miscellaneous:

Total

Lodging, Meals and Transportation:

Destination	Type	Days	Cost	Number of Sponsors/ Students	Cost of Lodging	Cost of Meals
		Total		Total		

TOTAL ESTIMATED EXPENDITURES _____

* * * * *

MUSKOGEE HIGH SCHOOL
BUDGET FORM FOR ATHLETICS

Sport Requesting Budget

	AMOUNT REQUESTED	AMOUNT TO BE BUDGETED
1. EQUIPMENT:	_____	_____
2. COACHING SUPPLIES:	_____	_____
3. SUNDRY ITEMS:	_____	_____
4. TRAVEL TO GAMES AND SCRIMMAGES:	_____	_____
5. SCOUTING & MEALS:	_____	_____
6. OFFICIALS:	_____	_____
7. MEALS FOR TEAMS:	_____	_____
8. MISCELLANEOUS:	_____	_____
TOTALS:	_____	_____

Signature of Coach, Date

Please attach an itemized list for each of the above items.

All expenditures are subject to direct examination by Jim Buchanan, Principal and
J. R. Johnson, Assistant Principal in charge of Athletics.

J. D. Buchanan	Date	J. R. Johnson	Date

BULLETINS

See Also: ANNOUNCEMENTS; FLIERS; MEMOS

sample athletic information bulletin...

HEAVENER PUBLIC SCHOOLS
DALE ELLIOTT, Superintendent
P.O. Box 698
HEAVENER, OKLAHOMA 74937

HEAVENER WOLVES INFORMATION BULLETIN

Colors: Purple & Gold (Heavener wears Purple at home; White on the road)

Head Football Coach: Johnnie Gragg

Assist. Coaches: Jack Terry
Rod Turney
Marty Rogers
Danny Edwards

Football Team:	Visiting team will dress in the dressing room at the North end of the field (old gym).
Bus Parking:	An area will be reserved for all busses of the visiting team on the East side of the football stadium, behind the visitors' bleachers. All busses will need to enter the stadium via the East gate.
Band:	Visiting bands in uniform will be admitted free at the East gate. An area on the North end of the visitors' bleachers will be reserved for the band.
Pep Club:	Visiting Pep Clubs will be charged 50¢ per member in uniform, in a group, and accompanied by a sponsor. Pep Club busses will be permitted to enter the East gate without unloading members. The sponsor should collect from each member and turn it in to the East gatekeepers. Cheerleaders are admitted free. An area on the North end of the visitors' bleachers will be reserved for the Pep Club.

General Admission:

High School . . . . Adults -$2.50
Student-$1.00

Jr. Varsity . . . . Adults -$1.00
Student-$1.00

Jr. High . . . . Adults -$1.50
Student-$1.00

Administration:

Superintendent - Dale Elliott ... 653-4436
H.S. Principal - James McMillin 653-4307

BUS

See Also: TRANSPORTATION; TRAVEL AND TRIPS

pick-up schedule form...

MEMORANDUM
DEPARTMENT OF EDUCATION
WAIAKEA

_____
School or Division

To _____ Date: _____

From _____ Subject __Bus Pick-up times__

Date: Site: Veh: Pick-up time:

_____   _____   _____   _____

_____   _____   _____   _____

_____   _____   _____   _____

_____   _____   _____   _____

_____   _____   _____   _____

_____   _____   _____   _____

_____   _____   _____   _____

COMMENTS:

trip information form...

See: TRANSPORTATION, TRAVEL, AND TRIPS

trip permit...

See: TRANSPORTATION, TRAVEL, AND TRIPS

CASH FUND

ledger form...
(see next page)

CERTIFICATES

See: AWARDS

CHECK REQUISITION FORM

See: REQUESTS AND REQUISITIONS

CHEERLEADERS

parental permission form...

See: PERMISSIONS

tryout form for...
(see page 63)

LEDGER FORM

ACCOUNT TITLE

ACCOUNT NO.

| DATE | RECEIVED FROM OR PAID TO | PURPOSE | FOLIO | ACCT. NO. | TOTAL-TO-DATE | | BAL. FWD. |
					RECEIPTS	PAYMENTS	ACCOUNT BALANCE

SAMPLE CHEERLEADING TRYOUT FORM

Rating Scale   1 = Excellent
2 = Good
3 = Average
4 = Poor
5 = Unacceptable

| | GROUP CHEER | | | | INDIVIDUAL CHEER | | | | | JUMPS | | | GYM-NASTICS | | To be completed by sponsor | To be completed by sponsor | |
	Group Coordination	Enthusiasm	Smoothness	Leg & Arm Motion	Neatness (General Appearance)	Poise/Carriage	Body Coordination	Voice	Facial Expression	Elbow	Spread Eagle	Herkie	Cartwheel/Round-Off	Splits (Full or Dance)	Composite Academic Score (5 = best possible)	Average Citizenship Score (6 = best possible)	TOTAL POINTS
#1																	
#2																	
#3																	
#4																	
#5																	
#6																	
#7																	

COACHES

See Also: ASSISTANT COACH; ATHLETIC DIRECTOR; COACHING STAFF; HEAD COACH; SPECIFIC SPORT

application for ...

NAME: _____

ADDRESS: _____

Social Security #: _____ Phone #: _____ Date: _____

EDUCATIONAL BACKGROUND

	Name and Location	Graduation Date
High School	_____	_____
College	_____	_____
	_____	_____

College Major(s) _____ College Minor(s) _____

OTHER EDUCATION: _____

SPORTS EXPERIENCE AND PARTICIPATION

	Name and Location	Year(s)	Letter
High School	_____	___	___
	_____	___	___
	_____	___	___
College	_____	___	___
	_____	___	___
	_____	___	___

ANY RELATED ACTIVITIES AND/OR EXPERIENCES
(Include sports, community and recreational work, etc.)

_____
_____
_____

ANYTHING YOU FEEL SHOULD BE CONSIDERED IN EVALUATING THIS APPLICATION:

_____
_____
_____
_____

REFERENCES
(Give Name, Title, Address, Phone Number)

1. _____
2. _____
3. _____

PLEASE ANSWER ALL OF THE FOLLOWING QUESTIONS:

Do you hold a valid state health certificate? _____

Do you hold a valid state teaching certificate? _____

What is your citizenship? _____

18 years of age or older? _____

Are you available for an interview? _____

Most convenient time for interview? _____

associations...

PARTNERS IN
PROFESSIONAL PROGRESS

Memberships are available in two separate, national organizations formed through the National Federation of State High School Associations to serve the professional needs of the men and women who coach and/or officiate interscholastic athletics throughout the nation.

NATIONAL FEDERATION INTERSCHOLASTIC OFFICIALS ASSOCIATION (NFIOA) — An organization founded on the principles of professional growth and service for the high school sports official.

NATIONAL FEDERATION INTERSCHOLASTIC COACHES ASSOCIATION (NFICA) — An organization featuring specialized services and benefits that are tailored to the interests and needs of the high school coach.

Administered by high school coaches and officials in cooperation with the National Federation and state associations, the two organizations utilize an extensive committee structure to insure "grass roots" involvement and a viable communication path from the local, state and national levels.

Rather than being extraneous to the state and national bodies that have responsibility and authority for the administration of high school sports, NFIOA and NFICA are integral parts in the operation of these associations. In short, membership in the NFIOA and NFICA means active professional growth and participation on the inside, instead of on the outside looking in.

LINES OF COMMUNICATION

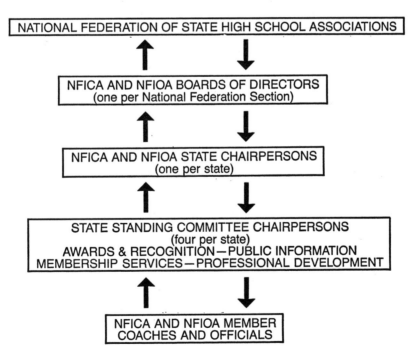

checklist for (two examples)...

COACHES CHECKLIST

___ 1. Roster for grade checks (eligibility) to be submitted to the AD day after turn outs.

___ 2. Physical exam cards completely filled out (Dr., parent's/student's signature, insurance) and collected prior to practice.

___ 3. Coaches/parent meeting scheduled no later than 1 week prior to first game. For Library usage, reservations must be made with Mrs. Tsuchiya at the main office.

___ 4. Official team roster with all pertinent information submitted to AD 2 weeks prior to the first game played.

___ 5. Forms required to be filled out and filed with the coach. Forms to be submitted to AD at end of the season.
   ___ NOCSAE form (headgear)
   ___ Parent Authorization for Travel with attachment
   ___ Permission to treat a minor

___ 6. Bus pick up time request to be submitted no later than 1 week prior to 1st game.

___ 7. Accident report forms to be filled out immediately and submitted to the school official.

___ 8. End of season requirements: Due no later than 2 weeks after the end of the season.

___ Athletic inventory	___ Athletic request for next year
___ Athletic Awards list	___ Recommendations for following year
___ Physical cards	___ Return of all keys signed out

   ___ Return of Uniforms — uniforms should be cleaned, folded and submitted by the coaches.

___ 9. Fund Raisers/Travel Requests due by June 1st for the following year.

* * * * *

STARTING THE SEASON RIGHT — A COACH'S CHECKLIST
(TAKEN FROM CIF HANDBOOK)

A little effort when you first meet your team will save hours, headaches and serious problems. It is strongly recommended that each coach develop a written hand-out covering the essentials of the season, i.e., practice schedules (holidays, in particular), team rules, required documents, parent information, etc.

The following, in outline form, may suggest topics you would want to include in your hand-out.

1. Parent Awareness

a. Practice Schedules	e. Insurance Information
b. Team Rules	f. Physical Exam Information
c. Parent Activities	g. Permission Forms
d. Transportation Policy	h. Eligibility Rules

2. NIAA, District and School Regulations

a. Who May Participate
b. Physical Exams
c. Medical Insurance
d. League Rules—Re: Practice and Games
e. Scrimmage—Definitions and Limits
f. Practice Days Allowed and Required
g. Practice Prohibitions—i.e., age, level, sport
h. Game Limits
i. Non-NIAA Contests
j. Supervision at Contests

3. Eligibility Requirements

a. Academic
b. Age
c. All Star Competition
d. Amateur Standing
e. Awards
f. Enrollment/Semesters/Participation
g. Exhibitions and skill contests
h. Ineligibles cannot compete
i. Outside Competition
j. Residential and Transfer Rules
k. Senior Privileges (No Such Thing)
l. Unofficial Competition (illegal!)
m. School Rules

contract for...

See: CONTRACTS

"creed"...

All coaches will follow the Nebraska Coaches Creed which reads:

I BELIEVE Interschool sports have an important place in the general educational scheme and pledge myself to cooperate with others in the field of education to so administer them that their values shall never be questioned.

I BELIEVE the other coaches of Interschool sports are earnest in their desire to keep the Interschool program high on the plane of citizenship training and I shall do all that I can to further their efforts.

I SHALL abide by the rules of the game in letter and spirit.

I BELIEVE in the exercise of all the patience, tolerance, and diplomacy at my command in my relations with all players, co-workers, game officials, and spectators.

I BELIEVE proper administration of all sports offers effective laboratory methods of development of high ideals of sportsmanship, qualities of cooperation, courage, unselfishness and self-control, desires for clean, healthful living and respect for wise discipline and authority.

I BELIEVE these admirable characteristics, properly instilled by me through teaching and demonstration, will have a long carry-over and will aid each one connected with the sport to become a better citizen.

I BELIEVE in and will support all reasonable moves to improve athletic conditions, to provide for adequate equipment, and to promote the welfare of an increased number of participants.

evaluation of...

See: EVALUATION

volunteer...

VOLUNTEER COACHING APPLICATION

NAME _____ Age _____ Wt. _____ Ht. _____

ADDRESS _____

POSITION APPLYING FOR: _____

1. High School Attended: _____ Yrs. _____

2. List high school sports participation record:

Sports Participation	Years	Letters Earned
A. _____	_____	_____
B. _____	_____	_____
C. _____	_____	_____
D. _____	_____	_____

3. College attended: _____ Major _____ Minor _____

   Yrs. _____

4. College sports participation:

	Years	Letters Earned
A. _____	_____	_____
B. _____	_____	_____
C. _____	_____	_____

5. Sports Participation other than college: Year

    A. _____   _____

    B. _____   _____

    C. _____   _____

6. List any paid experiences in sports, recreation or physical activities: Year

_____   _____

_____   _____

7. Do you have a valid First Aid Certificate? _____ If so, Date _____ No. _____

REFERENCES: Give name and address. (School district certificated personnel preferred.)

1. _____

2. _____

3. _____

Return to: Director of Athletics

COACHING STAFF

See Also: ATHLETIC DEPARTMENT; COACHES; EVALUATION; NUMBER OF STUDENTS PER COACHING STAFF

information sheet on ...

WAIAKEA HIGH ATHLETICS

RE: COACHING STAFF INFORMATION (To be submitted as soon as possible)

SPORT: _____

Name	SSN	Address	Phone	W-2 Marital	Depen.	Exemp.	Shirt Size

SUBMITTED BY: _____ DATE: _____

roster and credentials of ...

NEW MEXICO ACTIVITIES ASSOCIATION
Box 8407
Albuquerque, New Mexico 87198

ATHLETIC COACHING STAFF

SCHOOL   CARLSBAD JUNIOR HIGH SCHOOL

Each person engaged in coaching, girls or boys, in any phase of the athletic program must have a valid New Mexico Teaching Certificate. Please list each person and give their certificate number and type.

NAME	TEACHING CERTIFICATE	(Type and Number)

SIGNED _____

DATE _____

Please return to:

New Mexico Activities Association
Box 8407
Albuquerque, New Mexico 87198
DEADLINE: MUST BE POSTMARKED BY OCTOBER 15 OF CURRENT SCHOOL YEAR.

salary criteria of (two examples)...

DEMANDS MADE ON COACHES IN VARIOUS HIGH SCHOOL SPORTS

—A WEIGHTED COMPARISON TO BE USED IN ADJUSTING POINTS FOR SALARY SCHEDULE (based upon a survey made in 1973 of 15 athletic directors, representing 47 AAA high schools from all regions of the State of Washington.)

CRITERIA

(most often used in determining coaching salaries)

1. Hours involved in the sport
2. External pressures from spectators and the community
3. Number of participants to supervise
4. Degree of experience essential for the assignment
5. Equipment and facilities to supervise
6. Risk of injury to the participants
7. Environmental factors related to the sport

The scorecard listed 16 factors under the seven general areas. Points from 9 (highest) to 0 (lowest) were assigned to each factor in each of nine sports. A total of 144 was the maximum possible points any sport could receive.

* * * * *

CRITERIA FOR POINT WEIGHTING—COACHES' SALARIES

1. Student Time: Practice; dressing time; performance time; travel time.

1–30 hours = 1 pt.	151–180 hours = 6 pt.
31–60 " = 2 pt.	181–210 " = 7 pt.
61–90 " = 3 pt.	211–240 " = 8 pt.
91–120 " = 4 pt.	241–270 " = 9 pt.
121–150 " = 5 pt.	271– " = 10 pt.

2. Student Load per Coach: The number of coaches involved in the activity will be divided into the total number of students participating.

28+ = 4 pt.   11–18 = 2 pt.
19–27 = 3 pt.   1–10 = 1 pt.

3. Community Exposure to the Sport:

High = 7 pt.   Average = 3 pt.
Above Avg. = 5 pt.   Some = 1 pt.

4. Preparation Time: before season starts; scouting time; week-end and holiday time; time involved after season ends.

High = 7 pt.   Average = 3 pt.
Above Avg. = 5 pt.   Some = 1 pt.

5. Equipment Management:

High = 4 pt.
Average = 2 pt.
Some = 1 pt.

6. Assistants Supervised on a Regular Basis:

3 or more = 3 pt.
2 = 2 pt.
1 = 1 pt.

7. Skill Knowledge Necessary for Coaching the Sport:

High = 5 pt.
Average = 3 pt.
Some = 1 pt.

8. Travel Supervision:

Exceptional Amount = 3 pt.
Average Amount = 2 pt.
Some = 1 pt.

CODE

See Also: ATHLETE; BEHAVIOR POLICY

of ethics (two examples)...

CHAPARRAL HIGH SCHOOL CODE OF ETHICS

As a member of my school, I pledge myself

To demonstrate courtesy by

showing respect for the rights, privileges,
  and safety of fellow students and adults;
having proper hall conduct;
always being polite.

To aim for higher academic achievements by

attending school regularly and being on time
  for school and classes unless properly excused;
striving for good study habits;
being efficient in completing assignments;
always being honest and trustworthy in my actions;
setting a reasonable goal and striving to reach it.

To show respect for school property by

treating furniture and facilities as my own;
putting refuse into proper containers.

To practice sportsmanship by

upholding fair play;
being gracious in defeat and modest in victory;
being a worthy representative at all games.

To promote school spirit by

supporting team and cheerleaders;
attending extracurricular activities;
participating in pep rallies;
having pride in, and loyalty to, my school.

* * * * *

We believe that it is the duty of everyone concerned with school athletics to:

1. Stress the values derived from fair play.
2. Show respect for the integrity and judgement calls of officials.
3. Recognize that the purpose of athletics is to promote the physical, moral, mental, social and emotional well-being of the individual participants.
4. Become familiar with the rules of the game and the school's standards for eligibility.
5. View an athletic contest in perspective, as a game rather than a "do or die" effort.
6. Downplay those contingencies which tend to lessen the highest values of the game.
7. Stress the highest ideals of ethical conduct, sportsmanship, and fair play.
8. Show courtesy and respect to all visiting teams and officials.
9. Encourage the development of leadership, initiative, and good judgement in all team members.
10. Establish a cordial and friendly relationship between host team and visiting team.

COMPETITION AGREEMENTS

See: POLICIES AND PROCEDURES

CONSENT FORMS

See: PERMISSIONS

CONSTITUTION

See Also: HANDBOOK; RULES AND REGULATIONS

of a conference (an excerpt)...

HANDBOOK OF THE JUNIOR HIGH SCHOOL BORDER CONFERENCE

FOREWORD

BORDER CONFERENCE HANDBOOK AS REVISED SEPTEMBER 1983

The member schools of the Conference are as follows:

EIGHTH GRADE	NINTH GRADE
Colts-Carlsbad	Lovington
Heizer-Hobbs	Mustangs-Carlsbad
Highland-Hobbs	Heizer-Hobbs
Houston-Hobbs	Highland-Hobbs
Park-Artesia	Houston-Hobbs
Lovington	Park-Artesia

CODE OF ETHICS

This Conference can be no stronger than the spirit of cooperation and agreement that is displayed on the part of its individual members.

CONSTITUTION

Name: The association shall be known as the Border Conference.

Object: It is the purpose of this organization to establish common agreement on rules and regulations pertaining to junior high athletics and to insure harmonious relations among member schools. The conference will sponsor eighth and ninth grade basketball tournaments, annual track meets, and help individual schools facilitate scheduling of games in all sports.

MEETINGS

Organization:

Three annual meetings will be held as follows:

1. On Wednesday immediately following Labor Day
2. On the second Tuesday in December (general business-football schedule)
3. On the Friday before the start of the tournaments during the first week of February. (general business-basketball schedules-basketball tournaments-track schedule)

Special meetings may be called at the discretion of the group by the president.

Each Spring a new president and secretary will assume office at the conclusion of the last regular or special meeting of the year. Both officers will be from the same school. The conference president will be either the principal or vice-principal and the conference secretary will be the athletic coordinator of the school assuming office. It will be the duty of these two officers to conduct all business of the Conference, mail pertinent information to each member school, and serve as treasurer for the Conference. The athletic coordinator of each school shall mail weekly results to the president of the conference. The president will tabulate results and mail copies to each member school. It shall be the responsibility of the secretary to mail three (3) copies of the minutes of each meeting to each member school.

ROTATION

Heizer	81-82	Houston	85-86
Carlsbad	82-83	Lovington	86-87
Highland	83-84	Heizer	87-88
Park	84-85	Carlsbad	88-89

VOTING

Member schools will have one vote in meetings of the Conference. It will be the right of individual schools to designate it's own voting delegate at each meeting. All business and discussion will be open to all representatives of all member schools who attend meetings.

There will be one vote per member school for general business (affecting both teams).

Business affecting only 8th grade or 9th grade voting shall be one vote per team.

AMENDMENTS

A two-thirds majority vote of the member schools of the Conference will be necessary to amend the Constitution and/or By-laws. Each member school shall be entitled to vote.

FUNDS

Gate receipts from any joint event sponsored by the Conference will be retained in a Conference account. The account will be under the direct supervision of the president and secretary. The fund will be used to defray expenses of the Conference or otherwise used as voted upon by the general membership in business meetings. If other funds are needed to hold tournaments, track meets, or carry on Conference business, the expense will be divided equally among the members of the Conference.

General:

Any member school not able to or willing to comply with the rules and by-laws of the Conference may be expelled from the Conference by a two-thirds vote of the member schools.

BY-LAWS

ARTICLE I–Provisions Covering Contests

SECTION I

Officials are to be certified by the state association, when possible.

The Conference will use the same rules for contests as those used by senior high schools in this area with the exception of games as listed below.

SECTION II

Eligibility lists will be exchanged by all Conference schools at the beginning of each season. Lists are to be mailed by September 15 for football, and volleyball, November 15 for basketball, and by March 15 for track. Also include schedule for football, volleyball, and basketball. A self-addressed post card for confirmation of games should be mailed.

SECTION III

Host schools will see that adequate emergency provisions are made to care for possible injuries incurred during contests in their town.

SECTION IV

The maximum number of games in each sport is set by the state activities association. Maximum and minimum limits for contests will be as follows:

Football: Eight minute quarters for 8th and ten minute quarters for 9th grade.

Basketball: Six minute quarters for 7th and 8th grade and eight minute quarters for 9th grade.

Volleyball: Two out of three games; 15 points; win by two.

Agreements reached on tournaments and track meets are attached in the special appendices. These events will be conducted in accordance with the wishes of the Conference as indicated in the appendices. If changes are voted by the Conference, it will be the responsibility of the president to mail corrected copies to all member schools.

CONTEST

See Also: ACTIVITIES; OFFICIALS; PARTICIPATION

cancellation of a ...

CANCELLATION OF CONTESTS

1. Any coach wishing to cancel an athletic contest shall notify the Athletic Director.
2. It shall be the duty of the Athletic Director to cancel the contest, whether an away or home game.
3. The Athletic Director shall at once contact the coach of the opposing team.
4. The Transportation Department shall then be notified.
5. The Administration of the home school shall be notified and directed to announce the cancellation.
6. Officials for the contest shall be notified.
7. Local radio stations shall be notified, and if cancellation is one day or more prior to the contest, local newspapers shall also be notified.
8. These same procedures, in the same order, shall apply to a game cancelled by the opposing team coach.

number of ...

Length of Season, Number of Practices and Contests

Sport	Length of Season	Number of Practices	Number of Contests
Football	7.5 weeks	27	6
Basketball	9 weeks	30	9
Gymnastics	6.5 weeks	26	4
Swimming	6.0 weeks	22	5
Track	7.5 weeks	28	6
Volleyball	7 weeks	26	9
Wrestling	7.5 weeks	30	5-6

CONTRACTS

See Also: ACCEPTANCE; PARTICIPATION

for a coach ...

THIS AGREEMENT made this ____ day of ____, 198__ by and between the WAIAKEA HIGH SCHOOL ATHLETIC DEPARTMENT by JOHN SOSA, Principal, hereinafter referred to as "W.H.S.", and _____ whose address is _____, Hawaii, hereinafter referred to as "Coach",

W I T N E S S E T H:

The parties hereto in consideration of their mutual promises, covenants and conditions agree as follows:

1. Independent Contractor

W.H.S. agrees to appoint Coach as an independent contractor to provide instructions as coach of _____ for the _____ school year.

2. Payment

Coach shall be paid in accordance with the salary schedule for coaches and is based on the G-043-E column on form 435 of the State of Hawaii D.O.E. Allotment for coaches.

3. Athletic Handbook

The Athletic Handbook as amended from time to time shall be made a part hereof by reference and Coach shall abide by all of the terms and conditions of the said handbook. Coach further acknowledges that he has received a copy of the Athletic Handbook and is familiar with all of the terms and conditions of the said Athletic Handbook.

4. Termination of Agreement

This contract shall be for a term of one (1) school year, however, may be terminated prior to its expiration by agreement of the parties. Coach recognizes and agrees that W.H.S. may terminate this agreement based upon an unsatisfactory rating by the Athletic Director of W.H.S. or upon the breach of any of the terms of the agreement.

The execution of this agreement does not vest any rights upon Coach and the agreement may or may not be extended by W.H.S. despite a satisfactory rating by the Athletic Director during the following school year.

5. Best Effort

Coach agrees to use his best effort in executing his obligation as Coach for W.H.S.

WAIAKEA HIGH SCHOOL ATHLETIC
DEPARTMENT

By_____
JOHN SOSA, Principal

_____
Coach

for an athlete

See: ATHLETE

for officials...

See: OFFICIALS

for participants (two examples)...

Oklahoma Secondary School Activities Association
CONTRACT FOR ATHLETIC CONTESTS
(Make in Duplicate)

We, _____ School, party of first part, and _____
School, party of the second part, do this _____ day of _____, 19_____,
contract for _____ games of _____ to be played as follows:
One game at _____, 19_____, and
one game at _____, 19_____.
The home school in each case agrees to pay the visiting team _____

The school cancelling this contract without the consent of the other shall forfeit the sum of $_____ to the offended school.

Both parties agree that the rules of the Oklahoma Secondary School Activities Association are a part of this contract and that the suspension or termination of membership in this Association of either party shall render this contract null and void. Provided that this contract shall not be binding on either party unless a copy, properly signed, is returned to the party of the first part by _____ _____, 19_____,

_____ School,   by _____ Prin., Supt.
           Party of the First Part

_____ School,   by _____ Prin., Supt.
           Party of the Second Part

* * * * *

NEW MEXICO ACTIVITIES ASSOCIATION
CONTRACT FOR ATHLETIC CONTESTS

_____, New Mexico _____, 19_____

This Contract is drawn under the supervision of the New Mexico Activities Association, and must be used in arranging games participated in by schools of this Association.

THIS CONTRACT, Subscribed to by the Principals or Superintendents of the _____ High School and of the _____ High School, is made for _____ games of _____ to be played as follows:

One game at _____ on _____ at _____ P.M.
One game at _____ on _____ at _____ P.M.

All games to be played under the following stipulations:

The _____ High School agrees to pay to the _____ High School the sum of _____ dollars ($_____), and the latter school agrees that this sum shall cover all its claims arising by virtue of this contract.

1. The rules of the New Mexico Activities Association are a part of this contract.

2. The suspension or termination of its membership in the State Association by either of the parties to this contract shall render this contract null and void.

3. All officials used in football and basketball games must be registered by the New Mexico Activities Association and they shall be mutually agreed upon at least five (5) days before the contest.

4. Inter-state games should be scheduled on National Federation State High School Athletic Association contracts which may be obtained free of charge from the Association.

5. Unless otherwise specified, this contract shall call for a first team game.

6. This contract cannot be annulled without the consent of both parties.

7. If either party hereto fails to fulfill the obligation of any part of the contract, that party shall pay to the other party the sum of $_____ as forfeit, the remainder of the contract shall not be binding, and the breach of contract shall be reported to the Association.

Signed	Title	School
Signed	Title	School

CROSS COUNTRY

See Also: ELIGIBILITY; SEASON; TRACK AND FIELD

awards criteria...

See: AWARDS

meet...

See: MEETS

CROWD CONTROL

See: POLICIES AND PROCEDURES

CUSTODIAL ACTION REQUEST

See: REQUESTS AND REQUISITIONS

DANCE, REQUEST FOR

See: REQUESTS AND REQUISITIONS

DISTRICT ATHLETIC PROGRAM

See Also: ATHLETIC DEPARTMENT; ATHLETIC DIRECTOR; HEAD COACH

chain of command structure...

Within our District's Athletic Program, the following chain of command has been established. Except under extraordinary circumstances, individuals must not "skip" a step in the chain. Hopefully, this simple, linear structure will serve well for all necessary communications.

BOARD OF EDUCATION
|
SUPERINTENDENT OF SCHOOLS
|
DISTRICT ATHLETIC DIRECTOR
|
COACHES
|
ASSISTANT COACHES
|
PLAYERS

DUAL AND TRIANGULAR MEETS

See: MEETS

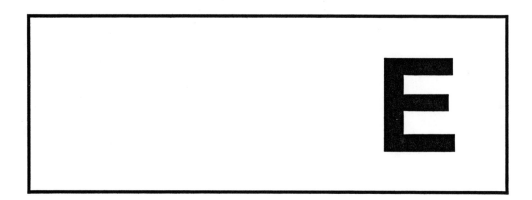

ECKMAN SYSTEM

See: EVALUATION

ELIGIBILITY

See Also: AMATEUR STANDING; ATHLETE; CODE; MEDICAL; POLICIES AND PROCEDURES; RULES AND REGULATIONS; WAIVER; SPECIFIC SPORT

academic progress report (two examples)...

ELIGIBILITY REPORT FOR 9 WEEKS AND 27 WEEKS	
Student _____ No. _____ Class _____	
SUBJECT	GRADE
_____	_____
_____	_____
_____	_____
_____	_____
_____	_____
_____	_____
Declared Eligible _____ Declared Ineligible _____	
Date _____ Asst. Principal _____	

PARKERSBURG HIGH SCHOOL
ATHLETIC DEPARTMENT
9 WEEK and 27 WEEK GRADE PROGRESS REPORT

Student _____ No. _____ Class_____

Subject _____ Teacher _____ Date _____

Progress Report
Current Grade _____

Addresses _____ Dates _____

Comments _____

_____

_____

_____

---

academic requirements for...

Scholastic Eligibility Requirements

This regulation shall apply to all regular education students who represent the schools by participating in any interschool competition or out-of-school or after school performance.

Special education students working for a regular diploma shall be subject to the same eligibility requirements as regular students.

Special education students working for an adjusted diploma or certificate of completion shall have eligibility requirements determined by an IEP committee, under guidelines developed by the Administrative/Special Student Services Division. Such guidelines will provide for consistency in the development and implementation of eligibility standards for special education students.

1. To participate in any interscholastic activity sponsored by the District, an individual must be officially enrolled in a member school of the District.

2. Students in grades 9-11 must be enrolled in courses having a minimum credit value of three (3) units. Students in grade 12 must be enrolled in courses having a minimum credit value of two (2) units.

certificate of (two examples)...

MIDDLETOWN TOWNSHIP PUBLIC SCHOOLS
MIDDLETOWN, NEW JERSEY
PHYSICAL ELIGIBILITY FORM

PLEASE CHECK: ☐ North   ☐ South   ☐ Bayshore   ☐ Thompson   ☐ Thorne

PERMISSION TO ENGAGE IN (Name Sport) _____

STUDENT'S NAME _____ BIRTH DATE _____

ADDRESS _____ TELEPHONE _____

PARENT OR GUARDIAN'S NAME _____

HEALTH QUESTIONNAIRE (Must Be Completed):

1. Has this student been told not to participate in any sport? ☐YES ☐NO
2. Has this student ever been unconscious, lost memory from a blow on the head? ☐YES ☐NO
3. Has this student ever had a fracture or dislocation? ☐YES ☐NO
4. Has this student ever had a knee or ankle sprain? ☐YES ☐NO
5. Is this student under a physician's care now? ☐YES ☐NO
6. Does this student take any kind of medicine every day? ☐YES ☐NO
7. Has this student ever fainted or "blacked out" during hard exercise? ☐YES ☐NO
8. Does this student have allergies? (hay fever, asthma, etc.) ☐YES ☐NO
9. Does this student have any cardiac history? ☐YES ☐NO
10. Has this student ever been in a hospital for an operation or other serious medical reason? ☐YES ☐NO
11. Does this student have a vision or hearing problem? ☐YES ☐NO
12. Is there a history of a family member dying suddenly? ☐YES ☐NO

EXPLAIN BELOW ANY QUESTIONS ANSWERED WITH "YES":

GIRLS: Menstrual Difficulties _____

The answers to the above are correct. I understand that any misrepresentation of any of the information contained herein will result in the student being denied the opportunity to participate. I hereby give my consent to the participation of

_____   in   _____
            (Full Name)   (Sport)

conducted by the school against other schools and within the school. Parents and guardians should be aware that such activity involves the potential for injury which is inherent in all sports. I/we acknowledge that even with the best coaching, use of the most advanced protective equipment and strict observation of rules, injuries are still a possibility. On rare occasions these injuries can be so severe as to result in total disability, paralysis, or even death. I/we acknowledge that I/we have read and understand this warning. I shall assume all responsibility and expense for any injury received in practice or participation. I give my permission for my son/daughter to be diagnosed and treated by the team physician should such service be necessary.

_____   _____
            (Date)   (Parent's or Guardian's Signature)

PHYSICALS AND STUDENT ELIGIBILITY

1. Students have the opportunity for a school physical on a specific date. This slip must be signed and turned into the coach beforehand. You have the right to have the student examined by your own physician at your expense. Medical exam forms are available from the School Nurse, this form must be used. Parents will be notified if the student is rejected in his/her physical.
2. The Middletown Schools eligibility rules are those endorsed by the N.J.S.I.A.A. The following rules are in effect for September 19XX. They are subject to change with rulings by the State Board of Education.
3. A student, in grades 7-12, must pass 23 credits to be eligible for September 19XX. To be eligible for the spring season 19XX, a student must be passing 11½ credits, as of January 31, 19XX.
4. If a student is eligible at the start of the season, he/she remains eligible for the entire sport season. Courses successfully made up during the summer 19XX, can be applied to satisfy requirements for September 19XX.

* * * * *

Oklahoma Secondary School Activities Association
SENIOR HIGH CERTIFICATE OF ELIGIBILITY
Certification to Executive Secretary

The following students are certified as eligible under the rules of the Association for the _____ semester 19 _____ 19 _____ (See Rule 9, Sec. 1; and Rule 3, Sec. 1).

ADDITIONAL CERTIFICATION BETWEEN SENIOR HIGH SCHOOLS
(See Rule 10, Section 2)

I further certify that these students have complied with the attendance regulation and at the close of the week _____ 19 _____ were passing in three solid credit subjects in work accepted for eligibility (See Rule 3, Sec. 1) and are eligible for the _____ contest to be played with _____ High School on _____ at _____.

School Colors _____ Team Nickname _____ Coach _____
Host school has secured the following officials which visitor's representative approved: _____

N-A-M-E Group by classes: Sr., Jr., etc. Alphabetize by last name first. Report boys & girls separately.	District in Which Parents Reside*	BIRTH Mo., Day, Yr. as 5-30-59	Date of first enrollment in ninth grade Mo., Day, Yr. as 9-13-1973	Credits made preceding semester & accepted for eligibility. (See Rule 3, Sec. 1)	IF MIGRANT— Give name of school and city where located	FOR USE ON EXCHANGE LISTS	
						Position	Jersey No.

*If parents reside in a district other than your district, please give the basis of the student's eligibility, such as Rule 8, Section 1 (c) in the "If Migrant" column.

list (two examples)...

JUNIOR HIGH ATHLETIC ELIGIBILITY LIST

School _____ School Number _____

Sport _____ Date _____

We hereby certify that the following students are eligible under the rule listed below:

Cross country, football, basketball, swimming, track, wrestling, and gymnastics for boys, and cross country, volleyball, basketball, swimming, gymnastics and track for girls will be grouped by grade. However, age grouping will be used to the following extent. If a seventh grade student is 14 as of September 1, 19XX, he or she must participate during the year on the eighth grade teams in these sports. An eighth grade student who is 15 as of September 1, 19XX must participate on the ninth grade teams—this applies to all sports. A freshman who becomes 16 before September 1, 19XX shall be ineligible for all freshman athletic competition; however special arrangements may be made that would allow participation on a non-varsity high school team. Please contact the Physical Education Office before making such arrangements.

Only repeat sex and grade if different from first entry line.
TYPE, PRINT OR WRITE LEGIBLY
PLEASE LIST ALPHABETICALLY, BY GRADE, BY SEX

STUDENT NUMBER	STUDENT'S NAME	BIRTHDATE Mo. Day Year	SEX B G	GRADE 7 8 9

I hereby certify that the above report is true and correct.

Terminal Operator _____

Loading Date _____ Terminal No. _____

_____
Administrator

* * * * *

PARKERSBURG HIGH SCHOOL ELIGIBILITY ———————— YEAR ———————— SEMESTER ————————

STUDENT	CL	GPA	4 SUB.	2 MAJORS	PREV. SC.	BIRTH	PARENTS OR GUARDIAN	RESIDENCE

policy on...

See: POLICIES AND PROCEDURES

END-OF-SEASON CHECKLIST

See Also: ATHLETIC DIRECTOR; COACHES; EVALUATION; SPECIFIC SPORT

sample form...

_____ HIGH SCHOOL
COACHES END-OF-SEASON CHECKLIST
(Due two weeks after end of sport season)

SPORT _____

COACH _____

1. All equipment put away and inventory turned in to _____.   —
2. Lost Equipment Form completed and turned in to _____.   —
3. Keys turned in to _____.   —
4. Coaches' lockers cleaned and vacated.   —
5. All team lockers cleaned and vacated, and combination locks turned in to the P.E. Office.   —
6. Sport Season Report completed and turned in to _____.   —
7. Arrangements made with _____ for awards.   —
8. Awards lists turned in to _____ one week prior to awards presentation.   —
    A. List of Varsity letter winners.   —
    B. List of participation certificates.   —
9. Athletic/Activity Budget Form for next year completed and turned in to _____.   —
10. Roll book turned in to _____.   —
11. Coach's evaluation completed and signed by _____.   —

ENTRY BLANKS

See: TOURNAMENT

EQUIPMENT

See Also: INVENTORY; NATIONAL OPERATING COMMITTEE ON STANDARDS FOR
ATHLETIC EQUIPMENT; REQUESTS AND REQUISITIONS; RULES AND
REGULATIONS; UNIFORMS; SPECIFIC SPORT

check-out forms (two examples)...

_____ HIGH SCHOOL
UNIFORM/EQUIPMENT CHECK-OUT CARD

NAME   GRADE PARENT/GUARDIAN

ADDRESS   HOME   PARENT BUSINESS PHONE
                        PHONE

ITEMS:	DATE OUT	DATE IN	SIGNATURE

Fines paid if any

_____

* * * * *

NAME _____
FOOTBALL CHECK-OUT LIST

LOCKER NO. _____   Birth Date _____
Telephone number _____   Home Address _____
Helmet _____
Shoulder Pads _____   Hand Pads _____
Hip Pads _____   Elbow, Arm Pads _____
Knee, Thigh Pads _____   Shoes (size) _____
Game Pants _____   Belt _____
Practice Pants _____   Neck Brace _____
Practice Jersey _____
Game Jersey Home _____
             Away _____

Insurance _____
Physical _____
Parent Permission _____

Signature _____
COMMENTS:

form for lost equipment (two examples)...

DATE: _____

THE FOLLOWING ATHLETE, _____, HAS FAILED TO HAND IN CERTAIN ITEMS OF EQUIPMENT.

EQUIPMENT LOST: _____

PRICE: _____

YOUR NAME HAS BEEN UP ON THE FINE LIST IN THE MAIN OFFICE. IF ARTICLE IS RETURNED, GET A NOTE FROM YOUR COACH, PRESENT IT TO THE MAIN OF-FICE, AND YOUR NAME WILL BE TAKEN OFF THE LIST. YOU MAY NOT PARTICI-PATE IN ANOTHER SPORT UNTIL THIS PROBLEM IS TAKEN CARE OF.

_____,

ATHLETIC DIRECTOR

* * * * *

_____ HIGH SCHOOL

LOST EQUIPMENT FORM

SPORT _____

COACH _____

NAME OF STUDENT	EQUIPMENT LOST/ DAMAGED	REPLACE-MENT COST	DATE PARENT CONTACT	DATE PAID

inventory forms (two examples)...

See Also: INVENTORY; TRACK AND FIELD; UNIFORMS

WAIAKEA HIGH SCHOOL ATHLETIC INVENTORY

SPORT _____ Check One: UNIFORM __ EQUIPMENT XX
COACH _____ DATE _____

Use one sheet for Uniform & one for Equipment ARTICLE	NO. ON HAND	CONDITION			DISCARD NO. TO REPLACE
		GOOD	FAIR	POOR	
E.G. Football helmets (blue)	47	30	7	10	10

* * * * *

INVENTORY SHEET

TEAM NAME _____   LEAGUE _____

DESCRIPTION	NO.	DATE ISSUED	CONDITION	DATE RETURNED	NO.	CONDITION	COMMENTS
Bats, wood							
Bats, alum.							
Balls							
Batting helmets							
Running helmets							
Catchers helmets							
Catchers masks							
Catchers mitts							
Chest protectors							
Shin guards							
Bases							
Base straps							
Base spikes							
First Aid kits							
Cold packs							
Scorebooks							
Misc.							

Manager's Signature _____   Director's Signature _____

notice...

Equipment and Uniforms

1. Athletic equipment is loaned to team members by the Athletic Department.
2. Athletes are responsible for equipment that is issued to them. Any lost items must be paid for by the athlete.
3. School uniforms are not to be used or worn at home or away from school unless on a team trip.
4. All uniforms will be washed and repaired by the Athletic Department.
5. Athletes are entitled to one school towel at a time. Exchange your dirty towel for a clean one.
6. Towel service costs $3.00 per sport and athletes are encouraged to make use of this service. Any athlete playing in three sports will be provided free towel service for the third sport.

return form for...

To the Parents of _____

Our records indicate that the soccer equipment listed below has not been returned. Unless these obligations are taken care of, we will recommend withholding the diploma of senior students and the report card of underclassmen. Please make checks or money orders payable to "Middletown Township Board of Education".

Very truly yours,

Mark Sessa
Soccer Coach

_____ $ _____

EVALUATION

See Also: ATHLETIC DEPARTMENT; OFFICIALS

of athletes...

See: ATHLETES

of coaches...

COACH'S EVALUATION

	Plan for Improvement	Proficient
A. Administration		
1. Care of equipment (issue, inventory, cleaning, etc.)		
2. Organization of staff		
3. Organization of practices		
4. Communication with coaches		
5. Adherence to district and school philosophy and policy (eligibility reports, inventories, budgets, follow-up, scores reported, etc.)		
6. Public relations		
7. Supervision		
B. Skill		
1. Knowledge of fundamentals		
2. Presentation of fundamentals		
3. Conditioning		
4. Game preparation		
5. Prevention and care of injuries (follow-up with parents)		
C. Relationships		
1. Enthusiasm		
a. For working with students		
b. For working with staff (support to other programs)		
c. For working with academic staff		
2. Discipline		
a. Firm but fair		
b. Consistent		

3. Communication with players
   a. Individual
   b. As a team

D. Performance

   1. Appearance of team on field or floor

   2. Execution of team on field or floor

   3. Attitude of team on field or floor

   4. Conduct of coach during game

E. Training and Experience

   1. Knowledge of sport/activity

   2. Education for injury treatment or prevention
     (Current First Aide Certification)

   3. Coaching/sponsoring experience

   4. Teacher certification

   5. Professional growth

   4. Evaluator Comments (Optional) Use
     additional page if necessary

   5. Evaluatee Comments (Optional) Use
     additional page if necessary

Number conferences held and dates: _____

_____   _____   _____   _____
Signature of Evaluatee   Date   Signature of Evaluator   Date

The evaluatee's signature does not mean agreement with the content of evaluation; however, the signature does acknowledge receipt of the evaluation.

of coaches (by the Eckman System)...

The Eckman Evaluation Instrument
A Tool to Evaluate Intercollegiate Athletic Coaches*

by Carol A. Eckman

Introduction

The recent decline of enrollments, escalation of budgetary demands due to inflation, related reduction of faculty and staff, and the strain on financial resources of educational institutions have resulted in an emphasis on accountability in education, and especially in higher education. Accountability has become an ongoing concern in education and, among other things, has led to a demand that there be a rigorous evaluation of teaching effectiveness. Coaches, especially, have become publicly accountable for their productiveness because of the important place that athletics holds in the American culture and the game by game score accountability. Likewise, recently, because of limited mobility of faculty and the demand for increased athletic competition, coaching expertise has become a focal point for administrators responsible for hiring and terminating coaches.

From the thorough review of the literature, it became apparent that a need exists for more attention to be directed toward the development of evaluation procedures to adequately assess coaching effectiveness. To date most of the evaluation of coaches has been done subjectively and informally. In too many instances, the won-loss record has served as the basis for decisions concerning the retention of coaches. An established coaching evaluation process could provide factual data to identify those coaches who are effective in the total coaching process. It could also serve to minimize the frequent use of the won-loss record as the sole measure of coaching effectiveness.

The development of an evaluative instrument could provide the cornerstone for a measuring process. Through appropriate utilization of an evaluative instrument, ineffective coaches could be brought to a more productive level and greater emphasis could be placed on the importance of coaching effectiveness. Clearly stated criteria for evaluation could also play a vital role in helping to eliminate the frequent atmosphere of anxiety and distrust commonly associated with the evaluation process. An evaluative instrument could be beneficial to coaches and administrators because it could provide for objectivity and a balanced emphasis in assessing coaching effectiveness. Additionally, such an instrument could be useful for purposes of self-improvement. A means for gathering factual data is essential for a fair evaluation of coaches.

PURPOSE

The purpose of this study was to develop a viable instrument for the evaluation of intercollegiate athletic coaches through the use of a modified form of the Delphi technique. More specifically, this investigation was designed to identify competency items appropriate for assessing coaching performance based on a consensus of opinion of selected experts.

Eckman Evaluation Instrument (EEI)

Rate the coach using the following scale of 1-5: (1) Hardly Ever,
(2) Occasionally, (3) Generally, (4) Frequently, (5) Almost Always.

A COACH...

Circle the Appropriate Number

I. PERSONAL AND PROFESSIONAL ATTRIBUTES

A. Personal Qualities
  1. Demonstrates self-confidence.   1 2 3 4 5
  2. Is enthusiastic.   1 2 3 4 5
  3. Presents a positive role model for the athlete, i.e., appearance, language, and sportsmanship.   1 2 3 4 5

B. Personal Conduct
  4. Exhibits ethical behavior.   1 2 3 4 5
  5. Maintains emotional control under stress.   1 2 3 4 5
  6. Places the welfare of the athlete above winning and would not sacrifice values/principles to win.   1 2 3 4 5

II. ADMINISTRATIVE PROCEDURAL ABILITIES

A. Practice Organization
  7. Conducts well-planned practice sessions.   1 2 3 4 5
  8. Utilizes the coaching staff competently.   1 2 3 4 5

B. Financial Resources
  9. Adheres to budget policies and procedures.   1 2 3 4 5
  10. Uses any supplemental funds in an accountable manner.   1 2 3 4 5
  11. Works within the constrants of the budget.   1 2 3 4 5

III. KNOWLEDGE AND PRACTICE OF MEDICAL-LEGAL ASPECTS

  12. Exhibits reasonable and prudent conduct in preventing and handling accidents and injuries.   1 2 3 4 5
  13. Follows the advice of the physician/trainer regarding the participation of injured athletes.   1 2 3 4 5
  14. Provides safe playing conditions and protective equipment.   1 2 3 4 5

A COACH...

Circle the Appropriate Number

IV. THEORY AND TECHNIQUES OF COACHING

A. Coaching Methods
  15. Applies knowledge of the skills, techniques and rules of the sport.   1 2 3 4 5
  16. Assists athletes in reaching their fullest potential.   1 2 3 4 5
  17. Demonstrates the ability to analyze and correct errors.   1 2 3 4 5
  18. Demonstrates the ability to teach fundamentals.   1 2 3 4 5
  19. Develops good team spirit and morale.   1 2 3 4 5
  20. Develops self-confidence and determination in athletes.   1 2 3 4 5
  21. Employs sound methods to teach skills and techniques.   1 2 3 4 5
  22. Maintains discipline in a firm and friendly manner.   1 2 3 4 5
  23. Provides an environment that makes participation enjoyable for the athletes.   1 2 3 4 5

B. Strategy
  24. Demonstrates the ability to evaluate the performance of athletes/teams.   1 2 3 4 5
  25. Is knowledgeable of a variety of tactics and strategies.   1 2 3 4 5
  26. Selects appropriate strategies and tactics.   1 2 3 4 5

C. Rules and Regulations
  27. Abides by the rules and regulations of the sport and appropriate governing bodies and complies with the academic policies of the institutions.   1 2 3 4 5
  28. Demonstrates a knowledge of the rules and officiating techniques of the sports.   1 2 3 4 5
  29. Enforces team rules in an equitable and consistent manner.   1 2 3 4 5

A COACH...   Circle the
                                        Appropriate
                                        Number

V. PERSONNEL MANAGEMENT

A. Recruiting
   30. Adheres to the policies and
       procedures of the appropriate
       governing body.   1 2 3 4 5
   31. Demonstrates effective utilization of
       scholarship funds.   1 2 3 4 5
   32. Demonstrates the ability to identify
       potential ability in athletes.   1 2 3 4 5
   33. Effectively uses the monies
       budgeted for recruiting.   1 2 3 4 5
   34. Utilizes a consistent and fair criteria
       in judging athletes' abilities. 1 2 3 4 5

B. Player Coach Relationships
   35. Demonstrates the ability to
       communicate effectively with all
       athletes.   1 2 3 4 5
   36. Develops and maintains a positive
       attitude among athletes.   1 2 3 4 5
   37. Is able to motivate athletes.   1 2 3 4 5
   38. Is concerned about the academic
       achievement of athletes.   1 2 3 4 5
   39. Respects the rights and individual
       differences of athletes as long as it is
       not a detriment to the rest of the
       team.   1 2 3 4 5
   40. Shows concern for the welfare of
       athletes.   1 2 3 4 5

VI. PUBLIC RELATIONS SKILLS
   41. Communicates effectively with
       assistant coaches.   1 2 3 4 5
   42. Cooperates with the athletic director
       in establishing and conducting a
       quality athletic program.   1 2 3 4 5

Possible Score-210   Total Score

seasonal report on coach...

SEASONAL EVALUATION OF COACH

NAME: _____ POSITION: _____ SCHOOL: _____

FOR THE 19___-19___ SEASON   DATE OF THIS EVALUATION:_____

S = Satisfactory   U = Unsatisfactory   NI = Needs Improvement

AREA:	S	U	NI
INTERPERSONAL AND PROFESSIONAL RELATIONSHIPS			
1. with students			
2. with faculty			
3. with school staff			
4. with parents and community			
5. with principal and vice-principal			
6. with athletic director			
7. with public relations personnel			
8. with coaching staff			
9. with team members			
10. with game officials			
11. with opposing coaches and teams			
12. with alumni organizations			
COACHING ABILITIES AND RELATED AREAS			
1. instructional techniques			
2. motivational techniques			
3. adherence to league and district policies			
4. organization of staff and support personnel			
5. evidence of pre-planning			
6. teaching of fundamentals			
7. maintenance of discipline			
8. evidence of professional growth (learning)			
9. supervision of participants (including injuries)			
10. ability to motivate			

COMMENTS: _____

OBSERVER: _____   COACH: _____

EVENTS CARD

See: TRACK AND FIELD

EVENTS VOUCHER

See: VOUCHER

EXAMINATIONS

See Also: ACCIDENT REPORT FORM; INJURY; MEDICAL; PERMISSIONS

health ...

ALASKA SCHOOL ACTIVITIES ASSOCIATION
HEALTH EXAMINATION FORM

(Please Print) LAST NAME   FIRST NAME   MI

Grade _____ Birthdate _____ Age _____ Height _____ Weight _____ Blood Pressure _____

Significant Past Illness or Injury _____

Eyes _____ R 20/_____; L 20/_____; Ears _____ Hearing R _____ /15; L _____ /15;

Respiratory _____ Cardiovascular _____ Liver _____ Spleen _____

Hernia _____ Musculoskeletal _____ Skin _____ Genitalia _____

Neurological _____ Laboratory: Urinalysis (As Needed) _____

Other _____ Comments: _____

Completed Immunizations: DPT _____ Polio _____ Measles _____ Rubella _____
              Date   Date   Date   Date

           Whooping Cough _____ Tuberculosis Tests _____: Results _____
                 Date   Date

I certify that I have on this date examined this pupil and find him (her) physically able to compete in supervised activities NOT CROSSED OUT:

BASKETBALL	CROSS COUNTRY	FOOTBALL	GYMNASTICS	ICE HOCKEY
SKIING	SWIMMING	TRACK	VOLLEYBALL	*WRESTLING

*Weight Loss Permitted To Make Lower Weight Class: Yes___ No___; if 'Yes' May Lose ___ Lbs.

Do you know of any reason why this individual should not participate in all sports? ☐ Yes   ☐ No

If "Yes" please explain _____ ALLERGIES TO MEDICATION? _____

KNOWN MEDICAL CONDITIONS _____ Examining Physician _____

Last Name: _____ First: _____ MI: _____ Grade _____ Birthdate _____ Date of Exam _____

_____

(Name) Last   First   MI

PARENT'S OR GUARDIAN'S PERMISSION

I hereby give my consent for the above student to engage in ASAA or School District approved interscholastic activities as a representative of his/her school, except those crossed out on the reverse side of this form (and if WRESTLING, approval of the weight loss listed) by the examining physician, and I also give my consent for the above named student to accompany the team or group as a member on its out-of-town trips.

I understand the local Board of Education or ASAA does not carry sports or activity insurance and will not assume responsibility for injuries sustained in the inter-school program. I also understand that accident insurance coverage is my responsibility.

Insurance Coverage: /   / Native Services   /   / Military   /   / Family
                /   / None: I will assume financial responsibility for injuries.

CONSENT FOR EMERGENCY TREATMENT FOR INTERSCHOLASTIC ACTIVITY INJURIES

I, _____ , parent or guardian of _____
In consideration of my _____ opportunity to participate in interscholastic activities hereby consent to emergency medical treatment, hospitalization or other medical treatment as may be necessary for the welfare of the above named child, by a physician, qualified nurse, and/or hospital, in the event of injury or illness during all periods of time in which the student is away from his/her normal residence as a member of an interscholastic activity team or group, and hereby waive on behalf of myself and the above named child any liability of the School District, any of its agents or employees, arising out of such medical treatment.

HOME PHONE: _____ EMERGENCY PHONE: _____
DATED IN _____, ALASKA THIS _____ DAY OF _____ _____
                                                    Signature of Parent
                                                     or Guardian

state standard physical form for...

CLARK COUNTY SCHOOL DISTRICT
NEVADA STANDARD PHYSICAL EXAMINATION FORM
(Please do not fold)

(Please Print)
PROGRAMS _____

PARTICIPANT'S NAME _____BIRTH DATE _____SEX _____

CITY _____SCHOOL _____GRADE _____

PARTICIPANT'S ADDRESS _____
                        Street   City   Zip
PARENT'S NAME _____ADDRESS (if different) _____

_____
City   State   Zip   Telephone
FAMILY PHYSICIAN'S NAME _____

ADDRESS _____TELEPHONE _____

FAMILY DENTIST'S NAME _____

ADDRESS _____TELEPHONE _____

                                                                            NO YES

1. Has this participant ever had hospitalization, surgery, or serious medical illness? .... ☐   ☐
2. Is this participant now under the care of a physician or taking medication? .... ☐   ☐
3. Does the participant have any allergies to medications, plants, food, animals, etc.? .... ☐   ☐
4. Has this participant lost consciousness during physical activity, had a concussion or at any
   time had a convulsion? .... ☐   ☐
5. Do you feel that there should be limits on your child's participation in activities because of
   symptoms of ILLNESS, INJURY, or ABNORMALITIES OF FAMILY HISTORY known to you or a
   physician? .... ☐   ☐

IF YOU HAVE ANSWERED ANY QUESTIONS "YES" PLEASE SPECIFY _____

_____

_____

I agree to the participation of my above-named son/daughter in the program/or programs that have been listed above. In addition, I consent to practice sessions and travel to and from the programs. I also agree to emergency treatment as deemed necessary by the medical personnel designated by the program authorities.

STUDENT _____PARENT OR GUARDIAN _____
DATED _____(Permission valid for 365 days unless rescinded.)

PHYSICIAN'S PHYSICAL ASSESSMENT

HEIGHT _____WEIGHT _____B.P. _____PULSE _____DATE _____

1. On the basis of a physical examination and a review of this individual's medical history, I find this individual to be in good health with the following exceptions:

2. This individual may participate in all physical activities with the following limitations:

3. Special instructions, i.e., diet, medications, precautions, allergies:

PHYSICIAN'S SIGNATURE

NAME AND ADDRESS (Please print or stamp)

DATE   TELEPHONE

EXPENSES

See Also: BID SURVEY; BUDGET; FUND RAISING; ORDERING; TELEPHONE; TICKETS; VOUCHER

and income sheet (sport specific)...

SPORT _____ NO. OF PARTICIPANTS _____ YEAR _____

INCOME:
- Gate Receipts _____
- Concessions _____
- Programs _____
- Adult Season Tickets _____
- Student Season Tickets _____
- Reserve Seat Tickets _____
- Pregame Ticket Sales _____
- Donations _____
- Fund Raising _____
- Radio & T.V. Fees _____
- Guarantees _____

TOTAL INCOME _____

EXPENSES:
- Equipment _____
- Laundry and Cleaning _____
- Repair and Reconditioning _____
- First Aid Supplies _____
- Transportation _____
- Meals & Lodging _____
- Officials _____
- Ticket Sellers _____
- Gate Helpers _____
- Police _____
- Film & Camera Person _____
- Other Helpers (Press Box Res. Seats) _____
- Maintenance _____
- Entry Fees _____
- Staff Development (Clinics) _____
- Scouting _____
- Insurance _____
- Band Transportation _____
- Cheerleader Transportation _____
- Cheerleader Uniforms _____
- Telephone _____
- Postage _____
- Field Supplies _____
- Other Expenses _____

TOTAL EXPENSES _____

NET INCOME OR LOSS _____

travel form for...

See: TRANSPORTATION, TRAVEL AND TRIPS

trip sheet for...

See: TRANSPORTATION, TRAVEL AND TRIPS

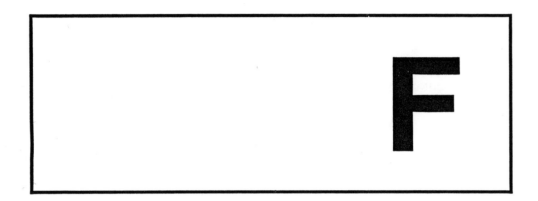

FACILITY

See Also: PROPERTY DAMAGE; VISITING SCHOOLS

bulletin on locker use...

PROCEDURES FOR THE USE OF THE VARSITY LOCKER ROOM

1. Lockers should be assigned by head coaches of the sports for a particular season.
2. Lockers are for athletes of current sports season.
3. Lockers should be used after the regular school day. The locker room will be kept locked during school hours.
4. Head coaches are responsible for keeping the room neat and clean.

maintenance checklist for...

FACILITY MAINTENANCE CHECKLIST

GYMNASIUM

| _____ EXHAUST FANS | _____ LIGHTING LEVELS |
| _____ LIGHT SWITCHES | _____ VENTILATION SYSTEM |

LOCKER ROOMS

| _____ SHOWER HEADS | _____ VENTILATION SYSTEM |
| _____ LIGHT LEVELS | _____ WATER THERMOSTAT |

POOLS

_____ VENTILATION   _____ WATER HEATERS
_____ FILTER SYSTEM   _____ WATER CLARITY

FIELDS

_____ MAINTENANCE   _____ WATERING PROCESS

usage permit...

CLARK COUNTY SCHOOL DISTRICT
SCHOOL FACILITY USE PERMIT—Non-Religious Purposes Only

Organization _____ Date _____
Address _____ Phone _____

Facility requested for the purpose of (check one):

☐ Conducting a (underline one) public, literary, scientific, recreational, or educational meeting.
☐ Presenting a (underline one) public, literary, scientific, recreational, or educational event.
☐ Conducting a precinct organizational or election meeting.
☐ Conducting an election.
☐ Holding personnel examinations. (Only public agencies are eligible.)

Detail or purpose _____
District facility requested _____ Location _____
Date requested _____ Hours to be used ____ a.m. to ____ a.m.
                                                              p.m.   p.m.

Charge for use of facility $_____ Number of students _____
Amount collected $_____ Number of adults _____

I understand that I am accepting the responsibility for the conduct of the organization indicated above who will abide by the rules and regulations that are effective relative to the use of school facilities. I agree that cost of repairing damage resulting from use of facility and/or equipment will be reimbursed to the District.

_____
REQUESTED BY

_____   _____
SCHOOL   TITLE

                                        _____
                                        ADDRESS

                                        _____
                                        PHONE NO.

usage, request for...

APPLICATION FOR USE OF SCHOOL FACILITIES

To the Red Bank Board of Education

The _____
(Name of Organization)

_____
(Address of Organization)

Wishes to make application for the use of the _____

_____
(Name of the School Facility & Room Desired)

on _____ from _____ to _____
(date)   (time)

For the following purpose _____

_____

THE FOLLOWING QUESTION MUST BE ANSWERED

Nature of the Organization _____
(Special Requirements)
(tables, chairs, etc.) _____

Use of profits if any _____
By signing this application, we hereby agree to comply with the regulations listed on the reverse side:

_____ (Signature)

Applicant: Name _____ Title _____

                  Address _____ Date _____

                  _____ Telephone _____

Rental payable in advance _____

Special requirements _____

Approved by Board of Education

_____
Secretary

_____
Date

usage schedule...

Uniforms, practice gear, any kind of practice or game equipment, belongs to the school district. It is not intended to be given to students and become a part of their daily wardrobe. Do not—under any circumstance—allow your students to use school property for their personal use.

FACILITY USAGE SCHEDULE

Month _____

Location _____(i.e. gym, locker room, weight room, etc.)

		A.M.						P.M.													
		6	7	8	9	10	11	12	1	2	3	4	5	6	7	8	9	10	11	12
Week 1	Monday																			
	Tuesday																			
	Wednesday																			
	Thursday																			
	Friday																			
	Saturday																			
	Sunday																			
Week 2	Monday																			
	Tuesday																			
	Wednesday																			
	Thursday																			
	Friday																			
	Saturday																			
	Sunday																			

FIELD TRIP

See: TRANSPORTATION, TRAVEL AND TRIPS

FINANCIAL REPORTS

See: POLICIES AND PROCEDURES

FLIERS

See Also: ANNOUNCEMENTS; BULLETINS; MEMOS

request for distribution of ...

REQUEST FOR DISTRIBUTION/POSTING OF FLIERS, ANNOUNCEMENTS

Description of flier/announcement/poster:

_____

_____

Distribution/Posting   approved _____   not approved _____
Date: _____

GUY M. SCONZO,
SUPERINTENDENT OF SCHOOLS

sample of ...

BYAA
—REGISTRATION—

DATES: Saturdays	BASKETBALL	BASKETBALL
September 29th		10 A.M.–2 P.M.
October 6th		10 A.M.–2 P.M.

LOCATION:

CROYDON HALL   1 Block from Bayshore Jr. H.S.
LEONARDO, N.J.   Leonardville Road, Leonardo, N.J.

AGE:

BOYS

	8-9-10	Biddy	(Includes End of Season
	11-12-13	Jr.	Tournament Play)

GIRLS

	8-9-10	Biddy
	11-12-13	Jr.

Games to be played at Croydon Hall Gymnasium on weekends. Practice time will be available prior to and during the season. Limited enrollments.

FOOTBALL

See Also: AWARDS; ELIGIBILITY; EQUIPMENT; INSPIRATIONALS; NATIONAL OPERATING COMMITTEE ON STANDARDS FOR ATHLETIC EQUIPMENT; SAFETY; UNIFORMS

announcer's form for ...

See: ANNOUNCER'S FORMS

equipment checklist form...

Day-To-Day Football Helmet Inspection Checklist

The National Federation of State High School Associations and the National Collegiate Athletic Association have both adopted rules making it mandatory, by 1980 and 1978 respectively, that all players wear football helmets meeting the standards of the National Operating Committee on Standards for Athletic Equipment (NOCSAE). Part of that standard is a recommendation that all previously certified models be tested, repaired as necessary, and recertified for continued use.

Each player has an important responsibility to make sure the helmet remains in certified condition. As part of a daily maintenance check, the following should be performed each day.

_____ Check that helmet fits tightly.

_____ Check for stress cracks in the plastic shell.

_____ Check for fixture cracks around the face protectors.

_____ Check for broken or loose chin straps and face protector fixtures.

_____ Check for face cages that have flattened out, or are holding the shell out of shape, causing a poor fit.

_____ Check for nose snubbers missing or defective.

_____ Check jaw pads for proper installation and snug fit.

_____ Check to be sure chin straps are adjusted properly and have not stretched out of shape.

_____ Check your particular helmet, as follows:

AIR & LIQUID

_____ Check that nylon rivets and velcro tabs are properly holding protective parts.

_____ Check that air sacs are holding air; and fluid sacs are holding liquid.

_____ Check that valves are operating properly and covered by protective tape when required by manufacturer.

SUSPENSION

_____ Check for rivets & rivet covers loose or missing.

_____ Check suspension for torn threads or stretched material. Stand-off distance to be sufficient at all points.

_____ Check crown rope for proper adjustment and tightly tied in square knot.

PADDED & AIR PADDED

_____ Check interior padding making certain it is near original condition and not deteriorating.

_____ Check for cracks in clear vinyl coating of air padded helmets.

_____ Check protective foam has not been cut away from padded parts.

CAUTION: In order to avoid damaging the helmet shell or adversely affecting its safety performance, select paints, cleaning agents and waxes carefully.

game checklist...

GAME CHECKLIST

Game Opponent: _____ Place: _____ Date & Time: _____

FOR OPPOSING TEAM, HAVE YOU:

(   ) PREPARED FACILITIES FOR THEM?
(   ) SEEN THAT TOWELS ARE PROVIDED?
(   ) CHECKED SEATING FOR VISITOR'S FANS?
(   ) ARRANGED FOR VISITOR'S PARKING?
(   ) PROVIDED AN INFORMATIONAL LETTER TO VISITOR'S COACH/SCHOOL?
(   ) MADE PROVISION FOR VISITING BAND?
(   ) MADE WELCOMING ARRANGEMENTS FOR VISITING COACHES?

FOR OUR TEAM, HAVE YOU:

(   ) ARRANGED FOR AND CHECKED GAME OFFICIALS?
(   ) NOTIFIED OFFICIALS OF TIME AND SET UP OFFICIAL'S ROOM?
(   ) ARRANGED FOR GAME DOCTOR?
(   ) CHECKED EQUIPMENT FOR READINESS?
(   ) ARRANGED FOR GAME AND TEAM SUPPLIES?
(   ) CHECKED THE FIELD FOR ACCURACY AND/OR CONDITIONS?

FOR THE GAME, HAVE YOU:

(   ) ENLISTED ANNOUNCER AND PROVIDED ANNOUNCING SCRIPT?
(   ) ARRANGED FOR SECURITY POLICE?
(   ) MADE PROVISIONS FOR MEDIA PERSONNEL?
(   ) ARRANGED FOR CHAIN CREW?
(   ) PREPARED TICKET PERSONNEL?
(   ) CHECKED PROGRAMS FOR SALE AND DISTRIBUTION?
(   ) PREPARED CONCESSIONS FOR OPERATION?
(   ) CLEARED HALF-TIME PROGRAM WITH DIRECTOR?
(   ) PROVIDED FOR TRAFFIC AND PARKING SUPERVISION?
(   ) ENLISTED FACULTY SUPERVISION WHERE NEEDED?
(   ) ARRANGED FOR GAME TIMER?

OTHER:

_____

_____

information sheet...

WESTVILLE HIGH SCHOOL
FOOTBALL INFORMATION SHEET

1. Nickname: Westville Yellowjackets
2. School colors: Purple and Gold
3. All home games will begin at 7:30 p.m.
4. Westville teams will wear PURPLE jerseys at home.
5. Visiting teams will dress in the gym. Please use the north door. The gym is located just north of the High School Building.
6. Officials will dress in the southeast dressing room of the gym.
7. All band members (in uniform) will be admitted free. They should enter at the south gate. Visitors will sit in the west stands.
8. All Pep Club members (in uniform) and Cheerleaders (in uniform) will be admitted free. Those not in uniform will be charged full price.
9. Buses ONLY will park inside the stadium. All other vehicles will park in parking lot east of stadium.
10. Admission prices will be: Adults–$2.00   Students–$1.00
    (OEA or faculty identification cards of visiting school will be accepted.)
11. Arrangements for broadcasting games by out-of-town stations should be made through the high school principal's office.
12. Westville Administration:
    Mr. Travis Slaton, Superintendent 918-723-3674
    Mr. Harold Phillips, HS Principal. 918-723-5511
    Mr. Darrell Stephens, JH Principal 918-723-5033
13. Westville Coaching Staff:
    Jackie Smith, Head Football Coach 918-723-3384
    Gary Tanner, Asst. Coach 918-723-5257
    Dennis Rhoads, Asst. Coach. 918-723-3657
    Dan Collins, JH & Asst. Coach 918-723-3755
    Norman Hall, Asst. Coach 918-723-3941
14. Schedule 1983-84:
    September 2. . . . . Stilwell . . . . Away
    September 9. . . . . Vian. . . . . Home
    September 16. . . . . Lincoln . . . . Home
    September 23. . . . . Prairie Grove. . . . . Home
    September 30. . . . . Hilldale. . . . . Away
    October 7. . . . . Heavener . . . . Home
    October 14 . . . . Panama. . . . . Away
    *October 21 . . . . Colcord . . . . Home
    *October 28 . . . . Kansas. . . . . Away
    *November 4 . . . . Salina . . . . Home

    *Conference games.

15. Pre-Game Schedule: 7:00–Warm-up
                        7:20–Clear Field
                        7:25–Coin Toss
                        7:25–Invocation
                        7:28–National Anthem
                        7:30–Kickoff

16. Halftime: Principals and Band Instructors

    All visiting bands are invited at halftime (excepting the 10-21-XX game with Colcord which is our Homecoming) to perform. If your program lasts longer than seven (7) minutes, please notify us at the beginning of the week prior to the game. Visiting bands will participate first in the halftime programs.

    We are looking forward to having you in Westville. If you have any further questions about the schedule or the game, please contact us.

safety in...

   #### See: SAFETY

scheduling guidelines...

FOOTBALL

1. Schedules shall be adopted at the December meeting.

2. When it becomes necessary to schedule two (2) games between schools, won-loss records of the last five (5) eighth grade games and the last five (5) ninth grade games will determine the Border Conference Champion.

3. When two schools have the same won-loss records, determination of the Border Conference Champion shall be based on the outcome of the regularly scheduled game between the two teams. The winner of that game shall be champion. If the regularly scheduled game between the two teams ended in a tie, the teams shall be co-champions.

4. On January 30, 19XX the Border Conference adopted the New Mexico Activities Association experimental rule allowing the coach on the field to talk to the entire team.

5. The starting date for junior high football practice is the third Tuesday before the first Thursday in September. Starting dates: 19XX, August 16; 19XX August 21; 19XX, August 20; 19XX, August 19; 19XX, August 18; 19XX, August 16.

season record form...

DATE	OPPONENT	SCORE HOME	OPP.	CONFERENCE STANDINGS		W.	L.	T.
				1st				
				2nd				
				3rd				
				4th				
				5th				
				6th				
				7th				
				8th				
				9th				
				10th				

SEASON _____

COACHES

Won ___ Lost ___ Tied ___ Total ___
AWARD HONORS: _____

DATE	J.V. RECORD	HOME	OPP.	DATE	FROSH RECORD	HOME	OPP.

J.V. COACHES   FROSH COACHES

Won ___ Lost ___ Tied ___ Total ___   Won ___ Lost ___ Tied ___ Total ___

FUND RAISING

See Also: HOME GAME ACTIVITY; POLICIES AND PROCEDURES

opportunity for, sign-up sheet...

RE: CONCESSION SIGN UP

Listed below are the football and basketball home games that teams may sign up for to earn monies for their travel. In signing up for the concessions, each coach must ensure that:

1. Team reports one-half hour prior to start of first game for assistance.
2. Coaching staff to be responsible for the team at all times, and to monitor the team in the booth.
3. Team remains until released by the concession personnel.
4. Extension cords, pans etc. are the team's responsibility.
5. Adult supervision/assistance provided by team.
6. Money-raising activity reflects the work done.

Football home games

6	Sep	Fri	Honokaa at Waiakea	_____
21	Sep	Sat	Honokaa (JV)/HPA (V) at Waiakea	_____
11	Oct	Fri	Kona at Waiakea	_____
2	Nov	Sat	Kona (JV)/Kau (V) at Waiakea	_____
9	Nov	Sat	Hilo at Waiakea	_____

Basketball home games

10	Jan	Fri	St Joe at Waiakea	_____
18	Jan	Sat	Hilo at Waiakea	_____
25	Jan	Sat	Kohala at Waiakea	_____
28	Jan	Tue	Pahoa at Waiakea	_____
14	Feb	Fri	Kona at Waiakea	_____
15	Feb	Sat	Pahoa vs Hilo, Laps at Waiakea 2 JV games/2 V games	_____

Note: 1. Do not be greedy; remember, there are 15 teams looking for fund raisers!
2. You may select 2 dates to work (primary and alternate date).
3. First come, first served.

report of fund-raising (example)...

THE FOLLOWING SPORTS HAVE EARNED FUNDS TOWARD THEIR PRESEASON TRAVEL CRITERIA:

1.	Baseball	1,227.08
2.	Basketball/boys	119.50
3.	Basketball/girls	—0—
4.	Bowling	140.50
5.	Cross Country	194.50
6.	Football	1,635.70
7.	Golf	45.50
8.	Judo	125.00
9.	Soccer	350.45
10.	Softball	670.68
11.	Swimming	460.86
12.	Tennis/girls	387.71
13.	Tennis/boys	22.50
14.	Track/boys	103.75
15.	Track/girls	128.47
16.	Volleyball	63.61
17.	Wrestling	787.75
18.	Cheerleaders	16.50
		6,480.06

solicitation activity report...

DEPARTMENT OF EDUCATION
MONEY-RAISING ACTIVITY

Date _____

School _____School Year _____

1. Requested By _____Gen. Excise Lic. No. _____
   (Name of Organization)

2. Place of Activity _____Date of Activity _____

3. Detail Plan of Program to be Supported by Profit from Activity:

   a. Planned Program

DESCRIPTION	ESTIMATED AMOUNT NEEDED	AMOUNT ALLOTTED
1)		
2)		
3)		
Total		

4. Means of Raising Funds (Describe in Detail—Ticket Sales, Hot Dog Sales, etc.):

   a. Revenues

DESCRIPTION	ANTICIPATED REVENUES	REVENUES REALIZED
1)		
2)		
3)		
Total Revenues		

   b. Cost of Project

DESCRIPTION	ESTIMATED EXPENDITURES	ACTUAL EXPENDITURES
1)		
2)		
3)		
4) General Excise Tax (4%)		
5) Use Tax—1/2% (Unlicensed mainland vendor)		
Total Expenditures		
c. Net Profit (a. minus b.)		

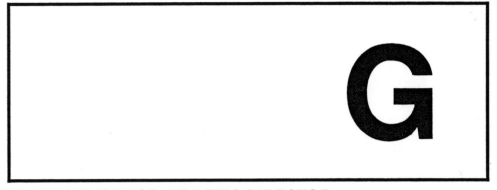

GAME CHECKLIST FOR ATHLETIC DIRECTOR

See: ATHLETIC DIRECTOR; GAME REPORT

GAME CLOTHING

See: UNIFORMS

GAME REPORT

See Also: OFFICIALS; SPECIFIC SPORT

form for (two examples)...

FOOTBALL LEAGUE GAME REPORT

Conference _____League _____Where Played _____

	Team	Score	Penetrations	First Downs
Home	_____	_____	_____	_____
Visitors	_____	_____	_____	_____

Winner by extra play _____

Details _____

_____

_____

Linesman _____Referee _____

Umpire _____Field Judge _____

Date _____Home Principal _____

These reports are to be MAILED to: U.G. Montgomery, Executive Secretary, Box 8521,
Albuquerque, New Mexico, 87108

WITHIN ONE DAY AFTER THE GAME HAS BEEN PLAYED.

* * * * *

MIDDLETOWN TOWNSHIP PUBLIC SCHOOLS
GAME REPORT

_____ vs _____   Date _____

Score   We _____   They _____   Sport _____

Officials: _____

Transportation:
(Briefly describe any problems; if okay please mark so.)

Rating of Officials: (Brief)   Game Problems:

Injuries:

To be turned in to Athletic Director via inter-office mail after each and every game (all levels) Please include vouchers for home games.

GOLF

See Also: AWARDS; ELIGIBILITY

season record form...

COACHES			SEASON		
		SCORE			
DATE	OPPONENT	HOME	OPP.	ROSTER	

WON _____ LOST _____   *LETTERMEN

AWARD HONORS: _____

CONFERENCE STANDINGS				DISTRICT STANDINGS			
SCHOOL	PTS.	SCHOOL	PTS.	SCHOOL	PTS.	SCHOOL	PTS.
1.		6.		1.		6.	
2.		7.		2.		7.	
3.		8.		3.		8.	
4.		9.		4.		9.	
5.		10.		5.		10.	

GYMNASTICS

See Also: INTRAMURAL PROGRAM; MEETS; SEASON

entry form for...

GYMNASTICS ENTRY FORM

School _____

Coach _____

ALL AROUND

1. _____
2. _____
3. _____

PARALLEL BARS

1. _____
2. _____
3. _____

FLOOR EXERCISE

1. _____
2. _____
3. _____

VAULTING

1. _____
2. _____
3. _____

RINGS

1. _____
2. _____
3. _____

SIDE HORSE

1. _____
2. _____
3. _____

HIGH BAR

1. _____
2. _____
3. _____

NOTE: Please return by Wednesday, March 20, 19XX.

meet (general information sheet)...

DUAL AND TRIANGULAR MEETS

Duals and triangulars will include both novice and all-city levels. They will be organized by the host school following these general procedures:

1. There may be 3 entries per event, per grade level from each school. For the first meet a school will be allowed to enter up to 4 in one event providing only 2 are entering another. If we do not finish these meets before 5 p.m. we will not allow the extra competitions at subsequent meets. Girls should be out of the building and on the buses by 5 p.m.

2. An individual girl may enter as many as three events if she qualifies. A girl who qualifies for All-City in one event must compete at this level in other events. Therefore, a girl may not participate in both the Novice and All-City levels at the same meet. Girls who are capable are encouraged to move up from the novice to the all-city levels as soon as possible.

3. Since judges will be volunteers, and possibly not real experts, do not try to calculate team scores. You may announce places if you wish. Compile results and get a copy to each visiting school as soon as possible.

ALL-CITY FINAL MEET

Entry Rules and Event Cards

1. Junior highs may enter two girls in each event at each grade level or a total of ten 7th; ten 8th; and ten 9th grade entries. To allow for some flexibility, they may enter up to three in one event providing only one is entered in another event. The total must not average more than two per event.

2. An individual girl may enter as many as three events if she qualifies. A girl competing in the All-City Meet should have participated at that level in at least one dual-triangular meet.

Levels

Three grades will compete (7th, 8th and 9th), each with separate routines. Age grouping will be used to the following extent: if a 7th grade boy is 14 as of September 1, 19XX he must participate on the 8th grade team. An 8th grade boy who is 15 as of September 1, 19XX may participate on the 9th grade team. A 9th grade boy who becomes 16 before September 1, 19XX is ineligible for all 9th grade athletic competition.

Events

Floor exercise, side horse, still rings, parallel bars, vaulting, horizontal bar, and all-around. NOTE: all around includes all events.

Routines

All events will have compulsory routines. Follow the written explanation and video tape prepared during the 1982-83 school year.

Entry Rules

Each school may enter three boys in each event including all-around. A boy may enter a maximum of four events. If four events are entered, one of the events must be all-around.

Scoring

Grade team scores will be kept in the finals. Scoring will be as follows: All contestants will score team points. Three judges' scores will be totaled then divided by 3 and the average will count toward the team scores.

Awards

A medal will be awarded to the champion in each event and ribbons will be awarded to the second through sixth place in each event. Ribbons will be distributed through the school mail following the final meet.

Judges

Judges will be Omaha Public Schools gymnastic team members plus other certified judges.

Entry Sheets

Entry sheets are enclosed. These sheets must be filled out and returned to the Physical Education Office in the school mail on the date listed at the bottom of the entry blank.

Order of Events

All events will be run simultaneously.

Rules of Competition

Floor Exercise—the routine will be performed on mats (60'0")

Side Horse—46" from mat to top of pommell

Still Rings—performer may be lifted to the rings

Parallel Bars—adjustable to accommodate individual performer

Vaulting—height of horse from floor to top of horse—

> 7th grade—48"
> 8th grade—48"
> 9th grade—48"—Long Horse

One vault will count in scoring.

Horizontal Bar—adjustable to accommodate individual performer *policy on...*

GENERAL PREPARATION AND PLANNING

1. Safety suggestions for teaching gymnastics and using the equipment should be reviewed with students and placed in a conspicuous wall space.

2. The Junior High Athletic Book should be reviewed for information pertinent to gymnastics and the general requirements regarding eligibility lists, physical examinations, etc.

3. Coaches of boys' and girls' teams should work together to plan equitable practice time on shared equipment.

4. Coaches should have available in each building the following supplies for the season:

    a. Videotapes and written explanations of current routines.
    b. Check lists for hosting dual/triangular meets.
    c. Event cards, novice certificates, score sheets for meets, and cassettes for novice floor exercise routines.

HALL OF FAME

See: AWARDS

HANDBOOK

See Also: PUBLIC RELATIONS AND THE PRESS

suggested outline form for...

STUDENT ATHLETIC HANDBOOK

A student Athletic Handbook can be of great value to the athletic department for delineating and explaining school policies, regulations and other facets of the sports program with which students ought to be familiar. The handbook also should be made available to the parents to enable them to be better informed concerning the operation of the athletic program.

The following outline for suggested organization of a student handbook may serve as a developmental guide for high schools in general, and made to fit a specific school with minor alterations and additions.

Suggested outline for material: STUDENT ATHLETIC HANDBOOK

I.   Statement of Purpose of Athletic Program
     (Produced within the school; superintendent or principal might write this; could be done by director or by representative committee of administration, faculty, and students.)

II. Rationale of the Athletic Program

III. Rules of Eligibility
    A. State
    B. District
    C. Conference
    D. Residence
    E. Definition of an Amateur
    F. Summary of NCAA "Guide"

IV. Regulation of Student Participation
    A. Forms to be filed:
        1. Physical examination
        2. Parental permission
        3. Physician's approval
        4. Insurance coverage
        5. A.S.B. Card
    B. Statement of responsibility for school equipment
    C. Copy of attendance regulations
        1. Class
        2. Turnout
    D. Copy of athletic code

V. Responsibility of Athlete to School District
    A. Conduct on and off the field
    B. Dress and appearance

VI. Discipline
    A. Activity discipline
    B. Suspension
        1. Short term
        2. Long term

VII. Requirements for Lettering

VIII. Directory of Coaches

table of contents of (partial sample)...

TABLE OF CONTENTS

Objectives 1
Rules & regulations 4
Eligibility 4
Requirements for participation 12
Conduct of athlete 13
Enforcement of regulations 15
Grooming and dress policy 15
General requirements for athletic letters 17

HEAD COACH

See Also: ACCEPTANCE, COACHING STAFF: CONTRACTS: EVALUATION; SPECIFIC SPORT

job description (two examples)...

JOB DESCRIPTION

Title:	Head Coach
Qualifications:	Full time teaching assignment in Middletown Township Public Schools.
	At least five (5) years of successful teaching experience in his or her chosen coaching area.
	Such alternatives to the above qualifications as the Board may find appropriate and acceptable.
Immediate Responsibility:	Athletic Director
Overall Job Goal:	Within the framework of the entire athletic program, provides leadership in the ongoing development and improvement of his coaching area through coordination, planning, evaluation, and implementation of programs.
Functions:	

1. Assists in the coordination of all programs (7–12).
2. Plans and administers staff responsibilities, staff plans, seasonal plans, and scouting duties if applicable.
3. Maintains liaison and active participation with other community acitivities, i.e., recreation, Pop Warner, MYAA.
4. Assists in the recruitment, screening, hiring, training, and assignment of coaching staff.
5. Assists in the ongoing evaluation of the coaching staff.
6. During Season
   a. Implement "Athletic Standards" as outlined in Athletic Handbook.
   b. Provide information for transportation, officials & game management.
   c. Assume responsibility for constant care of equipment & facilities being used.
   d. Follow carefully the procedure for initiating purchase orders.

e. Assume supervisory control over all phases of teams in his program.

f. Organize and schedule practice sessions on a regular basis with the idea of developing the athlete's greatest potential.

g. Apply discipline in a firm and positive manner as outlined in the Athletic Handbook.

h. See that building regulations are understood and enforced.

i. Emphasize safety precautions and be aware of best training and injury procedures.

j. Conduct himself and his teams in an ethical manner during practice and contests.

k. Report a summary of all contests and provide any publicity information that would aid his program and his athletes.

l. Instruct his players concerning rules and rule changes, new knowledge, and innovative ideas and techniques.

7. End of Season

a. Arrange for the systematic return of all school equipment and hold the athlete responsible for all equipment not returned.

b. Arrange for the issuance of letters and special awards.

c. Arrange for cleaning, sorting and inventory of all equipment.

d. Be concerned with the care and maintenance of his facility by making recommendations concerning additions and improvements.

e. Recommend concerning equipment needed to be purchased or repaired.

f. Maintain records of team and individual accomplishments.

* * * * *

OMAHA PUBLIC SCHOOLS
Job Description
High School Head Coach

I. General Statement of Responsibility

The head coach for each sport has the responsibility of carrying on the sport in the best interest of the school district by adhering to the Policies and Regulations of the School Board, as well as the practices and Procedures of the School Administration. Further, each head coach should have a working knowledge of individual building practices, the Metropolitan High School Activities Association rules, and the Nebraska School Activities Association rules.

II. Qualifications

A. Professional preparation: employment as a teacher with coaching preparation either through experience or college preparation.

B. Background experience: possess working knowledge of all aspects of the sport.

C. Personal: demonstrated interest in and an aptitude for performing tasks listed:

1. At every opportunity urge the student body to be polite, courteous, and fair to the visiting team.

2. Always display good sportsmanship, losing or winning.
3. Maintain poise and self-control at all times, especially at the contests.
4. Teach the team to play fairly. Games should be played hard but not as "blood and thunder" or "survival of the fittest" contest.
5. Be a good host to the visiting team, coach and spectators.
6. Discipline and, if necessary, dismiss players who disregard good sportsmanship.
7. Educate the players on the sidelines to the fact that it is unsportsmanlike conduct to yell intimidating remarks at the visiting team or officials.
8. Respect the officials' judgment and interpretation of the rules. If an interpretation appeal is necessary, follow appropriate procedures.
9. Let the officials control the game and the coach control the team.
10. Publicly attempt to shake hands with the officials prior to the game and the opposing coach before and after the game.

III. Specific Duties and Responsibilities

A. Program responsibilities

1. Has full responsibility for the overall supervision of the program, including sophomore and junior varsity teams.
2. Is in charge of assigning all duties of assistant coaches working under his/her supervision.
3. Is responsible for keeping practice periods for the sport within the confines of the time specified by the athletic director and with due consideration to the coaching staff and welfare of participants.
4. Is responsible for the general upkeep and protection of equipment under the jurisdiction of the program.
5. Reports periodically while the sport is in season to the athletic director with regard to developments in the program.
6. Is directly responsible for a complete inventory of the equipment used for the sport; to be made at the end of each season.
7. Writes at the end of the season an annual report evaluating the program with recommendation for improvements.
8. Is responsible for keeping records as requested by the athletic director.
9. Is responsible for recommending purchase of equipment, supplies, and uniforms as need demands.
10. Has a shared responsibility for striving to build good sportsmanship and developing good public relations in the school and community.
11. Plans and schedules a regular program of practice in season.
12. Works closely with the athletic director in scheduling interscholastic contests.
13. Oversees the safety conditions of the facility or area in which assigned sport in conducted at all times that athletes are present.
14. Promotes that sport by prompt and accurate score reporting to the local media.
15. Makes recommendation to the athletic director in matters of scheduling.
16. Cooperates with all other coaches in providing the optimum sports program possible under existing conditions.
17. Makes financial reports of all trips away from home where money has been advanced and keeps accurate records when expenses are to be repaid.
18. Turns in the following to the athletic director:
   a. an alphabetical squad roster as soon as the squad is set.
   b. a squad roster with all necessary personal data, at least one week before the first contest.
   c. an alphabetical list of award winners and score sheets immediately following the season.

19. Keeps abreast of new developments, innovative ideas and techniques by attendance at clinics, workshops, and reading in the field.
20. Performs other duties as related to his/her assignments as designated by the building principal and/or the building athletic director.

B. Personnel responsibilities
1. Coaches individual participants in the skills necessary for excellent achievement in the sport involved.
2. Helps to establish performance criteria for eligibility in interscholastic competition in all sports.
3. Enforces disciplined and sportsmanlike behavior at all times, and establishes and oversees penalties for breach of such standards by individual students.
4. Determines the system of play to be used.
5. Understands that he/she is continually on display and must exercise good judgment in protecting positive coaching behavior. Be reminded of the fact that you are responsible for your team's conduct during practice and traveling, as well as playing. All coaches would like athletic teams to project a "class image"—they should lead by example in that endeavor.
6. Encourages good sportsmanship and desirable pupil/teacher relationships.
7. Is certain that no athlete is permitted to participate until all appropriate "check-out" procedures have been completed.
8. Thoroughly explains eligibility requirements and participation rules to all squad members. If a violation occurs, make sure you discuss it with the athlete. Don't assume he/she knows the consequences, procedures and recourses. Due process must be utilized.
9. Is responsible for clearing with the athletic director, the departure time for trips that involve loss of school time; and for seeing that the faculty is given adequate and appropriate notice.
10. Should see that all participants have made necessary arrangements for their own transportation home when returning from road trips in late evening hours.

IV. Number of Students Involved

Sport	Minimum
Football 1 head coach 5 asst. coaches	24 per team (If total number falls below 72, reduce one assistant coach)
Basketball 2 head coaches 3 asst. coaches	10 per team
Baseball 1 head coach 1 asst. coach	15 per team
Track and Field (boys and girls combined) 2 head coaches 3 asst. coaches	10 per coach
Swimming (boys and girls combined) 1 head coach 1 asst. coach	Under 20 participants, head coach only
Wrestling 1 head coach 1 asst. coach	Under 20 participants, head coach only

Gymnastics
  (boys and girls combined)   Under 12 participants,
  1 head coach   head coach only
  1 asst. coach

Volleyball   10 per team—under 20 participants
  1 head coach   head coach only
  1 asst. coach

Cross Country
  1 head coach   7 boys; 5 girls (combined)
  1 asst. coach

Golf   6

Tennis   8

NOTE: The first contest date will be the date used to determine the coaching assignments for any given sport. Some discretion may be used in determining the number of coaches assigned.

V. Length of Season, Number of Practices and Contents

Sport	Length of Season	Number of Practices	Number of Contests
Football	11-13 weeks	67-70	9-12
Basketball	18-19 weeks	87-90	18-25
Baseball	11-12 weeks	55-60	15-18
Track & Field	12 weeks	55	13
Swimming	16 weeks	70-75	12
Wrestling	15 weeks	67	19
Gymnastics	13 weeks	57	13
Volleyball	12-13 weeks	54	13-15
Cross Country	10-11 weeks	43	13
Golf	9-11 weeks	42-50	12-14
Tennis	9-12 weeks	40-50	10-13

HEALTH CERTIFICATE

See: EXAMINATION

HEALTH EXAMINATION FORM

See: EXAMINATION

HEAT CHART

See: SAFETY

HIGH SCHOOL ATHLETIC CODE

See: CODES

HOME GAME ACTIVITY

> ***See Also:*** ANNOUNCERS' FORMS; FACILITY; OFFICIALS; PUBLIC RELATIONS AND
> THE PRESS; REQUESTS AND REQUISITIONS; TICKETS; VISITING
> SCHOOLS; SPECIFIC SPORT

home game activity checklist...

ACTIVITY _____ DATE _____

PLACE _____ TIME _____

SUPERVISOR OF ACTIVITY _____

FACULTY SUPERVISORS _____

_____

GAME OFFICIALS _____

_____

SUPPORT PERSONNEL (FIELD):
   SCOREKEEPER _____

   TIMER _____

   ANNOUNCER _____

   FILM/PHOTOGRAPHER _____

   CHAIN CREW _____
SUPPORT PERSONNEL (STADIUM):
   TICKET SALES _____

_____

   TICKET TAKERS _____

_____

   PROGRAMS _____

_____

   CONCESSIONS _____

_____

   OTHER: _____

_____

_____

HONORS, ATHLETIC

> ***See:*** AWARDS

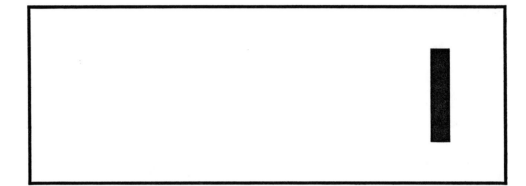

INCOME/EXPENSE SHEET

See: EXPENSES

INJURY

See Also: ACCIDENT REPORT FORM; EXAMINATIONS; LIABILITY, LEGAL; MEDICAL; PERMISSIONS; SAFETY

permission to treat a minor...

WAIAKEA HIGH SCHOOL ATHLETICS

To: Any Hospital, Clinic, or Physician

AUTHORIZATION TO TREAT A MINOR FORM

I (We), the undersigned parent, parents or legal guardian of _____

Minor's Name

authorize any hospital or clinic or licensed physician to treat my/our child, charge with any X-ray examination, anesthetic, medical or surgical diagnosis rendered under the general or special supervision of any member of the medical staff of the hospital/clinic or office of a physician who are licensed to practice in the State of Hawaii.

It is understood that this authorization is given in advance of any specific diagnosis, treatment or hospital care being required but is given to provide authority and power to render care when the physician in the exercise of his best judgement may deem advisable. It is understood that effort shall be made to contact the undersigned prior to rendering treatment to the patient, but that treatment will not be withheld if the undersigned cannot be reached.

_____   _____
Signature of Coach/Witness   Signature of parent/Legal Guardian

_____ _____   _____ _____
Date   Phone   Date   Phone

List any restrictions to your authorization to treat: _____

_____

Date minor received last tetanus/diphtheria booster: _____

List any allergies to drug(s) or food(s) minor may have: _____

Any special medication(s) or other pertinent information on minor: _____

_____

_____

_____

This consent shall remain effective until the end of the minor's participation in: _____
or until: _____
Expiration date

* * * * *

policy on (two examples)...

Student Injuries

If you have a student that gets injured, please use caution in administering any kind of first aid or in requesting trained medical assistance. We certainly want to emphasize the proper care of the injured and we urge you to use your discretion when handling an injured student. If you are not sure of what procedure to follow—ask for the assistance of another coach or sponsor. Anytime we have a serious injury, one so serious that you call a doctor or call an ambulance, please notify the Activities Director immediately.

CLARK COUNTY SCHOOL DISTRICT GUIDELINES
REGARDING ATHLETIC PHYSICAL EXAMINATIONS
AND INJURY REFERRAL

All students participating in athletics must have a current physical examination on file at their school. Schools should seek to establish a program for physical examinations available to students and assist students with information regarding such a program. Schools may contact local physicians and therapists for volunteer assistance with their programs.

If an injury occurs during a practice or contest, the coach responsible for the activity should:

1. Provide aid to the student with emergency assistance utilizing one or more of the following:

        a. available physician
        b. available ambulance/paramedic
        c. available coaches
        d. available physical therapist/trainer
        e. available nurse

2. After emergency procedures have been implemented, the coach should attempt to notify the parent or legal guardian of the nature of the injury and release the athlete to the parent.

3. If injury is of a serious nature, or in the opinion of the coach needs immediate attention, the coach has the authority to refer the athlete for medical transportation and emergency treatment to the closest local hospital emergency room.

4. Only if requested by the parent or legal guardian or student may the coach or person in charge of the activity recommend a personal preference of medical personnel.

5. If a physical condition or injury warrants a referral to a physician, a medical release from a physician must be filed at the school before the student will be permitted participation rights.

referral form for...

NAME OF INJURED ATHLETE: _____ DATE: _____

COACH: _____ ACTIVITY: _____

WHAT HAPPENED: _____

_____

_____

FOR ATTENDING PHYSICIAN:

DIAGNOSIS: _____

_____

RECOMMENDED TREATMENT (INCLUDING FOLLOW-UP): _____

_____

MAY STUDENT RETURN TO PRACTICE: _____ IF "YES", WHEN: _____

MAY STUDENT RETURN TO COMPETITION: _____ IF "YES", WHEN: _____

PHYSICIAN'S SIGNATURE: _____ DATE: _____

INSPIRATIONALS

...THINK LIKE A WINNER

What are the traits that make one person a winner and another person a loser? The big difference is in how a person thinks. The <u>attitude</u> will govern the actions. For instance...

A winner is always ready to tackle something new...a loser is prone to believe it can't be done.

A winner isn't afraid of competition...a loser excuses himself with the idea that the competition beat him out.

A winner knows he's sometimes wrong and is willing to admit his mistakes...a loser can usually find someone to blame.

A winner is challenged by a new problem...a loser doesn't want to face it.

A winner is decisive...a loser frustrates himself with indecision.

A winner thinks positively...acts positively...and lives positively...a loser usually has a negative attitude and a negative approach to everything.

So, if you want to be a winner, think like a winner...act like a winner...and sooner than you think...you will be a winner.

...WHAT WE EXPECT

WHAT DO WE EXPECT FROM OUR PLAYERS?

Proper conduct must be shown in school, at home and on the football field. Respect should be shown to all coaches and teachers.

You are responsible for all football equipment. Failure to return any equipment results in payment for that particular item. Take proper care of equipment.

Get into and stay in good physical condition. You must stay active after the season is over. To be in good condition, you must implement your own program. We can tell you, but you must do it!

You must obey the training rules concerning no smoking, drinking and curfew hours.

You must be in school. Get into the habit of being on time for school and for practice. If you cannot make practice, contact a coach.

You must spend time doing homework, studying, etc., for school. If you are doing poorly in school, notify the coaching staff. Remember, football has become a complicated game and you must be sharp and alert.

Show good sportsmanship.

Be proud to be a member of the football team!

...WHAT YOU RECEIVE

WHAT YOU WILL RECEIVE FROM THE COACHING STAFF

Constructive criticism on your performance on the field during practice sessions and games. You should expect criticism and accept it as an athelete. This is the only way a player can become successful.

Dedication to football and the football team. We will give 100% effort to develop a winning football team. Hours will be spent for preparation of games and improving individuals' on the field.

Communication from the coaching staff. You will be able to discuss with the staff problems at home, school and on the field. We believe with a sense of communication in a coach-player relationship this will lay the foundation for a successful football team.

Experience from the coaching staff. Everyone on the staff has played football beyond high school. We feel experience is the best teacher and this is something we can offer to you.

Fairness to all players. The coaching staff will have unbiased opinions and work with the player in the situation that occurs. The staff will justified all changes in the football program.

Attitude from the coaching staff will not be down in any situation. We will always be out to win and improve the team.

Confidence from the coaching staff will be shown to all players. Our main goal is to instill confidence to our players. We want to make you a better ballplayer than anyone else.

...YOU CAN DO IT

GENERAL REMINDERS

Remember, your success is measured in what the team accomplishes.

Victory goes to the team which is more aggressive.

The real star of a game has been the man who attained a high degree of excellence through voluntary drill.

This is your team, win or lose.

You will play like you practice.

Football is a game of hardy characters—for men who are tough in body and in spirit.

The most important ingredient in football is DESIRE.

A winner never quits and a quitter never wins.

We must stress 100% hard work during practice. Good performance begins in practice sessions.

Attitude is extremely important. You must want to do it and pay the price.

You must be able to accept a coach's criticism. This is part of football. To improve yourself, you must be told what you are doing wrong.

INSURANCE

See Also: LIABILITY, LEGAL; MEDICAL; PERMISSIONS

notice to parents on...

The school district has insurance available to students. If your students desire 24-hour coverage, it is available through the assistant principal's office. If students do not have insurance through the school, they must provide their own. Make your students aware that their family insurance will have to pay for an injury if they do not have school insurance. (24-hour coverage insurance).

policy statement to parents...

TO PARENTS OF STUDENTS WHO PARTICIPATE IN INTERSCHOLASTIC SPORTS

The policy of the Middletown Township Board of Education is as follows:

"It shall be the policy of the Middletown Township Board of Education that all students in interscholastic athletic competition shall carry appropriate insurance coverage under a plan underwritten by a private carrier."

This year all athletes participating in the interscholastic sports will be covered by the Board of Education on an excess policy by Bob McClosky Insurance. This excess policy means that your personal insurance will be liable first for any injuries incurred and then the Board's insurance will cover "excess" costs. OUR EXCESS INSURANCE HAS A MAXIMUM PAYMENT OF $250.00 FOR 1984-85 FOR PHYSICAL THERAPY TREATMENTS.

I can assure each parent that the utmost care will be taken at all times and that we would hope and work toward the end that there would be no accidents.

It should be understood that this insurance applies only to athletic activities and is not intended to substitute or replace regular voluntary student insurance offered through the regular school solicitations.

All claims and inquiries can be directed to Bob McCloskey Insurance, P.O. Box 390, Matawan, New Jersey 07747, (201) 591-9520. Claim forms are available in each secondary school.

> Paul W. Bennett, RSBA
> School Business Administrator

I hereby acknowledge that I have read the above and understand the coverage described.

| (Name of Student) | (Sport or Activity) |

(   ) I do have private insurance.
(   ) I do not have private insurance.

| (Private Carrier) | (Signature of Parent) |

INTEREST SURVEY

See Also: ALTHETE; INTRAMURAL PROGRAM; LETTER ON/TO; MEMOS;
PARTICIPATION; PHILOSOPHY

sample of...

NAME: _____ GRADE: _____ DATE: _____

HOMEROOM: _____ SEX: _____ HOME PHONE: _____

Please indicate your degree of interest in each of the following sports activities. This allows us to know your interests, in order that we may present a better athletic program for everyone. Thank you.

SPORT	NOT INTERESTED	NEED MORE INFORMATION	VERY INTERESTED
BASEBALL			
BASKETBALL			
CROSS COUNTRY			
FIELD HOCKEY			
FOOTBALL			
GYMNASTICS			
HOCKEY			
SOCCER			
SOFTBALL			
TENNIS			
TRACK & FIELD			
WRESTLING			

INTERSCHOLASTIC CONTESTS

See: CONTESTS

INTERVIEW

See Also: EVALUATION

checklist for (two forms)...

CANDIDATE: _____ DATE: _____

POSITION SOUGHT: _____

ITEM	OUTSTANDING · POOR
APPEARANCE	
ENTHUSIASM	
KNOWLEDGE	
MATURITY	
PERSONALITY	
RELATIONSHIP TO OTHERS	

* * * * *

(Designed for use on 8" × 5" card.)

INTERVIEW RECOMMENDATIONS

POSITION _____ DATE _____

NAME OF CANDIDATE _____

Circle one rating for each item:	Low 1	2	3	4	High 5
Interpersonal relations					
Knowledge of activity					
Personality					
Emotional Maturity					
Health and Stamina					
General Appearance					
Enthusiasm for the Job					

Overall Rating (Circle one)   1   2   3   4   5

Acceptable _____ Not acceptable _____

INTERVIEWER (signature) _____

Use reverse side for additional comments.

After all interviews have been completed, a discussion session should produce a recommendation from the committee to the superintendent, Board of Education or whomever is responsible for final action. A good idea is to recommend three choices so as to allow for exigencies such as the refusal of a candidate to accept the offer.

When the position has been filled, all applicants should be notified by letter, thanking them for their interest and recording the committee's action. Resumés of the top candidates might be kept on file for a reasonable period of time to facilitate action should more vacancies occur.

INTRAMURAL PROGRAM

See Also: ATHLETIC DEPARTMENT; INTEREST SURVEY; PARTICIPATION; PERMISSIONS; PHILOSOPHY; SPECIFIC SPORT

suggested activities in...

Suggested Activities

(Any addition to the following list will require written approval from the Department of Staff Personnel Services prior to offering the activity.)

A. Art
B. Basketball
C. Cheerleading
D. Chess Club
E. Chorus

F. Cross Country
G. Debate
H. Drama
I. Exercise Club
J. Flagball

K. Gymnastics
L. Individual Sports
M. Instrumental Music
N. Rhythms
O. 50 Mile Run Club
P. Soccer-Speedball
Q. Softball
R. Stagecraft

S. Student Government
T. Swimming
U. Synchronized Swim
V. Tennis
W. Volleyball
X. Weight Training
Y. Wrestling
Z. Newspaper

INVENTORY

See Also: EQUIPMENT

athletic inventory form (two examples)...

_____ HIGH SCHOOL
ATHLETIC/ACTIVITY INVENTORY FORM

SPORT/ACTIVITY _____
COACH/SPONSOR _____
DATE _____

ITEM	NUMBER	DESCRIPTION	CONDITION	DISCARD	ON HAND

* * * * *

UNIFORM INVENTORY FORM:
SPORT: _____   DATE RCVD: _____   GENERAL CONDITION: _____

DESCRIPTION (list brand, type, number)	DATE	TOTAL	S	M	L	XL	REPLACEMENT

COMMENTS:

ticket seller's inventory sheet...

See: TICKETS

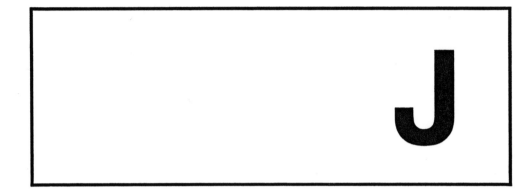

JOB DESCRIPTION

assistant coach...

See: ASSISTANT COACH

athletic director...

See: ATHLETIC DIRECTOR

head coach...

See: HEAD COACH

JUNIOR HIGH SCHOOL

eligibility list...

See: ELIGIBILITY

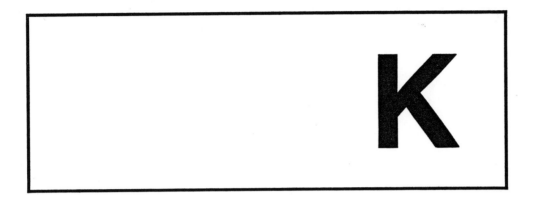

KEYS

See Also: THEFT

bulletin on ...

Keys are issued to advisors of school-sponsored activities on a "need" basis. Once issued, the keys become the responsibility of the person to whom they were given. Since some keys literally provide the entry to thousands of dollars worth of equipment, the loss of certain keys (either through negligence or theft) poses a problem of some weight. Therefore, advisors are never to allow a student to use these keys, whether supervised or unsupervised. Moreover, keys may not be passed from one advisor to another via a student courier. Any loss must be reported immediately to the main office.

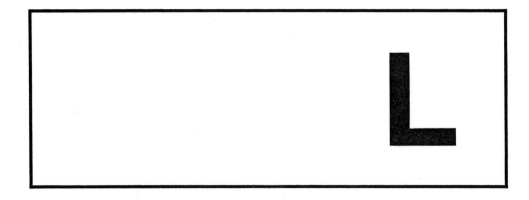

LETTER AWARD, VARSITY

See: AWARDS

LETTER OF RECOMMENDATION

See Also: PARTICIPATION

sample of a ...

Dear Coach,

I've had the pleasure of coaching Jim Finnerty on our Middletown Traveling Team and the misfortune of coaching against him in high school play. His high school team, C.B.A., was extremely good. It was ranked by the coaches association at the end of the season as the tenth in the entire state.

Jim was primarily a defensive player with good skill under pressure. He was always very calm, but very aggressive. He has the ability to recognize situations quickly and has the presence of mind to initiate the attack. He plays well in the air and has average speed. Jim is also an asset because of his ability to throw the ball in "far and accurate".

Jim is a personable young man who is both intelligent and coachable. His down to earth demeanor earns the respect of the other players. He is the type of player who leads by example.

I would strongly recommend Jim for college soccer. He has both the skill and the experience necessary.

Sincerely,

LETTER ON/TO:

See Also: INSURANCE; PARTICIPATION; PERMISSIONS

an official's conduct...

See: OFFICIALS

athletes...

Dear Parent and Football Participant:

The purpose of this letter is to welcome your son into our 19XX football program. We want him to enjoy his association with other members of the team, and learn all he can from our coaches.

Our main interest for your son concerns his safety and health while he is a participant in our football program. Even though all of our football staff are professionally trained coaches and will teach your son the proper skills, there is a chance of injury while he is playing football. We sincerely hope this does not happen, but because football is a contact sport we must warn, in writing, each player and parent or guardian of the possibility of an injury while playing football.

We need each participant and parent or guardian to sign this notice that acknowledges they have read this letter and do not hold the school district liable for any accident or injury that may occur while the undersigned participant is playing football for School District No. 25.

Sincerely,

BYRON TOONE
Director of Athletics

I have read this letter and do not hold the school liable for any accident or injury that may occur while playing football.

Player: _____

Parent or Guardian: _____

Date: _____

parents...

_____	_____
Student's Name	Class Period
_____	
Teacher's Name	

August 25, 19XX

Dear Parents:

This year at Carlsbad Junior High, the Physical Education classes will be stressing more physical fitness. This will include running, jumping rope, conditioning and basic skills in sports.

If for any reason your child cannot participate in running or strenuous activities please contact the Physical Education Department or the school nurse, Mrs. Peggy Townsend, immediately at

The approved physical education uniform is blue shorts with a white stripe, a white shirt with a blue striped sleeve and a pair of tennis shoes (any color). This uniform is required to provide safety and flexibility for students. Include your child's name on the back of the shirt and on the leg of the shorts. This is done so that if the uniform is lost or stolen, it will be easily recognized by the teachers.

If you have any questions or problems, please feel free to call.

_____

Parent's Signature

_____

Address

_____

Telephone Number

COMMENTS:

LIABILITY, LEGAL

See Also: INSURANCE

release form ...

WARNING, AGREEMENT TO OBEY INSTRUCTIONS, RELEASE, AS-
SUMPTION OF RISK, AND AGREEMENT TO HOLD HARMLESS

(Both the applicant student and a parent or guardian must read carefully and sign.)

SPORT: (Student must circle all sports he or she will participate in.)

Baseball	Cross Country	Soccer	Track
Basketball	Football	Softball	Volleyball
Bowling	Golf	Tennis	Wrestling

- -

STUDENT

I am aware that playing or practicing to play/participate in any sport can be dangerous in nature involving MANY RISKS OF INJURY. I understand that the dangers and risks of playing or practicing to play/participate in the above sport include, but are not limited to, death, serious neck and spinal injuries which may result in complete or partial paralysis, brain damage, serious injury to virtually all bones, joints, ligaments, muscles, tendons, and other aspects of the muscular skeletal system, serious injury to virtually all internal organs, and serious injury or impairment to other aspects of my body, general health and well-being. I understand that the dangers and risks of playing or practicing to play/participate in the above sport may result not only in serious injury, but in a serious impairment of my future abilities to earn a living, to engage in other business, social and recreational activities, and generally to enjoy life.

Because of the dangers of participating in the above sports, I recognize the importance of following coaches' instructions regarding playing techniques, training and other team rules, etc., and to agree to obey such instructions.

In consideration of the Clark County School District permitting me to try out for the Chaparral High School teams circled and to engage in all activities related to the team, including, but not limited to, trying out, practicing or playing/participating in that sport, I hereby assume all the risks associated with participation and agree to hold the Clark County School District, its employees, agents, representatives, coaches, and volunteers harmless from any and all liability, actions, causes of action, debts, claims, or demands of any kind and nature whatsoever which may arise by or in connection with my participation in any activities related to the Chaparral High School (indicate sport/sports) _____
team/teams. The terms hereof shall serve as a release and assumption of risk for my heirs, estate, executor, administrator, assignees, and for all members of my family.

> The following to be completed if sport is football, wrestling, or baseball:
>
> I specifically acknowledge that _____
> (indicate sport)
>
> is a VIOLENT CONTACT SPORT involving even greater risk of injury than other sports. _____
> (initial)

Date _____, 19____, _____
Signature of Student

(over)

PARENT

In consideration of the Clark County School District permitting my son/daughter to try out for the Chaparral High School _____ team
(indicate sport/sports)
and to engage in all activities related to the team, including, but not limited to, trying out, practicing or playing/participating in that sport, I hereby assume all the risks of my son/daughter associated with participation and agree to hold the Clark County School District, its employees, agents, representatives, coaches, and volunteers harmless from any and all liability, actions, causes of action, debts, claims, or demands of any kind and nature whatsoever which may arise by or in connection with his/her participation in any activities related to the Chapparral High School _____ team.
(indicate sport/sports)

The terms hereof shall serve as a release and assumption of risk for my son's/daughter's heirs, estate, executor, administrator, assignees, and for all members of his/her family.

I have read and understand the risks as detailed in the student section of this agreement on the opposite side of this card.

> The following to be completed if sport is football, wrestling, or baseball:
>
> I specifically acknowledge that _____
> (indicate sport)
>
> is a VIOLENT CONTACT SPORT involving even greater risk of injury than other sports. _____
> (initial)

Date _____, 19____, _____
Signature of Parent
or Guardian

LOCKER ROOM USAGE BULLETIN

See: FACILITY

LOCKERS, CLEANING OF

See Also: FACILITY; THEFT

notice for...

PROCEDURE FOR CLEARING ATHLETIC AND/OR P.E. LOCKERS

When a need is determined to remove school or personal items from a student's locker, do the following:

1. Make an inventory sheet recording:
   a. The date
   b. The student's name
   c. The lock number
   d. The locker number
   e. All school items removed
   f. All personal items removed.
2. Clear all student records, including the school bank, of school assigned items. (e.g. athletic uniforms and/or equipment, locks, etc.)
3. Attempt to contact the student or parents to claim the personal items. If they cannot be reached, maintain all personal items in a safe storage place until the end of the academic year. If not claimed by then, the items can be placed into general use or discarded.

loss of eligibility...

See Also: POLICIES AND PROCEDURES

LOST EQUIPMENT

See: EQUIPMENT

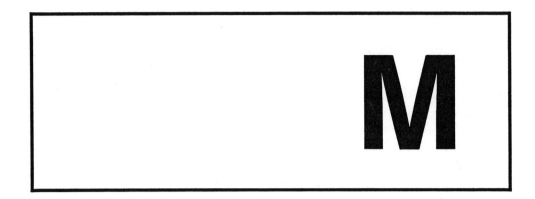

MAINTENANCE

facility checklist...

See: FACILITY

requisition form (custodial)...

See: REQUESTS AND REQUISITIONS

MEDICAL

See Also: ACCIDENT REPORT FORM; EXAMINATIONS; INJURY; INSURANCE; PARTICIPATION; PERMISSIONS

consent form...

HILLDALE HIGH SCHOOL
DIST. I-29
Muskogee, Oklahoma

MEDICAL CONSENT FORM

Athlete: _____

Permission is hereby granted to the attending physician to proceed with any medical or minor surgical treatment, X-ray examinations and immunizations for the above named student. In the event of serious illness, the need for major surgery, or significant accidental injury, I understand that an attempt will be made by the attending physician to contact me in the most expeditious way possible. If said physician is not able to communicate with me, the treatment necessary for the best interest of the above named student may be given.

In the event that an emergency arises during a practice session, an effort will be made to contact the parents or guardian as soon as possible. Permission is also granted to the athletic trainer to provide the needed emergency treatment to the athlete prior to his admission to the medical facilities.

Signature of Parent or Guardian _____

Date _____

Phone numbers where parents can be reached:

Office _____   Name of Family Physician

Home _____   _____

Other _____   Phone No. _____

report form (two examples)...

STUDENT'S MEDICAL HISTORY
(To be completed by parents or family physician)

Name of student _____ Birth date _____

Address _____ Tel. No. _____

1. Has had injuries requiring medical attention	Yes	No
2. Has had illness lasting more than a week	Yes	No
3. Is under a physician's care now	Yes	No
4. Takes medication now	Yes	No
5. Wears glasses	Yes	No
Contact lenses	Yes	No
6. Has had a surgical operation	Yes	No
7. Has been in hospital (except for tonsillectomy)	Yes	No
8. Do you know of any reason why this individual should not participate in all sports?	Yes	No

Please explain any "Yes" answers to above question:

_____

_____

9. Has had complete poliomyelitis immunization by oral vaccine (Sabin)(Salk)	Yes	No
10. Has had primary series of tetanus toxoid (DPT or DT) and a booster within the last 10 years	Yes	No

Date: _____ Signed: _____

(Parent or Physician)

PHYSICIAN'S CERTIFICATE

(To be filled in and signed by the examining physician)
(Separate examination and certificate required for each school year, July 1 through the ensuing June 30)
(Cooperatively prepared by the National Federation of State High School Associations and the Committee on Medical Aspects of Sports of the American Medical Association)

- -

(Please Print)

Name of Student _____City and School _____

Grade _____ Age _____ Ht _____ Wt _____ Blood Pressure _____

Significant Past Illness or Injury _____

_____

Eyes _____ R 20/   ; L 20/   ; Ears _____ Hearing R /15; L /15_____

Respiratory _____

Cardiovascular _____

Liver _____Spleen _____Hernia _____

Musculoskeletal _____Genitalia _____

Laboratory: Urinalysis _____Other: _____

Comments: _____

- -

I certify that I have on this date examined this student and find him/her physically able to compete in supervised activities NOT CROSSED OUT BELOW.

BASEBALL	GOLF	SOCCER	TRACK
BASKETBALL	GYMNASTICS	SOFTBALL	VOLLEYBALL
CROSS COUNTRY	RIFLERY	SWIMMING	*WRESTLING
FOOTBALL	ROWING	TENNIS	O T H E R S
			_____

*Weight loss permitted to make lower weight class: Yes _____ No _____ If "Yes," may lose ___ pounds.

Date of Examination: _____ Signed: _____, M.D.
(Examining Physician)

Physician's Address _____ Phone No. _____

* * * * *

CARLSBAD MUNICIPAL SCHOOLS
ATHLETIC MEDICAL FORM
(Below to be filled out by Legal Guardian)

Date _____

PRINT ALL INFORMATION

Name _____ Age _____ Birthdate _____

Address _____ Phone Number _____

Parents/Guardians _____

Family Doctor _____

Medications & Medical History: (Allergies _____ Injuries _____ Head & Neck Injuries _____;

Operations _____ Serious Illnesses _____)

COMMENTS: _____

_____

Parents/Guardians Signature _____

- -

(Below to be filled out by Physician)

Head, Eyes, Ears, Nose & Throat:	Height _____
	Weight _____
Cardio-Respiratory:	BP _____
	P _____
Abdomen, Hernia, Genitalia:	UR: Protein _____
Muscolo-Skeletal:	Sugar _____

Podiatric:

"I certify that I have on this date examined this student and that, on the basis of the examination requested by the school authorities and the student's medical history as furnished to me, I have found no reason which would make it medically inadvisable for this student to compete in supervised athletic activities.

Date _____

Examined By: _____

MEETS

See Also: ANNOUNCEMENTS; TOURNAMENT; SPECIFIC SPORT

assignments for swimming...

SWIM ENTRIES

1. Try to include every girl who has practiced regularly in one of the triangular meets. If possible, include them in exhibition events even though it will not count for their team's score.

2. Each school may enter two girls in each individual event and one team in each relay.

3. A girl may enter only three events, one of which must be a relay. A girl may not enter more than two individual events.

4. A girl may not enter both the 100 yard and 200 yard freestyle events.

5. Exhibition swimmers may be entered only if there are empty lanes available for them.

A contestant may enter no more than three events.

—one must be a relay
—diving does not count as one event
—a contestant may enter two relays

Only the boys that qualify in a qualifying meet may be entered in the city meet.

Scoring for individual events: 7 - 5 - 4 - 3 - 2 - 1
Scoring for relay events: 14 - 10 - 8 - 6 - 4 - 2

No substitutions are allowed except when a relay member becomes ill or is injured.

A medal will be awarded to each champion and a ribbon will be awarded to the second through sixth place champions.

Only boys who have had an opportunity to practice should be entered in any swimming or diving meet. Non-pool schools should arrange for practice time by calling the principal of the school where they wish to practice.

cross country, record form for...

CROSS COUNTRY

DATE: _____ DISTANCE: _____

PLACE AND COURSE: _____

ORDER OF FINISH	NAME	SCHOOL	TIME	POINTS
1.				
2.				
3.				
24.				
25.				

diving, notice of...

DIVING MEET

Each school may enter a total of six divers, 2 each from the 7th, 8th, and 9th grade. They will perform dives as listed below:

7th Grade	8th Grade	9th Grade
Any 4 dives from 4 different groups	Any 4 dives from 4 different groups	Any 5 dives from 4 different groups

Diving sheets from the finals will be mailed separately. Return to the Physical Education Office on Monday, February 11, 1985.

dual and triangular (types and schedules)...

SWIMMING

1. Coaches should have cards completed before the meet. Swimmers hold them while they wait in the "on deck" area then hand them to the lane timers when they are called to the starting blocks. If a school has extra girls who could swim exhibitions, turn the card over and write EXHIBITION in large letters on the back, with name and school. Do not fill out the front of the card for an exhibition swimmer so there is no delay or confusion in assigning to lanes, picking places, etc.

2. The coach at the host school will serve as meet director but will call upon other coaches to bring watches and perhaps serve as timers or judges.

3. Diving will be included in all dual and triangular meets.

4. Scoring

   a. Individual events in the triangular meet will be 6-4-3-2-1

   b. Individual events in the dual meet will be 5-3-1

   c. Scoring for relays will be 12-6 (triangular), 10-0 (duals)

   Final scores will be checked again after the meet and mailed to participating schools. They may be announced at the meet.

WRESTLING

1. Cheerleaders will not be allowed to cheer from the floor during tournaments. Hopefully this will eliminate the congestion near the mats.

2. A match will consist of three one-minute timed periods with a moderate rest between periods for eighth graders. The ninth grade team will wrestle 1-2-2 minute periods in all dual meets and tournaments.

3. There must be absolutely no weight cutting. This is the responsibility of the individual coaches. No boy will be permitted to wrestle up more than one weight classification. A wrestler cannot enter city tournament at a weight lower than lowest weight class wrestled during season. A wrestler entering city must have at least one dual meet at the weight class.

4. At the qualifying meets, weigh-in will begin at 2:00 p.m. and continue until finished. Weight will be taken in wrestling attire, excluding shoes. Weigh-in will not be conducted at the finals.

At all dual meets and qualifying meets, wrestlers will be allowed two pounds over their weight class with uniform on excluding shoes.

5. Scoring will be as follows:

   Overtime in districts and city finals will be three 30-second periods for both 8th and 9th grades.

6. Medals will be awarded to the champion and ribbons to the runner-ups at the city meet.

7. Officials are being assigned by the Physical Education Office for all meets. These assignments will be mailed to each principal and coach during the first week of November. Officials will be reimbursed at the rate of $14.00 for dual meets, $17.00 for 8th and 9th grade meets, and $22.00 for city meets.

8. All junior high wrestling coaches should attend the state rules meeting that will be held in the local area.

9. Students should not be cut from a wrestling squad.

NOTE: The use of head gear will be required.
   All weights are Top Limits at all meets.

Organizational Pattern

There will be four mats in use during 8th and 9th grade qualifying matches at Lewis and Clark and Mann. During the finals at Norris three mats will be used.

On December 5 and 6, 19XX, both sites will qualify one wrestler for each weight classification.

On December 10, 19XX, semi-finals and final matches will be necessary to determine champions.

Summary of Scoring

Dual Meet

Fall - 6 points
Forfeit - 6 points
Default - 6 points
Superior decision - 5 points
  (by 12 or more points)
Major decision - 4 points
  (by 8 to 11 points)
Regular decision - 3 points
Draw - 2 points

Tournament

Advancement - 2 points
Fall - 2 points
Default - 2 points
Forfeit - 2 points
Disqualification - 2 points
Superior decision - 1 point
Major decision - 1 point

entry forms for...

—gymnastics

See: GYMNASTICS

—track and field

See: TOURNAMENT

MEMOS

See Also: ANNOUNCEMENTS; BULLETINS; FLIERS

agenda...

To: All Head Coaches at Muskogee High School

From: J. D. Buchanan and J. R. Johnson

Date: February 18, 19

RE: Head Coach Meeting, Tuesday 2/22/XX, at 1:00 PM, in A-205

AGENDA

1. Oklahoma Six Conference Business

   a. Conduct of Coaches at Contests and Comments to Media.
   b. Oklahoma Six Banquet—Monday, 4/18/XX at Harrison's Steakhouse—MHS
      gets 15 tickets. Extra need cost $13.25 each.
   c. Conduct of Students/Athletes.

2. April 15 (Friday) Muskogee Invitational Track Meet

   a. Help!
   b. Substitutes for Coaches.

3. 1983-84 Athletic Budgets

   a. 1982-83 Revenue Projections vs Actual Receipts.
   b. 1983-84 Revenue Projections.
   c. 1983-84 Budgets.

4. Coaching Positions

5. Your Questions, Concerns, Comments.

athletic requirements...

To: All Coaches

From: J. R. Johnson, Assistant Principal, Athletics/Ron Wolff, Principal

Date: September 28, 19XX

RE: Athlete Requirements

It is imperative that each student who is participating in any sport in any way must meet the requirement or a physical examination, a completed contract, and either insurance as made available through the school or signed statement by the parents that they have adequate insurance for coverage for the student.

Guidelines:

1. All students must have physical examinations, insurance clearance, and a completed contract before the competitive season begins and/or before physical contact begins.

2. The coach is responsible for this process. Each head coach should make sure the information is completed and submitted to the athletic director.

3. The athletic director is responsible to inservice each new head coach on the process outlined above. He is also responsible to make sure that each coach has turned in "something" for each sport.

_____

James R. Johnson

_____

Ron Wolff

meeting summary ...

To: All Head Coaches and J. R. Johnson

From: J. D. Buchanan

Date: October 19, 19XX

RE: Written Summary of 10/19/XX Coaches Meeting on Budget

To cut down expenses we will do the following:

a) Use fewer police at 10/28/XX home football game.

b) Establish schedule for coaches to assume gate keeper and ticket-taker duties at home basketball and wrestling contests, thereby, eliminating paid employees.

c) Limit athletic purchases to absolute necessities until further notice. Each coach must submit those necessities to Mr. Buchanan in writing and Mr. Buchanan will forward any orders to vendors.

To raise revenue Mr. Buchanan will approach Mr. Gaines about several ideas raised in the meeting and report back to the group in a future meeting.

multiple activities ...

To: All Coaches

From: Dean Forrest, AD

On: STUDENT INVOLVED IN MULTIPLE ACTIVITIES AND/OR ATHLETICS

We are all aware that most active and talented students involve themselves in many activities with the result that occasionally there will be a conflict in practices and/or performances. It is our responsibility to help guide and direct students in their choices so these conflicts will be minimized. However, we should not discourage students from developing and demonstrating multiple talents and abilities.

The following guidelines are provided to help students, parents, advisors, and coaches to deal fairly and consistently with conflicts that arise with these multi-talented students.

A. In the event a student is scheduled for a practice and a performance on the same day or evening, the performance should always take precedence with no penalty to the student in the activity in which he/she cannot participate.

B. In the event a student is scheduled for activities of equal classification (i.e. two practices/rehearsals or two performances occurring simultaneously) the student should be allowed to make a choice without pressure or penalty from either of the coordinating adults of the two activities.

sports banquet...

MUSKOGEE HIGH SCHOOL

MEMORANDUM

DATE _____ May 13, 19XX _____

TO _____ All Coaches _____

FROM _____ J. R. Johnson _____

SUBJ. _____ All-Sports Banquet _____

In order that there may not be any misunderstanding about who may attend the All-Sports Banquet, for each sport all students who played the entire season, managers, statisticians, bookkeepers, and trainers are eligible to attend without cost.

NATIONAL INTERSCHOLASTIC ATHLETIC ADMINISTRATOR'S ASSOCIATION (NIAAA)

See Also: ATHLETIC DIRECTOR

general information on...

STATEMENT OF PURPOSE...

A NATIONAL PROFESSIONAL ORGANIZATION, administered by and for high school athletic administrators for the purpose of:

● PROMOTING the professional growth and image of interscholastic athletic administrators;

● PROMOTING the development and prestige of state athletic administrators organizations which will contribute, in cooperation with their state high school associations, to the interscholastic athletic program of each state;

● PROVIDING an efficient system for the exchange of ideas between the National Federation of State High School Associations and state athletic directors organizations and individual athletic administrators; and

● PRESERVING the educational nature of interscholastic athletics and the place of these programs in the curricula of schools.

NIAAA MEMBERSHIP CATEGORIES...

Regular Membership is open to anyone employed by a school or school district in the United States who has among his/her responsibilities the administration of interscholastic athletics.

Associate Membership is open to anyone who:

(a) is involved in some phase of school, or athletic administration in the United States or a foreign country, or

(b) is a student or instructor in athletic administration.

Associate members receive all benefits and services afforded a regular member, except voting or holding office.

Retired Membership is open to any retired person who has been a regular member of this association. Retired members receive all benefits (except insurance) and services afforded a regular member including opportunities to serve on NIAAA committees, but may not vote or be elected to office.

Organizational Membership is open to state athletic directors associations. Organizational members receive the Annual National Directory of State Athletic Directors Associations, the use of the NIAAA logo, Speakers Resource Book, and the privilege of appointing delegates to the NIAAA Representative Assembly.

*DUES

Regular and Associate Membership	$20.00**
Retired Membership	$10.00**
Organizational Membership	$25.00 per delegate**

The NIAAA is a non-profit professional organization exempt from federal income tax under section 501(c)(3) of the Internal Revenue Code.
*Membership dues and contributions are tax deductible.
**(*Figures here are as of June 1, 19XX and may change.*)

NIAAA MEMBERSHIP BENEFITS...

1. Interscholastic Athletic Administration magazine: A quarterly professional journal written by, and for, athletic administrators such as yourself.

2. National Federation News: A monthly magazine that includes the latest information on rule changes, interpretations and questionnaires on proposed rule changes, as well as, a wealth of timely articles that will benefit you and your entire coaching staff.

3. Proceedings: A bound report of the presentations from the National Federation's Annual Conference of High School Directors of Athletics.

4. *Insurance Benefits: That cover you while you are fulfilling your responsibilities as athletic director, including travel to or from an activity for which you are responsible as an athletic administrator.
    $1,000,000 Personal Liability
    $50,000 Excess Major Medical
    $5,000 Death Benefit

5. A $10 Discount: On the registration fee for the National Conference of High School Directors of Athletics, to be held in Milwaukee, Wisconsin, on December 9-12, 1984.

6. *Other Discounts to NIAA Members:
    Howard Johnson and Best Western Hotels
    Avis and Hertz Car and Truck Rentals
    Conference Speaker Tapes

7. An Athletic Sure Rate Card: Good at more than 300 participating Holiday Inns for individual or team travel.

8. Your Opportunity to participate in the nation's largest professional organization, whose activities are directed exclusively to high school athletic administration.

*Toll-free numbers for reporting insurance claims, or making hotel reservations, as well as the appropriate ID numbers that qualify you for these discounts, are printed on the back of each membership card for easy reference.

HOW THINGS GET DONE...
QUARTERLY MAGAZINE

The National Federation's Interscholastic Athletic Administration magazine has been adopted as the official publication of the National Interscholastic Athletic Administrators Association. A section of the magazine is devoted to news of the NIAAA including meeting announcements, proposed changes in the Constitution and Bylaws, financial reports, election notices, committee appointments, proposed resolutions, and much, much more. NIAAA reports are also reported in the National Federation NEWS.

THE ANNUAL MEETING

The National Federation hosts the NIAAA Annual Meeting in conjunction with its National Conference of High School Directors of Athletics. This affords the NIAAA members the opportunity to participate in:

Sectional Caucuses—Committee Meetings
Business Meetings—Formal and informal sessions with outstanding athletic
administrators from throughout North America.

LEGISLATIVE BODY

The REPRESENTATIVE ASSEMBLY is the legislative body that elects members to the Board of Directors, and frames the national policy for the NIAAA. It consists of delegates elected by the Organizational Members, the individual state athletic director associations.

NATIONAL OPERATING COMMITTEE ON STANDARDS FOR ATHLETIC EQUIPMENT (NOCSAE)

See Also: EQUIPMENT; SAFETY

questions and answers concerning (bulletin on)...

NOCSAE has, since its inception in 1969, received numerous questions concerning the policies and procedures of the organization. Following is a list of questions and answers that represent the most common concerns of all involved.

1. What is NOCSAE?
NOCSAE (pronounced "noxey") is the acronym for the National Operating Committee on Standards for Athletic Equipment. The group was formed in 1969 in response to a need for a safety standard for football helmets. In 1973, the NOCSAE Football Helmet Standard was developed; and the 1974 helmet models were the first to undergo the NOCSAE tests. The baseball batting helmet standard was released in 1981, and the 1983 helmet models were the first to undergo NOCSAE tests. The baseball standard has now been designated as the baseball/softball batting helmet standard. In addition to testing baseball and football helmets, NOCSAE conducts tests on other athletic equipment to explore the feasibility of establishing safety standards.

2. Who belongs to NOCSAE?

The members of NOCSAE are the National Collegiate Athletic Association, National Association of Intercollegiate Athletics, National Federation of State High School Associations, National Junior College Athletic Association, Sporting Goods Manufacturing Association, American College Health Association, National Athletic Trainers Association, National Sporting Goods Dealer Association, National Athletic Equipment Reconditioners Association, and Athletic Equipment Managers Association. In addition, the National Football League Players Association is an associate member.

3. What are the NOCSAE Helmet Standards?

They are voluntary test standards that have been developed to reduce head injuries by establishing minimum requirements of impact attenuation for football helmets and baseball/softball batting helmets.

4. How are football helmets tested?

The NOCSAE Test Standard involves mounting a football helmet on a synthetic head model and dropping it a total of 16 times onto a firm rubber pad including two each from a height of 60 inches onto six locations at ambient temperatures. Two 60-inch drops onto the front corner also are conducted immediately after exposure of the helmet to 120°F for four hours. Shock measurements are taken to determine if the helmet meets an established Severity Index for concussion tolerance and thereby passes the NOCSAE Football Helmet standard test.

An equivalent to the 60-inch drop test would occur if a player running at 17.9 feet per second (12.2 mph) ran into a flat surface which stopped his head in less than one inch. Most players run faster than this, i.e., the average speed of a player running 40 yards in 4.8 seconds is 25 feet per second, but very rarely would the head be stopped in such a short distance on the football field.

5. Who tests football helmets for compliance with the NOCSAE test standard?

Manufacturers test their own and competitors' helmets as they are produced. Qualified reconditioners partial test used helmets in the recertification process. The principal investigator tests new and used helmets in the event of controversy.

6. How are baseball/softball batting helmets tested?

These batting helmets are tested in a manner similar to football helmets, except that instead of dropping the helmet and head form onto a hard surface, an air cannon is used to fire a baseball at the helmet at specific speeds, angles and locations. Shock measurements are taken and the Severity Index is calculated and compared with the NOCSAE Standard to determine if the helmet meets the Standard.

7. Are all helmet sizes tested?

No. It would not be feasible to test all helmet sizes. Therefore, the most critical sizes (6 ⅝, 7 ¼ and 7 ⅝) are tested in the three common shell sizes used by most equipment manufacturers. The sizes have the least amount of standoff distance from the shell and if these shell sizes pass the NOCSAE Standard, it is reasonable to assume the other helmet sizes in that particular shell also would pass.

8. Does a helmet model have to pass in all three test sizes?

Yes, if offered for sale in those sizes. If a helmet fails to pass the test in any of the models, it will not be listed on the NOCSAE Helmet Certification list and will not bear a NOCSAE seal.

9. Does a certified helmet attenuate shock better than a noncertified helmet?

Yes, according to laboratory test results certified helmets should perform at Severity Indexes significantly lower on the average than predecessors, due to size adjustments, materials and design changes and elimination of many models.

10. Would making the NOCSAE test more severe produce helmets which perform better in the field?

Quality of materials, methods of fabrication and design concepts now available for manufacturing helmets would tend to increase the weight, size and stiffness of helmets if the tests were made more severe. All of these factors could increase the risk of injury to the wearer and to opponents. NOCSAE is continually studying all types of helmets and test conditions.

NUMBER OF STUDENTS PER COACHING STAFF

See: SPECIFIC SPORT

notice on ...

Number of Students Involved

Sport	Minimum
Football 1 head coach 1 asst. coach	20 (If total number falls below 20, reduce one assistant coach
Basketball	10 per team
Gymnastics 2 head coaches	10 per team
Swimming 2 head coaches	10 per team
Track & Field 2 head coaches 1 asst. coach (for combined boys & girls)	(If total number falls below 30, reduce one assistant coach)
Volleyball	10 per team
Wrestling	15

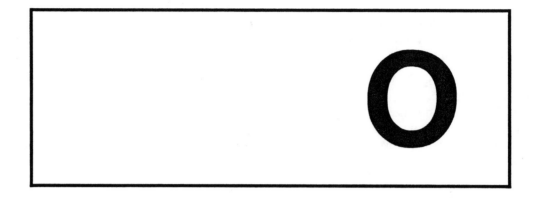

OFFICIALS

See Also: ANNOUNCERS' FORMS; CONTEST; GAME REPORT; HOME GAME ACTIVITY; VISITING SCHOOLS

conduct of, improper...

Dear Mr.

I was dissatisfied with the decisions that were made in our game on 9/19/ , at High School. The two officials, of your association, that were assigned to the game were Mr. and Mr.

The first quarter time was kept by a student from . Mr. had the back-up time and noticed that it had gone 2 minutes past the required 20 minutes. He decided to keep the time in the second quarter. had scored three goals in the second quarter and as time continued, scored a fourth. Mr. stopped his watch at 20 minutes, 9 seconds gone for the fourth goal. The student timer had approximately 2 minutes more to go in the second quarter. A discussion between Mr. , Mr. , and the coach continued for 5 minutes. I then came to ask for a decision. The matter was explained to me and I asked Mr. for a decision. The decision was to award the fourth goal and play 51 seconds more. The second quarter totaled 21 minutes and I believe that time was to be cut short later. This was a violation of Rule No. 7, Articles 1 and 2.

Later in the game, a ball was crossed from our left wing, through the goal mouth of , to our right wing. Mr. apparently mistook a football yard line for the soccer goal line. The whistle blew and the players stopped. Mr. realized his mistake but awarded a goal kick. A mistake is understandable but I think the correct call was a drop ball.

I pride myself in my behavior as a coach. I try to be an example to my players in respecting the referees and their decisions; but, when the decisions are not in accordance with the rules as stated, it is hard to teach respect.

Mr. _____, would you please put this matter before your professional standards committee. Also, kindly inform me about any actions that your body may take.

Sincerely,

contract for...

New Mexico Activities Association
CONTRACT FOR OFFICIALS

_____ New Mexico _____, 19_____

The _____ High School and _____
(Official's Name and Address)
_____, an official registered with the New Mexico Activities Association, hereby enter into the following agreement: The said official agrees to be present and officiate _____
(NAME OF SPORT)
games or meets to be played with _____ High School.

	Date	Hour	Place	Position	Fee and Expenses
1.	_____	_____	_____	_____	_____
2.	_____	_____	_____	_____	_____
3.	_____	_____	_____	_____	_____
4.	_____	_____	_____	_____	_____

1. It is mutually agreed that the official shall be regarded as an independent contractor and holds registration card No. _____ in said association.

2. The said school will pay the said official the amount stated above for his services, provided that the obligation of the school ceases if and when the official ceases to be a registered official or if the contest is cancelled because of unfavorable weather, epidemics or other emergencies.

3. The Association reserves the right to drop an official whose dues are not paid, who is unfair and biased and whose conduct on or off the field or floor unfits him to act as an official.

4. If either party hereto fails to fulfill the obligation of any part of the contract, that party shall pay to the other party the sum of $_____ as damages, the remainder of the contract shall not be binding, and the breach of contract shall be reported to the Association.

Principal _____   Date Signed _____, 19_____

Official _____   Date Signed _____, 19_____

report on...

**OKLAHOMA SECONDARY SCHOOL ACTIVITIES ASSOCIATION
REPORT ON OFFICIATING**

_____ SCHOOL _____ year 19_____ 19_____
(Sport)

_____
(Signature and Title of Person Making Rating)

This is a confidential report to the Board of Directors on all officials used in all contests during the season. Please list officials in alphabetical order. Show total number of games used and give a composite rating for each official.

THE FOLLOWING FACTORS SHOULD BE CONSIDERED IN MAKING EVALUATION.

- Knowledge and application of Rules and Mechanics
- Speed and endurance in following play.
- Consistency in judging infractions of rules.

- Cooperation with other officials
- Leadership and ability to control game situations.
- Friendliness, courtesy, firmness, self-control, dependability and neatness.

RATING KEY: S-Superior; G-Good; F-Fair; U-Unsatisfactory; P-Poor   (Reason must be given on back side when rating is poor.)

OFFICIALS FULL NAME	NO. OF GAMES	COMPOSITE RATING	OFFICIALS FULL NAME	NO. OF GAMES	COMPOSITE RATING
HOME			AWAY		

use of movies to check calls of (notice on)...

It should be recognized that slow motion study of controversial decisions by officials is far different from on-the-spot decisions which must be made during the course of a game. To show critical plays to sportswriters, sportscasters, alumni, and the public which may incite them to label officials as incompetents must be considered unethical conduct.

ORDERING

See Also: ATHLETIC DIRECTOR; BID SURVEY; BUDGET; PURCHASE ORDER; REQUESTS AND REQUISITIONS; UNIFORMS; VOUCHER

rulebooks...

PLEASE ENTER MY ORDER FOR THE FOLLOWING RULEBOOKS AND FORWARD THEM AS SOON AS AVAILABLE.

BOOK		PRICE EACH		QUANTITY	TOTAL
FOOTBALL RULEBOOK		$2.25			
FOOTBALL CASEBOOK		2.25			
FOOTBALL HANDBOOK		2.25			
FOOTBALL OFFICIALS' MANUAL		2.25			
FOOTBALL SIMPLIFIED AND ILLUSTRATED		2.25			
SOCCER RULEBOOK		2.25			
VOLLEYBALL RULEBOOK		2.25			
VOLLEYBALL SCOREBOOK	Picked-Up $2.00	3rd Class $2.50	1st Class $3.00		
BASKETBALL RULEBOOK		2.25			
BASKETBALL CASEBOOK		2.25			
BASKETBALL HANDBOOK		2.25			
BASKETBALL OFFICIALS' MANUAL		2.25			
BASKETBALL SIMPLIFIED AND ILLUSTRATED		2.25			
WRESTLING RULEBOOK		2.25			
WRESTLING OFFICIALS' MANUAL		2.25			
SOFTBALL RULEBOOK		2.25			
SWIMMING RULEBOOK		2.25			
GYMNASTICS RULEBOOK (BOYS)		3.25			
TENNIS RULEBOOK		2.25			
TRACK AND FIELD RULEBOOK		2.25			
TRACK AND FIELD OFFICIALS' MANUAL		2.25			
TRACK AND FIELD CASEBOOK		2.25			
BASEBALL RULEBOOK		2.25			
BASEBALL UMPIRES' MANUAL		2.25			
BASEBALL CASEBOOK		2.25			

CHECK ONE (✔)   1. Payment Enclosed _____   2. Bill the School _____

Ship to: _____   _____
                      (Name)   (School)

scheduling of...

MEMORANDUM

TO: PRINCIPALS
        OTHER ADMINISTRATORS

FROM: Gynna Thornton, Purchasing

DATE: March 7, 19XX

SUBJECT: PURCHASE ORDER CUT-OFF DATES

THE CUT OFF DATES FOR 19XX ARE AS FOLLOWS:

OUT-OF-TOWN ORDERS	APRIL 1, 19XX
UNDER $25.00 PURCHASE ORDERS DUE IN PURCHASING OFFICE	MAY 31, 19XX
IN-TOWN ORDERS	JUNE 10, 19XX
FINAL WAREHOUSE ORDERS DUE (Orders received after this date will be charged to 19XX/XX Budget)	JUNE 18, 19XX
OUTSTANDING ORDERS CANCELLED	JUNE 1, 19XX

Any needs for supplies between May 31, and June 10, 19XX, can be handled directly through the Business Office by submitting a request sheet. After June 10, 19XX, purchases will only be approved in special circumstances.

PLEASE SHARE THIS INFORMATION WITH ACTIVITY SPONSORS, LIBRARIANS, AND OTHER APPROPRIATE PERSONNEL.

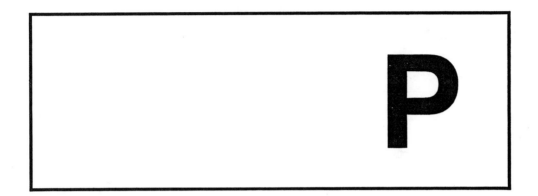

PARENTS

letters...

> *See:* LETTER ON/TO

release form...

> *See:* LIABILITY, LEGAL

PARTICIPATION

> *See Also:* CONTRACTS; PERMISSIONS; PERMITS; POLICIES AND PROCEDURES; REQUESTS AND REQUISITIONS; RULES AND REGULATIONS; SPECIFIC SPORT

athletic contests, contract for...

STUDENT PARTICIPATION AGREEMENT

Student's Name _____ School _____
　　　　　　　Last　　　　　　First　　　　Middle Initial
Birth Date _____ Place of Birth _____ Date _____

This application to compete in interscholastic athletics for the above high school is entirely voluntary on my part and is made with the understanding that I have not violated any of the eligibility rules and regulations of the State Association. I will adhere to the rules and regulations set forth by the school and the Nebraska School Activities Association. Furthermore, I understand that I will be held responsible for athletic equipment checked out to me. I recognize that it is a privilege to compete in athletics and will strive to earn respect for myself, school and community.

_____
Signature of Student

PARENT'S OR GUARDIAN'S PERMISSION

"I hereby give my consent for the above named student (1) to represent the school in athletic activities, except those crossed out below, provided that such athletic activities are approved by the State Association:

BASEBALL　　FOOTBALL　　BASKETBALL　　CROSS COUNTRY　VOLLEYBALL　　GOLF
GYMNASTICS　SWIMMING　　TENNIS　　　　TRACK　　　　　WRESTLING

(2) to accompany any school team of which he/she is a member on any of its local or out-of-town trips. I authorize the school to obtain, through a physician of its own choice, any emergency medical care that may become reasonably necessary for the student in the course of such athletic activities or such travel. I also agree not to hold the school or anyone acting in its behalf responsible for any injury occurring to the above named student in the course of such athletic activities or such travel."

ATHLETIC INSURANCE COVERAGE

Your school, acting for members of the athletic squad, makes available an Athlete Injury Benefit Plan approved by the Omaha Board of Education. The total premium is paid for by the student or parent. The purpose of such coverage is to assist in the cost of treatment of accidental injury. Payments are in addition to any payment by another company for the same injury.

Check the statements which apply:

SQUAD MEMBERS MUST HAVE INSURANCE COVERAGE TO PARTICIPATE.

_____ I shall participate in the Athletic Benefit Injury Plan. Information brochures, if not attached, are available from the school office upon request.
_____ I have accident injury coverage with the _____insurance company.

POLICY NO. _____ Signature of Parent or Guardian _____

Date _____ Address _____

Note: This form is to be filled out completely and filed in the office of the school before student is allowed to practice and/or compete.

PEP CLUBS

See: BOOSTERS

PERMISSIONS

See Also: ACCIDENT REPORT FORM; MEDICAL; TRANSPORTATION, TRAVEL, AND TRIPS

parental (four examples)...

CLARK COUNTY SCHOOL DISTRICT
SOLICITATION OF FUNDS
PARENT PERMISSION SLIP FOR

TO: _____ DATE: _____
　　　　　　　Parent or Guardian Name

I hereby give my consent for my son/daughter _____
　　　　　　　　　　　　　　　　　　　　　　　Student Name

to participate in the solicitation of funds for the authorized school project identified below.

1. ACTIVITY _____

2. ORGANIZATION _____

3. DATE OF PROJECT _____

4. SCHOOL _____

I understand that my son/daughter will be involved in this fund-raising project for the purpose and during the dates cited above, and they may or may not be on the school campus during all times during the completion of this project.

_____　_____
SIGNATURE OF PRINCIPAL　　　　　　SIGNATURE OF PARENT OR GUARDIAN

I do not wish my son/daughter to participate in this activity as identified from this Clark County School District form.

　　　　　　　　　　　　_____
　　　　　　　　　　　　SIGNATURE OF PARENT OR GUARDIAN

* * * * *

CARLSBAD MUNICIPAL SCHOOL DISTRICT NO. 20

In consideration of the Carlsbad Municipal School District No. 20 permitting _____ to participate in _____ a sanctioned New Mexico Activities Association activity, we hereby give permission and consent for: _____ _____ to participate in such activity, including participation in all out-of-town contest pertaining to such activity, and we further agree as follows:

1. We understand and agree that this activity is elective, and therefore, because our child has choosen to participate in this activity, we hereby accept the responsibility for payment of all medical bills, including, but not limited to, charges for doctors, hospitals and drugs which our child may incur by reason of participation in such activity, except we shall not be obligated to pay those medical bills which are paid for as a result of our participation in a group athletic insurance plan hereinafter mentioned.

*____ 2. We hereby agree to participate in any group activity insurance plan which the Carlsbad Municipal School District No. 20 may recommend from time to time, and agree to pay all insurance premiums required for our child to have insurance coverage and protection.

*____ 3. We are insured with _____ Policy # _____, and agree to maintain this coverage for the tenure of his/her participation in any school activity.

4. We hereby waive any claims or causes of action against the Carlsbad Municipal School District No. 20 which may arise by reason of injuries to our child because of such participation and agree that said School District is released and forever acquitted from all and any claims of liability to us or our child, or both for injuries sustained by our child because of such participation, excepting any claim for injury which may arise as the sole result of negligence on the part of said School District. We further hereby agree to hold harmless and to indemnify said School District of and from any and all actions, causes of action, claims liabilities, costs and expenses, including attorney fees, on account of, or in any way growing out of injuries sustained by our child because of such participation, excepting those which may arise as the sole result of negligence on the part of said School District.

WITNESS our hands and seals this ____ day of _____, 19____.

_____
(Parent)

_____
(Parent)

STATE OF NEW MEXICO } SS
COUNTY OF EDDY

The foregoing instrument was acknowledged before me this _____ day of _____, by _____ and _____ husband and wife.

My commission expires _____

_____
Notary Public

*Initial #2 or #3

* * * * *

STATE OF HAWAII
DEPARTMENT OF EDUCATION
HONOLULU, HAWAII

PARENT AUTHORIZATION FOR STUDENT TRAVEL
SAMPLE

Name of Student _____ School __Waiakea High__

Home Address _____ City _____ Home Phone _____

We (I), the undersigned, hereby grant permission, for our (my) daughter/son named above (hereinafter referred to as "said student") to participate in the following student travel activity:

_____

_____

Destination (s): _____

_____

We (I) grant permission for said student to participate in the planned activities of the travel, and to travel by car, bus, train, airplane, and other means of transportation as required.

Travel Period: from ___Indicate start of season date___ to ___End of season date___ 19_____

In the case of illness or injury to said student we (I) hereby consent to and authorize such medical or dental treatment as deemed necessary, and agree to pay for such medical and dental costs if incurred.

My child has medical coverage: _____ Yes _____ No; if Yes, check appropriate boxes:

☐ HMSA ☐ Kaiser ☐ Military
☐ Other (specify) _____

AUTHORIZATION:

Print or type Mother's/Guardian's Name	Mother's/Guardian's Signature	Date
Print or type Father's/Guardian's Name	Father's/Guardian's Signature	Date

Parents Comments:
Parents, specify any special medical or other such instructions you would want considered.

NOTE: VALUABLES OR LARGE SUMS OF MONEY SHOULD NOT BE TAKEN ON SCHOOL TRIPS.

* * * * *

MIDDLETOWN TOWNSHIP PUBLIC SCHOOLS
MIDDLETOWN, NEW JERSEY

PLEASE CHECK: _____ North _____ Bayshore _____ Thorne
              _____ South _____ Thompson

PERMISSION TO ENGAGE IN (Name Sport) _____
NAME _____GRADE _____BIRTH DATE _____
ADDRESS _____TELEPHONE _____

MEDICAL HISTORY (Please Give Dates of the Following):

Any serious accidents and/or injuries (Type) _____

Present Medication _____	Reason _____
Surgical Operations _____	Convulsive Seizures _____
Allergies _____	Hernia _____
Eyes (Vision) _____	Diabetes _____
Serious Medical Diseases _____	Chest Diseases _____
Ears, Nose, Throat _____	Hypertension _____
Cardiac (Heart Defects) _____	Orthopedic _____

ANY PREVIOUS REJECTION FROM COMPETITIVE SPORTS (Date & Reason)

_____

GIRLS: Menstrual Difficulties _____

PARENT'S FORM

The answers to the above are correct. I understand that any misrepresentation of any of the information contained herein will result in the student being denied the opportunity to participate. I hereby give my consent to the participation of

_____ IN _____
(Full Name)   (Sport)

conducted by the school against other schools and within the school. Parents and guardians should be aware that such activity involves the potential for injury which is inherent in all sports. I/we acknowledge that even with the best of coaching, use of the most advanced protective equipment and strict observation of rules, injuries are still a possibility. On rare occasions these injuries can be so severe as to result in total disability, paralysis, or even death. I/we acknowledge that I/we have read and understand this warning. I shall assume all responsibility and expense for any injury received in practice or participation. I give my permission for my son/daughter to be diagnosed and treated by the team physician should such service be necessary.

_____   _____
(Date)   (Parent's or Guardian's Signature)

PHYSICIAN'S SIGNATURE

_____   _____
(Date)   (Medical Inspector's Signature)

Height _____ Weight _____ Blood Pressure _____

This form is to be turned in to the School Nurse. Parents will be notified if rejected and a statement from the student's physician certifying his or her physical ability to participate will be necessary. Final decision, however, will be made by the School Medical Department.

PERMITS

See Also: PARTICIPATION; PERMISSIONS; TRANSPORTATION, TRAVEL, AND TRIPS

for activities...

ACTIVITY CLEARANCE SLIP

Date _____

Listed below are students who are scheduled to attend the following activity:

_____ on _____

(date and time)

If any of these student's grades or attendance is unsatisfactory, please so indicate by circling their names and returning this sheet to the sponsor of the activity by 3 p.m. today. Be sure to initial this page in order for the sponsor to know who has responded.

_____
Sponsor of Activity

SENIORS: JUNIORS: SOPHOMORES:

This list will be alphabetized, typed, run off and placed in the teachers' boxes by the sponsor of the activity at least one week before the scheduled activity. Three days before the activity, send one copy of this page to the Assistant Principal in charge of Activities. This copy will be used for typing the students' names on the Daily Bulletin. Be sure to mark off any student who was not cleared by his teachers. After returning from the activity, please turn in a list of the names of any students who did not attend the activity. The Daily Bulletin for the next day will carry a list of these students who did not attend and are not to receive an unrecorded, school-related absence.

to participate...

SCHOOL DISTRICT NO. 25
OFFICE OF THE ATHLETIC DIRECTOR

Dear Parents:

Your son or daughter is a candidate for one of the athletic teams sponsored by secondary schools of School District No. 25.

Participation of all athletic activities is voluntary, and therefore we would like to have your approval before the first practice session. In addition to your permission, it is necessary for your son/daughter to have one physical examination, followed by a yearly interim questionnaire filled out by the parents. They will not be permitted to practice or play until a satisfactory report has been filed with their coach. Even though the school district provides the best available equipment and trained supervision, the nature of athletic activities makes some injuries possible. The Pocatello School District No. 25 is not liable for bills incurred for physical examinations, or as a result of athletic injury. Such bills are the responsibility of the parents.

To protect the parent from financial hardship and to insure that the athlete receives proper medical treatment, it is required that each athlete purchase accident benefit insurance. The insurance plans listed below will provide protection at a reasonable cost. Payments are made according to a schedule and cover only specified injuries occurring during any school-sponsored activity. The benefit payments usually do not provide full reimbursement for medical expenses. If you have another insurance for health and accident, this school policy will pay only a limited amount after your other policy pays.

Byron Toone, Director of Athletics

CONSENT FORM

We have read and understand the conditions under which our son/daughter _____
(Please Print)
becomes a member of an athletic squad at school and give our consent to his/her participation.

LISTED BELOW ARE THE INSURANCE COVERAGES:

* * NOTE: This is not a contract. Refer to Certificate of Insurance for actual coverage and cost details.

PLEASE CHECK THE COVERAGE DESIRED

ALL SCHOOL ACTIVITIES INCLUDING FOOTBALL .... $13.00 _____
24 HOUR PLAN .... $36.00 _____
INCLUDING INTERSCHOLASTIC FOOTBALL

Please pay by check to Massachusetts Indemnity

ALTERNATIVE AGREEMENT

If you do not wish for your child to be a participant in the described insurance program, and in lieu of participation in any of the above plans, would prefer to use your own personal insurance to protect your child in case of any athletic injury, please read carefully, check and sign the following:

——
—— I, _____ hereby certify that I do have personal
(Parent's name)
insurance which would adequately cover interscholastic athletics, and I shall assume full financial responsibility for any athletic injury of my child requiring treatment beyond the facilities of the school, and that I shall not expect or request any financial aid from the school or any agency representing School District No. 25.

_____   _____   _____
(Student's Signature)   (Date)   (Parent's Signature)

THIS IS TO BE KEPT ON FILE IN THE PRINCIPAL'S OFFICE

PERSONNEL

See: HOME GAME ACTIVITY

PHILOSOPHY

See Also: ATHLETIC DEPARTMENT; INSPIRATIONALS; INTRAMURAL PROGRAM

activities checklist...

STUDENT ACTIVITIES PHILOSOPHY

The primary purpose of the Student Activities program is to meet those school-related interests and needs of students that are not provided for by the curricular program of the school. The activities program refers to clubs, classes, intramurals, fine arts and interscholastic programs. The following is a list of objectives for the activities for all students:

1. Help all students to learn how to use their leisure time more wisely.

2. Help all students to increase and use constructively their unique talents and skills.

3. Help all students to develop new avocational and recreational interests and skills.

4. Help all students to develop more positive attitudes toward the value of avocational and recreational activities.

5. Help all students to increase their knowledge of and skill in functioning as leaders and/or as members of a group.

6. Help all students to develop a more realistic and positive attitude towards themselves and others.

7. Help all students to develop a more positive attitude toward school as a result of participation in the student activities program.

8. Help all students to understand and participate in the democratic processes of an organization.

All school-sponsored interscholastic activities of member schools are conducted in accordance with ASAA By-laws, Rules and Policies. Additional standards may be established by each school for its own students.

athletic department (two examples)...

ATHLETIC DEPARTMENT PHILOSOPHY

The coaching staff of Bonanza High School has dedicated itself to the development of the total student athlete. Both the physical and psychological growth of each person is conscientiously considered when planning and implementing our athletic program.

Our professional staff is aware of the individual needs of youth as well as the social implications of being able to work as a member of a team. Students will be given the opportunity through extensive training, excellent equipment and good coaching to reach their maximum potential, athletically, if they dedicate themselves to our program.

Our goals are to produce young men and women who have the capacity to be successful citizens in our highly competitive society. We are committed to achieve this goal. We also want students to leave Bonanza and be able to say that they were proud to have been a part of Bonanza Athletics.

* * * * *

OUR PHILOSOPHY OF ATHLETICS

A great tradition is not built overnight. It takes the hard work of many people over many years. Through the years Anchorage teams have won many league, tournament and state championships. Many records have been set by individuals and teams, and further distinction has been earned through district and state competition.

Members of an interscholastic team have a definite responsibility to contribute to that tradition for their school, thereby gaining personal satisfaction.

The role in contributing to a tradition which brings honor to students, school, and community is worthy of the best efforts of all concerned.

PHYSICALS

See: EXAMINATIONS

POLICIES AND PROCEDURES

See Also: SPECIFIC TOPICS

activities...

CLARK COUNTY SCHOOL DISTRICT
Application and Information Guidelines Regarding Student Activities Participation for Secondary Schools

The Clark County School District sponsors a varied activities program for all students enrolled in the secondary schools. Student participation in one of these programs is governed by rules and regulations established by the District and the Nevada Interscholastic Activities Association. These guidelines have been developed to provide for:

—The uniform organization and management of each sponsored activity.

—The safety and welfare of each student participant.

—The protection of individual student rights.

—The instruction in the essential skills and attitudes needed for participation.

Establishment of Initial Secondary Student Eligibility

A. SCHOLASTIC ELIGIBILITY REQUIREMENTS

This regulation shall apply to all regular education students who represent the schools by participation in any interschool competition or out-of-school or after-school performance.

Special education students working for a regular diploma shall be subject to the same eligibility requirements as regular students.

Special education students working for an adjusted diploma or certificate of completion shall have their eligibility requirements determined by an EEP committee, under guidelines developed by the Administrative/Special Student Services Division. Such guidelines will provide for consistency in the development and implementation of eligibility standards for special education students.

1. To participate in any interscholastic activity sponsored by the District, an individual must be officially enrolled in a member school of the District.

2. Students in grades 9-11 must be enrolled in courses having a minimum credit value of three (3) units. Students in grade 12 must be enrolled in courses having a minimum credit value of two (2) units.

3. A student in grades 9-12, except a first-quarter ninth grader, must have earned a grade point average (GPA) of 2.0 for all classes during the immediate preceding nine-week grading period. A student earning less than a 2.0 GPA will be ineligible for participation for the ensuing nine-week grading period.

4. Students have an opportunity to make up a fourth-quarter GPA deficiency during the regular summer school program. Summer school grades may be averaged with grades from the immediate preceding fourth quarter.

5. All student participants in interscholastic athletic activities must be officially registered with the Nevada Interscholastic Activities Association.

6. In all cases, student eligibility will begin at the close of school the last day of the nine-week grading period.

B. RESIDENCE REQUIREMENTS

Residence eligibility is determined by the established attendance zone for each secondary school. A student establishes zone residency when the parent or legal guardian of the student resides within the specific zone attendance boundaries and the student physically resides with the legal guardian in all cases in this regulation. The word "parent" refers to parent(s) who hold legal custody of the student. For the purpose of eligibility, a legal guardian is a person with whom the student physically resides and who:

1. Has been appointed by a court of competent jurisdiction.

2. Holds a written power of attorney and has made application for appointment by a court of competent jurisdiction.

C. SCHOOL OF FIRST ENROLLMENT

The school of first enrollment shall be defined as the school which, during the current semester enrolls a student living with a parent or legal guardian in the school's specified attendance boundaries as set forth by the Board of School Trustees.

Transfer of Student Interscholastic Athletic Eligibility

A. CHANGE IN RESIDENCE BY PARENT OR LEGAL GUARDIAN

1. A student shall be eligible in the zone where the parent or legal guardian resides. Any change of residence of the parent or legal guardian shall require that the student apply for the re-establishment of eligibility in the new zone. The application must include proof of abandonment of previous residence and proof that the student physically resides with the parent or legal guardian in the new residence.

2. Applicants for reinstatement of eligibility should submit a Student Eligibility Transfer Waiver to the Director of Student Activities.

3. Any senior high school student enrolled in a secondary school (grades 11 and 12) who completes one full. semester of enrollment, and whose parent or legal guardian changes residence during the period of this enrollment, retains original school eligibility.

B. CHANGE OF SECONDARY SCHOOLS BY MEANS OF A ZONE VARIANCE

1. Any student, regardless of age, who receives a zone variance to a high school in a zone other than the one in which the parent or legal guardian resides, shall not be eligible to participate for one calendar year from the date of enrollment. This would not include a student who received a zone variance to remain in the school of first enrollment.

C. TRANSFER TO SOUTHERN NEVADA VOCATIONAL-TECHNICAL CENTER

1. Any student who transfers to the Southern Nevada Vocational-Technical Center at the start of grades ten or eleven is considered as meeting the qualifications for eligibility for enrollment purposes.

2. Any student transferring to Southern Nevada Vocational-Technical Center after grade eleven will be ineligible. Exceptions to this would be those students who transfer to Southern Nevada Vocational-Technical Center from outside the District.

D. TRANSFERS FROM PUBLIC TO PRIVATE AND PRIVATE TO PUBLIC SCHOOL

1. A student entering the ninth grade of the public school he/she is zoned to attend or any nonpublic school has established his/her eligibility to participate in that zone. At the time of entering the school of the student's choice at the ninth grade level, the student comes under the transfer rule of eligibility.

2. A student who transfers from public to private or private to public school thereafter loses one year of eligibility from the date of transfer. Rules of eligibility must be presented in writing to the student from the school to which he has transferred at the time of enrollment. All interpretations of eligibility are subject to appeal procedures. Student athletes have the right of due process and may appeal any ruling according to the Clark County School District Activities Appeal Procedure Regulation 5135.6.

E. TRANSFERS FROM SCHOOLS OUTSIDE OF THE CLARK COUNTY SCHOOL DISTRICT

1. A student who transfers into the District must show evidence of having successfully met the eligibility requirements of the school of last attendance.

2. If the student also meets the eligibility requirements established by the District and the Nevada Interscholastic Activities Association, he/she may apply for eligibility by submitting a Student Eligibility Transfer Waiver to the Director of Student Activities.

F. OTHER TRANSFERS

1. Any student who transfers within the District, after beginning the seventh or eighth semester of high school attendance, shall be eligible only in the school in which the student first enrolled during the seventh or eighth semester.

2. Regardless of any District transfer rule, no student shall participate, practice, or play for more than one school within the county during any one sport season. The three sport seasons, as defined by the Nevada Interscholastic Activities Association, are fall, winter, and spring.

Rule-Violations for Students Participating in Interschool Athletics

A. RECRUITING

1. The primary obligation of each coach is to those students who are enrolled in that coach's school. Any coach found guilty of recruiting students from outside that school's zone shall be suspended from coaching duties for one calendar year.

2. Recruiting is defined as inducing, soliciting, or in any manner using undue influence for the purposes of securing or encouraging a student and/or a student's parent or guardian to withdraw the student from his present school for purposes of enrolling in a different school for athletic reasons. Undue influence is defined by the Nevada Interscholastic Activities Association to mean "offers of or acceptance of financial aide to parents, guardians, or student, reduced or eliminated tuition and/or fees, any special privileges not accorded to other students, whether athletes or non-athletes, transportation allowances, preference in job assignments, room, board, or clothing."

B. SCHOOL SHOPPING

1. School shopping shall be defined as the process by which a student athlete, or parent, or legal guardian or a student athlete, attempts to circumvent any eligibility rule, or solicits or seeks enrollment in a school for the purpose of participating in interscholastic athletics in return for favorable conditions or treatment.

2. Any student found guilty of "school shopping" shall be ineligible for one calendar year.

C. TRANSFER OF INELIGIBLE STUDENTS

A student who has been declared ineligible for violation of training or citizenship rules carries this ineligibility to any school in the District to which the student transfers. Such transferring student shall not become eligible until the end of the ineligible period as specified by the principal of the school of original enrollment; except that in cases where the period of ineligibility extends beyond six (6) weeks after transfer, the principal of the school of attendance may submit the record of the student for possible reconsideration by the principal of the school where the ineligibility originated.

D. FALSIFICATION OF REGISTRATION RECORDS

Falsification of any part of the registration record by the student shall result in the student's permanent ineligibility. (Reference: NIAA Handbook, Chapter 13, Section 20(b).)

Maintenance of Student Interscholastic Athletic Eligibility

A. All students participating in interscholastic athletics, except first semester ninth graders, must have been enrolled in classes and successfully completed work granting two (2) units of credit for the immediate preceding semester.

B. First quarter ninth graders must have passed four (4) classes during the last semester of the eighth grade year. With the approval of the principal, one credit earned in summer school or through correspondence will apply towards fulfilling this requirement.

C. A student must maintain a passing academic grade and a satisfactory grade in citizenship in all courses during the sports season. A weekly record will be maintained by each school. (NIAA regulation)

   If a weekly record reflects that a student is failing any course or has an unsatisfactory grade in citizenship in any course, that student shall be ineligible for the entire week.

Loss of Interscholastic Athletic Eligibility

A. VIOLATION OF TRAINING RULES

   1. Smoking—Any student using tobacco will be denied the privilege of participation in all extracurricular activities for a minimum of one (1) week.

   2. Alcoholic Beverages—Any student using or in possession of an alcoholic beverage will be denied the privilege of participation in all extracurricular activities for a period not to exceed six (6) months. A student may appeal for full eligibility after a three-month suspension.

   3. Controlled Substance and Narcotics—Any student using or in possession of a controlled substance and/or narcotic will be denied the privilege of participation in all extracurricular activities for a period of one (1) calendar year. A student has the right to appeal for full eligibility after a six-month suspension.

Additional Eligibility Requirements for all students Impacted by This Regulation

A. POOR ATTENDANCE

   1. Absence—Any student absent from class on the day of an activity will not be permitted participation that day or evening unless an excuse has been granted, in advance, by the principal.

   2. Truancy—Any student who is declared truant will be ineligible for a period of one (1) week after the infraction is discovered.

B. GOOD CITIZENSHIP

   1. School Discipline Referral—Any student referred to the office for school rule violations may be denied the privilege of participation in all extracurricular activities for a period to be determined by the school principal. This eligibility suspension will not exceed one (1) school year.

   2. School Law Enforcement Referral—Any student referred to law enforcement authorities by school officials for school rule violations may be denied the privilege of participation in all extracurricular activities for a period determined by the principal. This eligibility suspension will not exceed one (1) school year.

   3. Arrest—Any student who is arrested for a felony or gross misdemeanor during school hours, school functions, and on the way to or from participating in a school event may be denied the privilege of participation in all extracurricular activities for a period determined by the principal. This eligibility suspension will not exceed one (1) school year.

C. PARTICIPATION ON INDEPENDENT TEAMS

1. Participation—If, during the school year and while a member of a high school team or squad, the student participates on an organized team engaged in the same sport, he shall be ineligible for any further participation in that sport for the remainder of that season.

D. ADDITIONAL INDIVIDUAL SCHOOL REQUIREMENTS

   1. I will meet any special requirements adopted by my school.

E. STUDENT APPEAL PROCEDURES

   1. I understand that all Clark County student athletes have the right of due process and may appeal any ruling according to the Clark County student appeals procedure.

attendance...

School Attendance Requirements:

A. A student must be in school the entire day in order to participate in an activity that day. An exception would be made if the student had an approved medical appointment; in which case, the student must present to the attendance supervisor, a signed statement from the doctor regarding the absence.

B. If a student is absent the last school day of the week, and the competition is on a non-school day, the student must bring to the coach a signed statement from the parent that permission is given to participate. It is recommended that the coach call the parent regarding the absence.

C. A student who has been injured and has had medical treatment cannot participate again until the date indicated by the student's doctor.

D. Non-valid absences from classes during the season will result in:
   1. First offense: Suspension for one contest.
   2. Second offense: Suspension for the remainder of the season.

budgets...

See: financial report, notice on...

competition agreements (three examples)...

Seventh and Eighth Grade Boys' and Girls' Competition

Competition consists of the following:

1. Three dual matches, plus the All-City Wrestling Tournament for boys. Seventh grade boys will be allowed to participate in the wrestling program on eighth grade teams.

2. For eighth grade only in basketball.

3. Three dual or triangular meets and a city gymnastics meet will include seventh and eighth grade boys and girls. Boys will be allowed to participate in both gymnastics and swimming.

4. Two dual or triangular swim meets, a district qualifying meet, a relay meet, a final swim meet, and a final city diving meet will be scheduled for seventh and eighth grade boys and girls. Boys will be allowed to participate in both gymnastics and swimming.

5. Four dual or triangular track meets and an all-city meet will include seventh and eighth grade boys and girls.

6. For eighth grade girls only in volleyball.

* * * * *

Additional Competition Requirements:

1. An athlete will not be eligible for junior high athletics in the same sport if he or she participates at the high school varsity level.

2. After the athlete has made his/her high school choice and has "tried out" for that high school team, that will remain the athlete's high school choice for the school year 19XX.

3. Transportation to and from all high school practices and contests will be the responsibility of the athlete and his/her parents.

4. The first dates for the sport seasons are as follows:

   Fall: August 13, 19XX

   Winter: November 5, 19XX

   Spring: February 25, 19XX

   All athletes should be "cut" by Friday of the first week of the season if the high school coach deems the athlete to be less than a varsity performer.

5. If the athlete is cut from the high school team, he or she may return to the junior high program immediately and be eligible for interschool competition after five school days. If after making the high school varsity team an athlete decides to return to the junior high program, he or she would be eligible for interschool competition after five school days; however, the athlete may not return to the high school program once he or she participates in the junior high program.

6. An announcement should be placed in the daily circular prior to the beginning of each sport season concerning the opportunity for eligible ninth graders to participate at the high school level during the fall, winter or spring sport season. (Please Note: this office will furnish the wording of this announcement to make certain it is transmitted exactly the same way to all junior high students.)

7. Senior high school coaches are prohibited from contacting any junior high athlete regarding this opportunity.

8. No junior high athlete is permitted to practice with the senior high squad unless he has been cleared as per Step I, II and III.

* * * * *

Freshman Athletic Participation at the High School Level

FALL:

The following procedures are outlined allowing eligible 9th graders the opportunity to participate at the high school level during the fall sport season of the 1984-85 school year: Participation in varsity football, cross country, tennis, and gymnastics will be open to boys while participation in volleyball, cross country, golf and gymnastics will be open to girls.

WINTER:

The following procedures are outlined allowing eligible 9th graders the opportunity to participate at the high school level during the winter sport season of the 1984-85 school year: Participation in varsity basketball, wrestling and swimming will be open to boys, while participation in varsity basketball and swimming will be open to girls.

SPRING:

The following procedures are outlined allowing eligible 9th graders the opportunity to participate at the high school level during the spring sport season of the 1984-85 school year: Participation in varsity baseball, track and golf will be open to boys, while participation in varsity track and tennis will be open to girls.

crowd control (bulletin on) . . .

COACHES' CONDUCT:
CROWD CONTROL

Section 1: The conduct of the coach in view of the spectators and players is the single most important factor in crowd control.

Section 2: If coaches as professional educators cannot exercise emotional control under stress, then they cannot expect it from the immature youngsters on their team nor from the heterogeneous combination of spectators in the stands.

Section 3: It is not enough to be a good sport when there is no pressure.

Section 4: The coach is usually a stabilizing influence in an emotionally charged situation. In the present social climate, coaches must always assume this important responsibility.

Section 5: No one should be coaching who does not have a strong desire to win.

Section 6: No one should be coaching who does not realize that the future of high school athletics is more important than the winning or losing of a particular game.

eligibility . . .

SUBJECT: Student Activity Eligibility Policy

A. Academic Requirements:
   To participate in activities each student will be required to pass a minimum of five (5) subjects: Three (3) of these must be core subjects; e.g. math, English, literature, science and social studies.

B. Use of Chemicals:
   To participate in activities students shall not: (1) Use or have in his/her possession any alcoholic beverage; (2) use, or have in his/her possession any form of tobacco; (3) use, or have in his/her possession any controlled substance considered to be illegal, including marijuana; (4) buy, sell, or give away any of the above noted items.

   First Violation:
   The student will be ineligible for the next two (2) consecutive events. In addition, the student will be subject to the policy outlined in the District Discipline Policy Handbook.

Second Violation

(If the Board expels the student or held in abeyance of second offense, the following applies:)

The student will be ineligible for the next four (4) consecutive events. In addition, the student will be subject to the policy outlined in the District Discipline Policy Handbook.

C. Infractions leading to major discipline and/or truancies will be treated the same as the first violation and second violation described in the preceding paragraph.

D. A Student expelled from school is automatically dropped from activities. When the student re-enters he/she is ineligible the remainder of that semester plus the following semester. This is cumulative for all grades 7-9.

NOTE: Each student will abide by these activity standards at all times; on or off school time. Penalties during any particular activity will extend into the following activity or into the following school year.

- -

PARTICIPANT:

Having read and understood the above noted policies, I/We agree to follow the policies as stated.

Date: _____Student _____

Date: _____Parent(s) _____

financial report, notice on ...

FINANCES

A. Admission Prices:

GENERAL ADMISSION	$3.00
*STUDENTS with Activity Cards	2.00 (away events)
*STUDENTS with Activity Cards	FREE (home events)
STUDENTS—7th & 8th grade	2.00
Elementary and Pre-School	FREE if accompanied by a parent

*Activity cards must be presented or general admission must be paid for both home and away events.

B. Family season tickets will be available for admission to home contests in basketball and/or wrestling. The cost will be $45.00 for each sport. This does not include tournaments. A hockey pass may be available and cost determined by the Anchorage High School Hockey Association.

C. The home school will admit without charge all competitors, cheerleaders (in uniform), coaches, and managers of the visiting school.

D. Activity Cards

1. Activity cards will cost $20.00 each and will admit students to all home athletic contests including those designated at locations which are not on school property i.e., Anchorage

Football Stadium, Boeke Sports Arena, etc. Activity cards will also admit students to contests at other Anchorage schools for $2.00 admission. Non-activity card holders will be charged $3.00 or full adult price. Activity cards may also be used for admittance or reduced rates to dramatic, social, cultural events.

2. Activity card use shall be standardized on an annual basis.

3. Activity cards will not be discounted in any way.

4. Refunds for activity cards of students leaving school will be $10.00 during the first semester only. Cards may be purchased second semester for $7.50.

fund-raising agreement...

FUND RAISING

A. Submit Sales Request Form to the student activities office. Written notification will be sent the advisor as to the approval/disapproval of the proposed fund-raising activity.

B. Order merchandise and arrange for delivery and safe storage.

C. If solicitations or sales are to be held outside of the school, or off school property, secure a Solicitations Permit as prescribed in the Clark County School District Administration Rules and Regulations Manual (5132.2). Applications are available from the student activities office.

D. Conduct the activity without the loss of school time.

E. Arrange with the school banker for payment of bills, charges, and a final accounting of the activity in a ledger kept by the appointed officer of the organization.

F. A completed and approved Sales Request Form must be on file in the student activities office before a fund-raising activity is begun. Those groups proceeding with a fund-raising project without the approval of the student activities office will be forced to close down the activity until the proper procedures are followed. Your cooperation is imperative so that fund-raising opportunities can be provided all groups desiring to raise money.

injury...

See: INJURY

insurance...

See: INSURANCE

loss of eligibility notice ...

VIOLATION OF RULES

A. Smoking—Any student using tobacco will be denied the privilege of participation in all extracurricular activities for a minimum of one (1) week.

B. Alcoholic Beverages—Any student using or in possession of an alcoholic beverage will be denied the privilege of participation in all extracurricular activities for a period not to exceed six (6) months. A student may appeal for full eligibility after a three-month suspension.

C. Controlled substance and narcotics—Any student using or in possession of a controlled substance and/or narcotics will be denied the privilege of participation in all extracurricular activities for a period of one (1) calendar year. A student has the right to appeal for full eligibility after a six-month suspension.

D. School Law Enforcement Referral—Any student referred to law enforcement authorities by school officials for school rule violations may be denied the privilege of participation in all extracurricular activities for a period determined by the principal. This eligibility will not exceed one (1) school year.

E. Arrest—Any student who is arrested for a felony or gross misdemeanor during school hours, school functions, and on the way to or from participating in a school event may be denied the privilege of participation in all extracurricular activities for a period determined by the principal. This eligibility suspension will not exceed one (1) school year.

participation ...

PARTICIPATION GUIDELINES

I. TRAINING RULES

   A. BASIC TRAINING RULE—An athlete will be ineligible for athletic participation or practice for that sport season for the following:

      1. Smoking
      2. Influence or possession of alcohol
      3. Influence or possession of illegal drugs
      4. Drug abuse

   B. Immediate dismissal from the team will result from any of the following:

      1. Violation of eligibility rules
      2. Violation of basic training rule

   C. Denial from participating with the team for a period of time to be determined by coach/principal may result from the following:

      a. Insubordination
      b. Obscene gestures; swearing
      c. Provocation

d. Fighting

e. Stealing

f. Other disciplinary situation which may arise

D. An athlete who is removed from a team for disciplinary reasons will not be eligible to practice or play another sport during the season of that sport.

E. Athletic uniforms and equipment are not to be worn or used by any student except during a practice of school sponsored event in which he/she participates.

F. Equipment issued to an athlete is his/her responsibility for return or replacement. If the equipment is neither returned, replaced or paid for, the letter award shall not be awarded nor any further equipment issued to the participant for any sport.

G. With administrative approval, coaches may establish additional training rules, schedules, curfews, etc. for each sport.

II. Participation Limitations

A. No basketball player shall participate in more than six quarters of basketball in one day (excluding tournaments).

B. No hockey player shall participate in more than three (3) game periods in one day, or change levels of teams during the same week, excepting JV goalies.

C. No wrestler shall participate in more than twenty-five individual matches per season (excluding regional and state tournaments).

practice bulletin...

PRACTICE ON "OFF" DAYS:

Teams may practice on weekends if the coach deems it necessary. It is the coaches responsibility to clear it with the building principal. It is his responsibility for the supervision of his team and building. All lights and showers must be off and doors locked when he leaves.

Practice on snow days is the sole responsibility of the coach. We do not play home games on these days. If the weather prevents school, it also prevents athletic contests. We, at this point, have no policy to cover whether practice may go on or not. It is a very serious decision to have athletes drive to practice over hazardous roads, therefore the coach must confer with principal and athletic director for permission to schedule practice on these days.

An organized practice shall be defined as:

Football—organized practice shall mean more than five players under the direct supervision of a sponsor.

Basketball and Volleyball—An organized practice shall mean more than four players under the direct supervision of a sponsor.

Track and Wrestling—An organized practice shall mean more than three players under the direct supervision of a sponsor.

recruiting guidelines...

1. The primary obligation of each coach is to those students who are enrolled in that coach's school. Any coach found guilty of recruiting students from outside that school's zone shall be suspended from coaching duties for one calendar year.

2. Recruiting is defined as inducing, soliciting, or in any manner using undue influence for the purposes of securing or encouraging a student and/or a student's parent or guardian to withdraw the student from his present school for purposes of enrolling in a different school for athletic reasons. Undue influence is defined by the Nevada Interscholastic Activities Association to mean "offers of or acceptance of: financial aid to parents, guardians, or student; reduced or eliminated tuition and/or fees; any special privileges not accorded to other students, whether athletes or nonathletes; transportation allowances; preference in job assignments, room, board, or clothing."

rules and regulations...

See: RULES AND REGULATIONS

scouting notice...

It will be considered unethical under any circumstances to scout any team, by any means whatever, except in regularly scheduled games. Any attempt to scout practice sessions will be considered unethical. The head coach for each sport will be held responsible for all scouting. This will include the use of moving pictures.

student managers...

Members of the corps of student managers should be considered by the athletic director and coaches as an important part of the athletic staff. A well trained, dedicated manager can be likened to an additional assistant coach.

The acquisition of good student managers seldom happens by chance. A sound recruitment and on-the-job training program must be projected to assure the continued presence of a competent corps. The entire coaching staff must actively engage in the training and orientation program, in developing a high degree of morale and esprit de corps and in providing adequate reward and recognition for jobs well done. Awards ought to parallel those earned by the participants in the sports. It is also true that some schools pay their student managers which makes an entirely different basis of operation.

A well organized program should encourage participation by as many individuals as possible so that doubling in sports may be kept at a bare minimum—ideally no more than two sports per person at the most. Assistants should be encouraged, especially in the major sports such as football and track where numbers can run to three or four if available. Freshmen should be motivated to continue in the program so as to work up to head manager through the years. From the P.E. classes, instructors should make recommendations to the coach and talk with likely prospects from the class. Counselors should discuss manager jobs with prospective candidates and should put them in touch with the coaches. Coaches, too, should encourage students who do not make the team to turn out as managers.

Coaches should be impressed with the importance of accepting the responsibility for putting into writing the general and specific duties for the managerial staff in each sport. This is a must if coach and manager are to work well together. Some thought should be given to the matter of dress so that the managers may be easily identified as they work with the teams. A badge or logo on a T-shirt or jacket might serve the purpose.

PRACTICE

See Also: PARTICIPATION; POLICIES AND PROCEDURES; SAFETY; SCRIMMAGE

time of, guidelines for...

As a general rule practice for our athletic teams begins at 2:15 p.m., because of the number of teams participating in some practices, especially junior varsity, may be held at a later time.

Practices are limited to six days per week unless approved by the school board or the NIAA. No practices or interscholastic activities will be permitted on Sundays.

The coaching staff is responsible for organizing and implementing the practices and the length of time they are to be held. Daily practices are expected with the average time of 2 to 2½ hours.

PROPERTY DAMAGE

See Also: FACILITY

report form...

PROPERTY DAMAGE REPORT

Playground _____

    Date of Damage _____Approx. Time _____

    Date report made _____Supervisor _____

Nature of damage:

    Cause of Damage:

    Persons responsible for damage: (Indicate full names and addresses)

_____

_____

_____

_____

_____

PUBLIC RELATIONS AND THE PRESS

See Also: ANNOUNCERS' FORMS; HANDBOOK

policy on (two examples)...

Media Outlets

When we schedule an event or have some type of public relations information we would like to release to the media—we must notify the following: Activities Office, Administration Office, KROE, KWYO, Sheridan Press, Principal's Office and the Assistant Principals' Office.

* * * * *

PUBLIC RELATIONS

Section 1: Sportswriters and Sportscasters. The responsibility of coaches to accredited writers and radio and television commentators is to provide them news about their team and players. They should be treated with courtesy, honesty, and respect. Derogatory and misleading statements should be avoided. Direct questions should be answered honestly or not at all. If good judgment indicates that an honest answer to a question would be prejudicial to the best interest of the game, ethical procedure demands that it not be answered. In such cases, "no comment" is entirely justifiable. Coaches should assume responsibility for and stress the importance of ethical procedures in teaching their players how to conduct themselves in player interviews in the best interest of the athletic program.

Section 2: Good Judgment. It will be questionable practice for coaches to stress player injuries, disciplinary measures, academic difficulties, eligibility problems, and similar personal items, with the press, radio, and television. Disciplinary problems should be a "family affair," to be solved between the coach and players involved. Injuries are essentially a province of the team physician and trainer. No good purpose can be served by emphasizing such matters.

Section 3: Alumni, Booster, and Quarterback Organizations. Such organizations can be of value to the athletic program if they have proper objectives. It will be unethical for coaches to use such groups to attempt to defeat or obstruct administrative or institutional athletic controls or to encourage violation of established rules and regulations in order to strengthen existing athletic programs. It will likewise be unethical for coaches to make demands, financially or otherwise, upon such groups which are not in keeping with the letter and spirit of existing controls or in any other manner misuse such strength and power in violation of accepted rules and regulations.

press releases (three examples)...

press release to newspapers:

DATE:	March 19, 19XX
FROM:	Parks and Recreation Department 32 Monmouth St., Red Bank, N.J. 07701 Mary Anne Gaul, Director
FOR RELEASE:	Immediate
RE:	Easter Egg Hunt

The Parks and Recreation Department in Red Bank will sponsor its Annual Easter Egg Hunt on Saturday, April 6, 19XX, at Count Basie Park (formerly Memorial Park). The Hunt will begin promptly at 11:00 AM.

Youngsters 10 years and under are eligible to participate in this event. Areas will be sectioned off according to ages. Prizes will be awarded for those children finding the special eggs.

Participants should bring a bag to hold their goodies.

Further information can be obtained by calling the department at 530-2782.

* * * * *

sample page from public relations newsletter:

RECREATION NEWS

The Recreation Commission would like to take this opportunity to thank every member of the community that supported our programs through their participation, especially to those parents who volunteered their service and time. As we all know, it is the volunteer who is the "heart" of any successful program and we appreciate you.

During the past year the Commission set out to improve its existing programs, as well as introduce new programs that would be of interest to our residents. We are pleased to report that we have exceeded our expectations and hope to continue to add new programs as they are needed.

New Programs

This past year we introduced a number of new programs that were most successful, please keep them in mind for next year:

1. Indoor Soccer which runs from mid January to the end of March. It was one of the most popular programs introduced with over 75 participants. The program was divided into the following groups: grades 6-8 coed, high school girls, high school boys, and adults over 18.

2. Open Basketball which was started in February, was received very well. It was divided into 2 main groups: grades 5–8 and grades 9–12. We had over 50 participants in our first year. Next year we hope to start in January.

3. Bowling, organized by Sigrid Blankley, had approximately 25 children participating in the Saturday morning activity. Again, providing diversified activities with the assistance of parents.

4. Volleyball (adult coed) meets every Wednesday from 7:30-9:30 P.M. at Swimming River School gym. The program is open to all adults over 19 and it runs through June. Come on out for a night of fun.

Present Programs—Update

As well as introducing new programs, we have a number of programs that have been with us due to their popularity. We have also made some changes in some of these programs for the better.

1. Aerobic Dance...we run 3 six-week sessions during the year (coed).

2. Men's Over 30 Basketball...meets one night throughout the winter.

3. Baseball Program...for ages 9–15 years.

a. CAP LEAGUE (9–12 years)...19XX looks to be our most exciting year ever. We have a completely new look...for the first time we have completely new uniforms, enthusiastic coaches, and we are now in a league with 8 other teams. Our home games will be played at the Tinton Falls School on Monday/Thursday at 6:00 P.M. The league is filled for 19XX.

* * * * *

form for gathering public relations information:

PARKS AND RECREATION DEPARTMENT
BOROUGH OF RED BANK
NEW JERSEY

PLAYGROUND _____ NEWSPAPER REPORT   DATE _____

Past Week—Interesting events and winners:

PURCHASE ORDER

See Also: ORDERING; VOUCHER

purchase order receiving ticket...

CARLSBAD MUNICIPAL SCHOOLS
103 West Hagerman Street
Carlsbad, New Mexico 88220

PURCHASE ORDER RECEIVING TICKET   One Copy to Business Office

Directions: Attach shipping ticket if possible. If your order has been completely received, the items need not be enumerated. Only a statement that it has been received is needed. If only a few items are lacking, kindly list these and so indicate along with the fact that the balance of the order has arrived. Time element is important.

Date _____Received from: _____

Purchase Order Number _____Date of Purchase Order _____

Comments: _____

_____

Number Units	Unit	Items	Condition of Delivery

Signed: _____
Principal or Representative

* * * * *

(There are no entries for the letter "Q.")

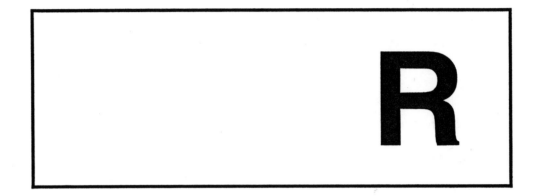

RECOMMENDATION, LETTERS OF

See: LETTERS

RECRUITING

See: POLICIES AND PROCEDURES

REQUESTS AND REQUISITIONS

See Also: BUDGET; EQUIPMENT; MAINTENANCE; ORDERING

budget form for...

BUDGET ALLOCATION REQUEST

Submit this original copy to the
Athletic Director. Keep a copy
for your files. Due _____

_____
Building/Location

CONSUMMABLE SUPPLIES AND SOFTWARE PRIORITY REQUEST

This request form is to be used to identify consummable supplies, that are essential for the operation of your athletic activity. Include in this request such items as tape, cloth wear, basketballs, etc. (DO NOT include on this sheet equipment such as blocking sleds, pitching machines, etc.)

ITEM AND DESCRIPTION: SUGGESTED SOURCE: EST. COST:

_____

_____

_____

_____

_____

_____

_____   _____
Signature of Principal   Signature of Coach

for a check...

Check No. _____
Date Pd. _____
Activity Account _____

HILLDALE PUBLIC SCHOOLS

CHECK REQUEST FORM

I hereby request a check be written

TO: _____

FOR: _____
      (P.O. Number)

AMOUNT: _____

INVOICE NUMBER _____

Activity Account: _____

Signed: _____
                 Principal

Date of Check Request: _____

Disposition of Check:

Return to Principal/Sponsor _____

Mail: _____

Address: _____
          Street/Route

_____
City—State—Zip Code

APPROVED FOR PAYMENT

By: _____

Date: _____

for activities...

REQUEST FOR ACTIVITY

_____
Date submitted

1. _____
   Organization

2. _____
   Activity

From: _____ To: _____
Time of Activity

3. _____
   Date of Activity

Admission Charge $_____

4. _____
   Area of school to be used

5. _____
   Brief Description of Activity

6. Equipment needed: Check to indicate

   _____ P A System
   _____ Record Player
   _____ Tape Recorder
   _____ Projector
   _____ Tables ( )
   _____ Chairs ( )
   _____ Heat or Air Conditioning needed

   _____ Special set-up
   (attach plan)
   _____
   OTHER

7. Will a custodian be needed?   Yes____ No____

8. Doors or exits to be open: _____

9. Other: _____

_____
Signature of Sponsor

APPROVAL

Approved—Director of Activities (Yes   No) _____
                                            Jack Mannion

_____
Head Custodian

Distribution: Original - Activity Director
          Pink   - Organization's copy
          Green -Head Custodian copy
          Yellow -Other as indicated below-

_____

_____ From: _____ To: _____
Heat

_____ From: _____ To: _____
Cooling

for athletic participation from parents...

ATHLETIC PARTICIPATION REQUEST

Dear Coach _____ Date _____

My son/daughter _____ is interested in trying out for _____
                                                                    Activity or team

at Pocatello—Highland High School this season.
    (Circle one)

       Since each junior high student is the responsibility of the junior high principal there will be need of his signature to acknowledge his permission.

       Since each junior high student is a possible candidate for the junior high team and the junior high coach is granting permission for the junior high student to become a member of the high school team, there will be need of his signature to acknowledge his permission.

       If my child is granted permission to try out I am fully aware and will support the eligibility requirements set forth by the State Idaho High School Activities Association.

Signed _____
             Parent or Guardian

_____
             Address

_____
             Phone Number

Signed _____Signed _____
             Junior High Principal   Junior High Coach

Signed _____Signed _____
             High School Principal   High School Coach

       This is to be returned to the District Athletic Directors Office for final approval prior to student's participation.

Date _____
             District Athletic Director

for custodial action...

REQUEST FOR CUSTODIAL ACTION

_____
Date

_____   _____
Teacher   Room

I request the following services (please be specific and include room/area):

1. _____

_____

_____

Scheduled Completion Date

2. _____

_____

_____

Scheduled Completion Date

3. _____

_____

_____

Scheduled Completion Date

ROUTE TO ACTIVITIES OFFICE

_____
Administrative Approval Signature

_____
Head Custodian Signature

_____ Work assigned to school district maintenance. You will be notified when job has been scheduled.

for distribution of fliers...

See: FLIERS

for equipment...

Date_____

School or Office _____   Authorized Purchaser _____

Del.	Out	Quantity	Unit	Article	Unit Price	Extension Price
				Total		

Approved _____ Received by _____ Date _____

form for general use...

Requisition   Hilldale Public Schools   Requisition

ALL INFORMATION MUST BE
COMPLETED BEFORE ORDER
CAN BE PROCESSED

Complete separate requests when
ordering for more than one subject
or grade level. Also use separate
requests if ordering furniture or
equipment and supplies.

Individual completing request
should keep pink copy. Person
making initial approval should keep
yellow copy and forward the white
copy to the finance office.

☐ General   ☐ Activity Account No. _____

☐ Cafeteria   ☐ Other _____

☐ Special Program Title _____

Requested by _____ Date _____
School Location ☐ Ele. ☐ MS ☐ HS ☐ Adm.

Grade _____ Subject _____

VENDOR: _____
ADDRESS: _____   CITY: _____   STATE: ____ ZIP: ____

Quantity	Item (Be sure to give color, size, catalog number, etc.)	Price Each	Total Amount

TOTAL AMOUNT [   ]

APPROVAL TO ISSUE P.O.   Date

INITIAL APPROVAL:
   Special Program Director _____ ____
   Principal _____ ____
FINAL APPROVAL:
   Superintendent _____ ____

NOT APPROVED _____ ____

OFFICE USE ONLY

Code _____
Vendor Number _____
P.O. Number _____ Date Ordered _____

for program information...

Eastwood School System

NOVEMBER 15, 19XX

DEAR COACH,

ENCLOSED IS THE BASKETBALL SCHEDULE AND ROSTER FOR THE 19XX SEASON.

WOULD YOU PLEASE SEND ME A ROSTER OF YOUR BOYS AND GIRLS AS SOON AS POSSIBLE. WE ARE PRINTING PROGRAMS AND MUST HAVE THIS INFORMATION TWO WEEKS PREVIOUS TO GAME DAY.

OTHER INFORMATION THAT MIGHT BE HELPFUL:

1. GAMES WILL BE PLAYED AT THE UNIVERSITY OF OKLAHOMA MEDICAL SCHOOL, LOCATED AT 29TH AND SOUTH SHERIDAN ROAD.

2. ENTER THE FIELD HOUSE ON THE SOUTH SIDE.

3. OUR SCHOOL COLORS ARE: RED, BLACK, AND WHITE.

4. SCHOOL NICKNAME: KNIGHTS.

5. NOTE: OUR ADDRESS AND PHONE NUMBER ARE LISTED BELOW.

HOPING TO SEE YOU SOON.

VERY TRULY YOURS,

for transportation...

See: TRANSPORTATION, TRAVEL, AND TRIPS

ROSTERS

form ...

SCHOOL _____

HEAD COACH _____ J.V. COACH _____

COLOR OF UNIFORMS: Home _____ Away _____

| NAME | NUMBERS | | | HT. | CLASS | LETTERS |
	POS.	LT.	DRK.			
1.						
2.						
3.						
4.						
5.						
6.						
7.						
8.						
9.						
10.						
11.						
12.						
13.						
14.						
15.						

JV ROSTER	POS.	LT.	DRK.	HT.	CLASS	LETTERS
1.						
2.						
3.						
4.						
5.						
6.						
7.						
8.						
9.						
10.						
11.						
12.						
13.						
14.						
15.						

Please type and place numbers in numerical order.

RULES AND REGULATIONS (BULLETINS)

See Also: POLICIES AND PROCEDURES; SPECIFIC TOPICS

concerning equipment and uniforms...

EQUIPMENT AND UNIFORMS

1. Athletic equipment is loaned to team members by the Athletic Department.

2. Athletes are responsible for equipment that is issued to them. Any lost items must be paid for by the athlete.

3. School uniforms are not to be used or worn at home or away from school unless on a team trip.

4. All uniforms will be washed and repaired by the Athletic Department.

5. Athletes are entitled to one school towel at a time. Exchange your dirty towel for a clean one.

6. Towel service costs $3.00 per sport and athletes are encouraged to make use of this service. Any athlete playing in three sports will be provided free towel service for the third sport.

concerning trips...

See: TRANSPORTATION, TRAVEL, AND TRIPS

for athletes...

INDIVIDUAL ELIGIBILITY RULES

Attention, Athlete! To be eligible to represent your school in any interscholastic athletic contest You—

must be a regular bona fide student in good standing of the school.
must have enrolled not later than tenth day of current semester.
must have earned at least 2 units of credit the previous semester (summer school excluded).
must have attained an overall "C" (2.00) average. Summer school may be included.
must not have reached your 16th (JH) or 19th (HS) birthday before September 1 of the current school year.

must be a resident of the school zone from which your HS or JHS receives its students.

must be residing with parent(s) or legal guardian as specified by Rule 7 and Rule 8.

    unless parents or guardians have made a bona fide change of residence during school term as provided by 7-0-4.

    unless an AFS or other Foreign-Exchange student (one year of eligibility only).

    unless the residence requirement was met by the 120 instructional days attendance prior to participation.

    unless you have been in attendance in this school zone for the three immediate preceding years without any change of residence to another attendance zone at any time during those three years.

must have not transferred from a private to a public or public to a private member school without forfeiting 120 instructional days of athletic eligibility.

must be an amateur as defined by Rule 14.

must have submitted to your Principal before becoming a member of any school athletic team an athlete Participation/Parental Consent/Physician Form, completely filled in and properly signed, attesting that you have been examined and found to be physically fit for athletic competition and that your parents or guardian consent to your participation. (See exceptions under Rule 11).

must not have transferred from one school to another for athletic purposes as a result of undue influence or persuasion by any individual or group of people.

must not have received in recognition of your ability as a HS or JHS athlete any award not presented or approved by your school or the WVSSAC.

must not, while a member of a school's team in any sport, become a member of any other organized team or as an individual participant in an unsanctioned meet or tournament in the same sport during the school sport season.

must not participate in any all-star contest between teams whose players are selected from more than one school.

must not have been enrolled in more than eight (8) semesters in grades 9 to 12. Must not have been enrolled in more than four (4) semesters of grades 7 and 8. (See Rule 5).

Eligibility to participate in interscholastic athletics is a privilege you earn by meeting not only the above listed minimum standards, but also all other standards set by your school and the WVSSAC. If you have any questions regarding your eligibility or are in doubt about the effect any activity or action might have on your eligibility, check with your principal or athletic director. They are aware of the interpretation and intent of each rule. Meeting the intent and spirit of WVSSAC standards will prevent athletes, teams and schools from being penalized.

for athletics...

WAIAKEA HIGH SCHOOL
ATHLETICS

RE: Rules & Regulations SAMPLE

Golf Team

General:
1. All federal, state and county statutes, laws and ordinance apply to all golfers in school or on school sponsored activities.
2. Display good sportsmanship on and off the golf course.
3. Meet physical requirements.
4. Meet BIIF eligibility requirements.
5. All training rules covered by the Athletic Handbook of Waiakea High School.

Expulsion from the team if:
1. Use of alcoholic beverage or illegal drugs—on or off campus.
2. Cheating on the golf course
    a. intentionally turning in wrong scores
    b. disregarding USGA rules

3. When coach feel that a golfer is a detriment to the team or school.
4. 2 practice cuts/2 non-playing cuts (written excuse from parents required for all absences).
5. Guilty of stealing.
6. Smoking
   a. 1st offense—warning and suspension from participation on next scheduled match.
   b. 2d offense—expulsion from the team.

Academic requirements:
1. Passing grade in all courses required by the D.O.E.
2. Failing grade in not more than one elective course.
3. Student will not participate in a given match if administration so requests.

Lettering:
The individual will qualify for the BIIF Individual Championship or the State High School Championship.

— —

I have read the above and understand the rules and regulations as stated, and understand that to be a member of the team, I must comply with the above stated items.

| Student Athlete | Date | Parent/Guardian | Date |

SAFETY

See Also: INJURY; NATIONAL OPERATING COMMITTEE ON STANDARDS FOR ATHLETIC EQUIPMENT; SCRIMMAGE

heat/humidity chart...

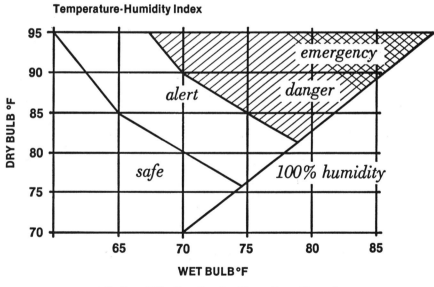

Temperature-Humidity Index

emergency

danger

alert

safe

100% humidity

DRY BULB °F

95 — 90 — 85 — 80 — 75 — 70

WET BULB °F

65   70   75   80   85

+ National Weather Service Operations Manual

When Is It Too Hot to Exercise?

Three factors determine the severity of a hot day: temperature, humidity, and wind speed.

When the outside temperature soars to 90°F. or more and the humidity climbs close to 90 percent with little or no wind velocity, there's the ever-present danger of heatstroke and heat exhaustion. Even though it doesn't measure wind speed, the simplest method of measuring the danger of hot day is with a combination wet and dry bulb thermometer. One thermometer, a standard one, measures air temperature; the other, covered by a wick that is dipped in water, is used to measure humidity. They can be bought at any hardware store at minimal cost.

By using the Temperature-Humidity Index graph, you can determine how dangerous it will be to exercise in the heat.

Read the wet bulb thermometer and record the point on the horizontal axis of the accompanying graph. Record the reading of the dry bulb thermometer on the vertical axis.

helmet...

TO: Athletes and Parents
SUBJECT: NOCSAE STANDARDS

SHARED RESPONSIBILITY FOR SPORTS SAFETY

Participation in sport requires an acceptance of risk of injury. Athletes rightfully assume that those who are responsible for the conduct of sport have taken reasonable precautions to minimize the risk of significant injury. Periodic analysis of injury patterns continuously leads to refinements in the rules and/or other safety guidelines.

1. Serious head and neck injuries leading to death, permanent brain damage or quadriplegia (extensive paralysis from injury to the spinal cord at the neck level) occur each year in football. The toll is relatively small (less than one fatality for every 100,000 players and an estimated two to three nonfatal severe brain and spinal cord injuries for every 100,000 players), but persistent. They cannot be completely prevented due to the tremendous forces occasionally encountered in football collisions; but they can be minimized by manufacturer, coach and player compliance with accepted safety standards.
2. The NOCSAE seal on a helmet indicates that a manufacturer has complied with the best available engineering standards for head protection. By keeping a proper fit, by not modifying its design and by reporting to the coach or equipment manager any need for its maintenance, the athlete also is complying with the purpose of the NOCSAE Standard.
3. The rules against intentional butting, ramming or spearing the opponent with the helmeted head are there to protect the helmeted person much more than the opponent being hit. The athlete who does not comply with these rules is the candidate for catastrophic injury. For example, no helmet can offer protection to the neck; and quadriplegia now occurs more frequently than brain damage.

    The typical scenario of this catastrophic injury in football involves lowering one's head while making a tackle. The momentum of the body tries to bend the neck after the helmeted head is stopped by the impact, and the cervical spine cannot be splinted as well by the neck's muscles with the head lowered as with the preferred "face up, eyes forward, neck bulled" position.

    When the force at impact is sufficient, the vertebrae in the neck can dislocate or break, cause damage to the spinal cord they had been protecting and thereby produce permanent loss of motor and sensory function below the level of injury.
4. Because of the impact forces in football, even the "face up" position is no guarantee against head or neck injury. Further, the intent to make contact "face up" is no guarantee that that position can be maintained at the moment of impact. Consequently, the teaching of blocking/tackling techniques that keep the helmeted head from receiving the brunt of the impact are now required by rule and by coaching ethics. Coaching techniques that help athletes maintain or regain the "face up" position during the course of a play must be respected by the athletes.

HELMET WARNING STATEMENTS

In an effort to warn players of the risk of injury, the NOCSAE Board of Directors has developed a warning statement which is found on all football and baseball/softball batting helmets. The statements are intended to warn participants of the possibility of severe head or neck injury despite the fact a NOCSAE approved helmet is being worn. The helmet is designed to give protection to the head. Neither the football or baseball/softball batting helmet can protect the player's neck.

NOCSAE urges that the warning statement be shared with members of the football, baseball and softball squads and that all coaches alert participants to the potential for injury.

FOOTBALL HELMET WARNING STATEMENT

Do not use this helmet to butt, ram or spear an opposing player. This is in violation of the football rules and can result in severe head, brain or neck injury, paralysis or death to you and possible injury to your opponent.

There is a risk these injuries may also occur as a result of accidental contact without intent to butt, ram or spear. NO HELMET CAN PREVENT ALL SUCH INJURIES.

BASEBALL/SOFTBALL BATTING HELMET
WARNING STATEMENT

Do not use this helmet if the shell is cracked or deformed or if interior padding is deteriorated.

Severe head or neck injury, including paralysis or death, may occur to you despite using this helmet. No helmet can prevent all head injuries or any neck injuries a player might receive while participating in baseball or softball.

I have read the extract from the NOCSAE Manual and fully understand the possibilities of injuries in athletics. I will comply with the standards as set forth.

Athlete: _____ Parent/Guardian: _____
                 Signature   Signature
Date: _____ Sport: _____

how to kill a player...

1. Schedule practice sessions between 2:30 and 6 each afternoon so that players will be exercising during the hottest part of the day.
2. Provide no water during training sessions or make it so unpalatable that no one will drink it. This assures that players will have no way to replace the fluid they lose through perspiration.
3. Encourage players to swallow salt tablets before practice. This promotes dehydration and increases thirst.
4. Help overweight linesmen lose weight rapidly by making them exercise while wearing plastic suits. This guarantees that they will perspire profusely and exposes them to the risk of dangerous dehydration of body cells.

5. Make players wear full uniforms complete with helmets during hot weather to help promote overheating.

6. Don't stop wind sprints at the end of each practice session until a sizable number of players vomit, have muscle cramps or collapse.

7. Attempt to improve players' performances with amphetamines. The drugs prevent a player from realizing when he is fatigued and assure that he will keep trying long after physical exhaustion dictates that he should quit.

treatment administered, form for recording...

DAILY LOG

DATE/TIME	NAME	DESCRIPTION

DAILY TREATMENT

DATE	TREATMENT

SCHEDULES

See Also: TRANSPORTATION, TRAVEL, AND TRIPS; SPECIFIC SPORT

bus pick-up...

See: BUS

change of athletic schedule (two examples)...

MIDDLETOWN TOWNSHIP BOARD OF EDUCATION
Middletown, New Jersey 07748

Date _____

Time _____

ATHLETIC SCHEDULE CHANGE

School _____Sport _____

Your contest with _____on _____

is changed to _____at _____

Bus @ _____

P.A. BRAUN
Athletic Director

* * * * *

ATHLETIC SCHEDULE CHANGE

This request complies with the Student Activities Procedures Manual, pages 5.61 and 5.64. (Procedures for Changing Approved Schedules) ☐ Yes ☐ No

SCHOOL _____ DATE _____

SPORT _____

Please check appropriate box: ☐ Addition ☐ Deletion ☐ Revision

PRESENT SCHEDULE	CHANGE YOU WISH TO MAKE

Reason for change _____
_____
_____

_____
Principal/Athletic Administrator

. . . .

Department of Student Activities: ☐ APPROVED ☐ DENIED

_____
Student Activities

When change is approved, the requesting school is responsible to notify Transportation, Media, Commissioner, Security, and all affected schools.

sample schedule...

MUSKOGEE HIGH SCHOOL

ATHLETIC DEPARTMENT—3200 EAST SHAWNEE—MUSKOGEE, OKLAHOMA
74401-(918)-683-4561

19XX-XX
Basketball Schedule
Boys and Girls

Date	School	Place	Time
Tuesday, November 20	Muldrow	Away	5:30, 7:00, 8:00
Saturday, December 1	Taft	Home	
Tuesday, December 4	Tulsa Washington	Away	
Friday, December 7	Broken Arrow	Home	
Tuesday, December 11	Muldrow	Home	
Friday, December 14	Taft	Away	
Tuesday, December 18	Tulsa East Central	Away	
Friday, January 4	Tulsa Washington	Home	
Tuesday-Saturday January 8, 9, 10, 11, 12	Shrine Tournament	Home	
Tuesday, January 15 Friday, January 18	Tulsa Memorial	Home	
Thursday, Friday, Saturday January 24, 25, 26	Tournament (Girls) Tournament Boys	Moore NEO	
Tuesday, January 29			
*Friday, February 1	Rogers	Home	
Tuesday, February 5	McLain	Away	
Friday, February 8	Broken Arrow	Away	
Tuesday, February 12	Tulsa East Central	Home	
Friday, February 15	Tulsa Memorial	Away	
Tuesday, February 19	Tulsa Rogers	Away	
Friday, February 22	Tulsa McLain	Home	
Tuesday, February 26			
Wednesday, February 27	Conference Selection Boys and Girls		

*Homecoming
Girls JV-4:00, Boys JV-5:00, Varsity Girls-6:30, Varsity Boys-8:00
Thursday-Saturday, February 28, March 1 and 2 - Regionals
Thursday-Saturday, March 7, 8, and 9 - Area
Thursday-Saturday, March 14, 15, and 16 - State

season...

See: SPECIFIC SPORT

sports programs...

ACTIVITY	START TIME	TOURNAMENTS DISTRICT	STATE	END DATE
Baseball				
Frosh				
Basketball - Boys				
- Frosh				
- Girls				
- Frosh				
Cross Country - Boys and - Girls				
Football				
- J.V.				
- Frosh				
Golf - Boys				
- Girls				
Gymnastics - Girls				
- Boys				
Soccer - Boys				
- Girls				
Softball				
Swimming - Girls				
- Boys				
Tennis - Girls				
- Boys				
Volleyball				
Wrestling				
- Frosh				
Track - Boys & Girls				
- Frosh				

SCHOLAR ATHLETE

See Also: ATHLETE; AWARDS

memo on (two examples)...

To: All Head Coaches
From: J. R. Johnson
Date: March 12, 19XX
RE: Scholar/Athlete Award

Please select your number one scholar/athlete and return this memo with that selection in writing to my office by March 14, 19XX.

Football: _____

_____
Signature of Coach

Basketball: _____

_____
Signature of Coach

Baseball: _____

_____
Signature of Coach

Wrestling: _____

_____
Signature of Coach

Cross Country: _____
Boy

_____
Signature of Coach

_____
Girl

Girls Track: _____

_____
Signature of Coach

Swimming: _____
Boy

_____
Signature of Coach

_____
Girl

Tennis: _____
Boy

_____
Signature of Coach

* * * * *

MUSKOGEE HIGH SCHOOL
3200 EAST SHAWNEE
MUSKOGEE, OKLAHOMA 74401

OFFICE OF THE PRINCIPAL

April 15, 19XX

Point System for Scholar-Athlete Award

100 Points as a Maximum

Scholarship . . . . 50 points
Athletics . . . . 50 points

Grade Point Average based upon 0 to 4.0 system.

For each one tenth point above 2.00 or major fraction there-of carried out to whatever decimal point necessary to break a tie: 2.5 points. Starting at 2.1 up to 4.0.

Point distribution for athletics:

One sport 30 points-for each additional sport 5 points per sport.

Grade Point Distribution example:

2.1 3.1
2.2 3.2
2.3 3.3
2.4 3.4
2.5 3.5
2.6 3.6
2.7 3.7
2.8 3.8
2.9 3.9
3.0 4.0

Athletic Points:

One Sport 30
Two Sports 35
Three Sports 40
Four Sports 45
Five Sports 50

Developed by James Roy Johnson,
Assistant Principal Athletics

SCOUTING

See Also: POLICIES AND PROCEDURES; SPECIFIC SPORT

baseball (two examples)...

RED BANK REGIONAL BASEBALL Scouting Report TEAM _____ VS. _____ DATE		
INFIELD		
OUTFIELD		
CATCHING		
PITCHING		
HITTING offensive plays		
ADDITIONAL		

* * * * *

VS. _____ AT _____ DATE _____

	2	3	4	5	6	7	8	9	Comments
B S P	B S P	B S P	B S P	B S P	B S P	B S P	B S P	B S P	
B S P	B S P	B S P	B S P	B S P	B S P	B S P	B S P	B S P	
B S P	B S P	B S P	B S P	B S P	B S P	B S P	B S P	B S P	
B S P	B S P	B S P	B S P	B S P	B S P	B S P	B S P	B S P	
B S P	B S P	B S P	B S P	B S P	B S P	B S P	B S P	B S P	
B S P	B S P	B S P	B S P	B S P	B S P	B S P	B S P	B S P	
B S P	B S P	B S P	B S P	B S P	B S P	B S P	B S P	B S P	
B S P	B S P	B S P	B S P	B S P	B S P	B S P	B S P	B S P	
B S P	B S P	B S P	B S P	B S P	B S P	B S P	B S P	B S P	
B S TP	B S TP	B S TP	B S TP	B S TP	B S TP	B S TP	B S TP	B S TP	

Key
B = Ball
C = Called Strike
S = Swing Strike
F = Foul
H = Hit

Example:

SBCS	B1
U	S3
K	P4

Batter struck out swinging on 4th pitch.

E	IP	R	ER	H	BB	SO	S	B	TP	W-L	SAV.	REC.	%S	P/IN.

basketball (two examples)...

INDIVIDUAL NOTES

PASS ------▶
DRIBBLE ～～▶
CUT ———▶

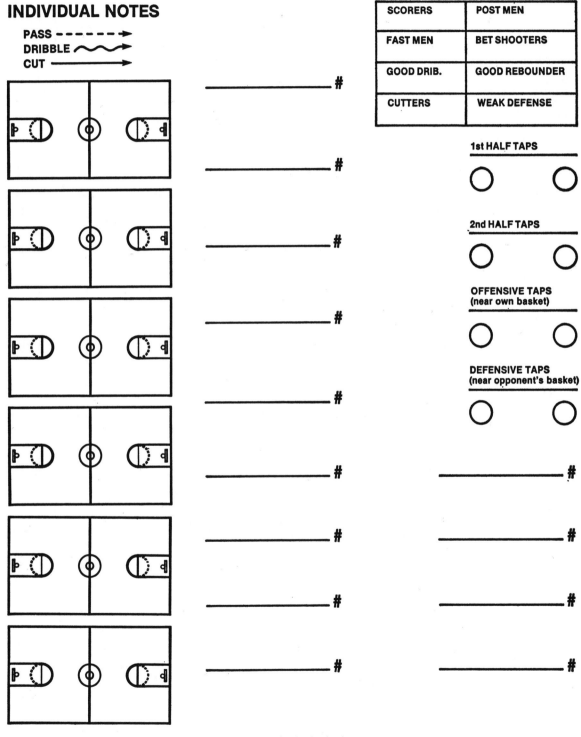

SCORERS	POST MEN
FAST MEN	BET SHOOTERS
GOOD DRIB.	GOOD REBOUNDER
CUTTERS	WEAK DEFENSE

————————— #

————————— #

————————— #

————————— #

————————— #

————————— #

————————— #

————————— #

1st HALF TAPS

○   ○

2nd HALF TAPS

○   ○

OFFENSIVE TAPS
(near own basket)

○   ○

DEFENSIVE TAPS
(near opponent's basket)

○   ○

————————— #

————————— #

————————— #

————————— #

* * * * *

TEAM CHARACTERISTICS INDIVIDUAL CHARACTERISTICS

General	Yes	No	General	#	#	#	#	#	#	#	#	#	#
Big?			Height										
Fast?			Weight										
Aggressive?			Good Condition?										
Good Condition?			Good Team Man?										
Competitive spirit?			Fast?										
Fight for rebounds?			Good rebounder?										
Reserves good?			Good competitive spirit?										
Offensive			**Offensive**										
Type?			Aggressive?										
The "post"?			Good?										
Plays where?			Good dribbler?										
How are passes made?			Dribbles through fast & hard?										
Shoot a lot?			Good ball handler?										
Good ball handling?			Good passer?										
Deliberate?			Pass to cutting teammates?										
Use a fast break?			"Up and unders"?										
"Cut" a lot?			"Give and goes"?										
"Give and go"?			Cut through hard and fast?										
"Up and under"?			Sleeper?										
Set up plays?			Deceptive?										
Use a sleeper?			Change direction on cuts?										
Shoot a lot?			Bump opponents into mates?										
Lot of set shots?			Screen for teammates?										
Many one-handed shots?			Good scorer?										
Tap-in rebounds?			Good set shooter?										
Dribbler through a lot?			Left-handed shots?										
			Right-handed shots?										
			Shoot a lot?										
			Good foul shooter?										
			Tap-in rebounds?										

TEAM CHARACTERISTICS   INDIVIDUAL CHARACTERISTICS (CONTINUED)

General	Yes	No	General	#	#	#	#	#	#	#	#	#	#
Defensive			**Defensive**										
Type?			Aggressive?										
Withdraw?			Good?										
Back fast?			Gets back fast?										
Zone?			Easily feinted out?										
All-court press?			Turn his head?										
Set Shooters-much room?			Watch the ball shots?										
How is "post" played?			Switch well?										
Do the men switch?			Fight for rebounds?										
Dribblers boxed out?			Ball hawk?										
Ball hawks?													
Slide well?													
Screens work?													
Turn their heads?													
Follow flight of shots?													
Aggressive?													
Rebound well?													

football (two examples)...

NOTES:

D_____, D_____.

POS.

PLAY

GAIN

D_____, D_____.

POS.

PLAY

GAIN

D_____, D_____.

POS.

PLAY

GAIN

* * * * *

ATTACH A GAME PROGRAM HERE.

This will permit you to check on names, numbers, heights, weights, ages and class status of all offensive and defensive starting personnel.

Defensive Unit

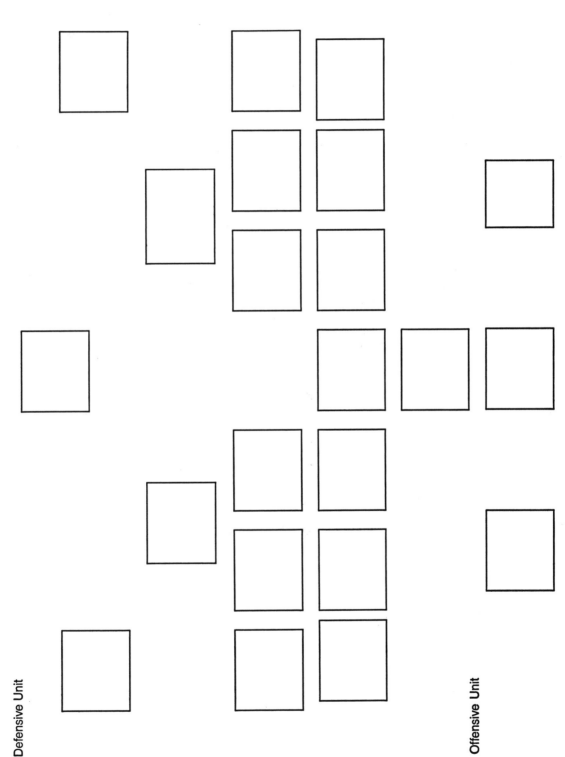

Offensive Unit

SCRIMMAGE

See Also: FOOTBALL; PRACTICE; SAFETY

schedule of...

MARCH

S	M	T	W	T	F	S
		P^1	P^2	P^3	P^4	P^5
P^6	P^7	P^8	P^9	P^{10}	P^{11}	P^{12}
O^{13}	P^{14}	S^{15}	P^{16}	S^{17}	P^{18}	S^{19}
O^{21}	P^{21}	P^{22}	S^{23}	P^{24}	S^{25}	S^{26}
P^{27}	P^{28}	S^{29}	P^{30}	P^{31}		

S—scrimmage
G—game
P—practice
O—off

SEASON

See Also: ATHLETIC DIRECTOR; END-OF-SEASON CHECKLIST; EVALUATION; SPECIFIC SPORT

length of...

Length of Season, Number of Practices and Contests

Sport	Length of Season	Number of Practices	Number of Contests
Football	7.5 weeks	27	6
Basketball	9 weeks	30	9
Gymnastics	6.5 weeks	26	4
Swimming	6.0 weeks	22	5
Track	7.5 weeks	28	6
Volleyball	7 weeks	26	9
Wrestling	7.5 weeks	30	5-6

record form...

See: SPECIFIC SPORT

report...

NEW MEXICO ACTIVITIES ASSOCIATION
SEASON REPORT—JUNIOR HIGH

Season Report _____Jr. High School for the 19 _____

sports seasons made to the Executive Secretary _____ 19_____
                                                                        (date)

NAME OF CONTESTANT (List Names Alphabetically)	DATE OF BIRTH	ENROLLMENT Month and year First Enrolled in 7th Grade.

I hereby certify that:

1. Each student passed a minimum of fifteen (15) hours of subject matter last semester and is passing a minimum of fifteen (15) hours of subject matter this semester;
2. No student has been enrolled more than six (6) semesters in grades 7-9;
3. No student has participated more than three (3) seasons in a given sport in grades 7-9.

COMMENTS:

_____

(Superintendent or Principal)

NOTE: This report due May 15 and will suffice for all sports.

SOCCER

See Also: AWARDS; INTRAMURAL PROGRAM; UNIFORMS

schedule...

	SUN	MON	TUES	WED	THURS	FRI	SAT	
M I D D L E T O W N S O U T H S O C C E R	19	20	21	22	23	24	25	**A U G**
	26	27	28	29	30	31	1	**S E P T E M B E R**
	2	3	4	5	6	7	8	
	9	10	11	12	13	14	15	
	16	17	18	19	20	21	22	
	23	24	25	26	27	28	29	

season record form...

TEAM: _____ SEASON: _____

COACH(ES): _____

TOTAL WON: _____ TOTAL LOST: _____ DISTRICT STANDING: _____

CONFERENCE STANDING: _____

DATE	AGAINST...	OUR SCORE	THEIR SCORE

AWARDS AND SPECIAL MENTIONS: _____

_____

_____

_____

_____

team rules...

MIDDLETOWN SOUTH SOCCER
TEAM RULES

It is an honor and privilege to represent Middletown High School South in Soccer. All players are required to follow the team rules outlined below. Knowledge of the rules is mandatory, as ignorance is no excuse. Failure to follow them will result in suspension from the team. A serious infraction will result in permanent removal.

SQUAD SELECTION:

A. Cuts are at the discretion of the coaching staff. These factors are considered in your selection: speed, physical condition, knowledge of the game, technical skill, aggressiveness, determination, ability to fit into the team, coachability and dedication.

B. You will be removed from the squad for disciplinary reasons.

C. If you quit the team, it is your responsibility to notify the coaching staff immediately.

PRACTICE:

A. Practice is essential for success. You will always do your best and attend every practice.

B. You will be on time for practice.

C. Vacations, employment, etc. should end by the first practice. Plan on playing until after Thanksgiving.

D. The only excuse for missing practice or games is absence from school. Your parent or guardian must notify the coaching staff ahead of time by phone for any other circumstances.

E. If you are absent from school you cannot practice or play in a game on that date.

F. Practice is held rain or shine unless otherwise noted by the coaching staff.

INJURIES:

A. All injuries of any nature must be reported to the coach at the time they occur.

B. After the coaching staff has been notified, you must report the injury to the nurse's office at the beginning of the next school day.

C. If you see a physician for treatment of an injury, you will not be permitted to return to the team to practice or play until you present the coach with a note signed by the doctor stating that you are physically able to play soccer.

PERSONAL CONDUCT:

A. Your schoolwork takes first priority. Always do your best to get good grades.

B. Stay out of trouble as it may interfere with your future on the team.

C. If you are assigned to ASP, you must come to practice and you will not play in the subsequent games, thereby hurting the team. The coaching staff will review the reasons for your transgressions and may decide on removal.

D. You are responsible for all equipment issued to you. The full replacement cost will be charged for any equipment lost, damaged, or stolen.

E. A clear, sharp mind is needed to play soccer effectively. Smoking, drinking, or the abuse of drugs will result in serious consequences or removal.

F. Coaches, players, referees and spectators must be treated with respect at all times.

G. Shin guards should be worn for all practices and games.

H. All players are subject to N.J.S.I.A.A. rules and regulations.

If you have any questions concerning these rules consult your coach.

I have read the attached rules and regulations and agree to comply with them during the current season.

I understand the consequences of failure to comply with these rules and regulations.

_____   _____
     Student's Signature   Date

_____   _____
     Parent's Signature   Date

SOFTBALL

> ***See Also:*** BASEBALL; SCOUTING

> ***season record form...***

> > ***See:*** SEASON RECORD FORM UNDER **SOCCER**

> ***team rules...***

> > ***See:*** TEAM RULES UNDER **SOCCER**

STUDENT MANAGERS

> ***information for (two examples)...***

INFORMATION FOR PROSPECTIVE STUDENT MANAGERS

There are in any school year, various team manager positions to be filled. Both head and assistant manager spots are available in the competitive team sports. Students who avail themselves of such an opportunity will find may special advantages such as making the acquaintance of new friends, making out-of-town trips with the team, working with faculty personnel in rewarding situations, having the satisfaction of contributing to the welfare of the team and being actively involved in the sports program.

QUALIFICATIONS for Head Managers:

1. Has the ability to take over responsibilities and to work with coaches.
2. Is able to work with participants and have their respect.
3. Can work with and supervise assistant managers without problems.
4. Is honest, reliable, trustworthy and dedicated.
5. Shows maturity in judgment and decision-making.
6. Is loyal to coaches and participants and motivates morale and team spirit.
7. Is willing to put in long hours without thought of thanks or recognition.

MAJOR RESPONSIBILITIES for All Managers:

Responsibilities will vary within school districts, will change with season, sport and individual coach, and depend to some degree on facilities available; but, in the end, there are certain procedures common to all.

* * * * *

KNOW WHAT THE COACH EXPECTS

<u>Prior to the Start of the Season:</u>

1. Meet with the coach to receive instructions on general and specific duties. Obtain a written list of duties to be performed and procedures to be followed.
2. Get acquainted with the location of all equipment and facilities. Understand responsibilities for storage, maintenance and security.
3. Understand precise procedures for check-out system and record keeping.
4. Ascertain responsibilities and duties involved with each home contest and with each out-of-town trip.

<u>During the Season:</u>

1. Schedule individual coach-manager discussion meetings prior to each contest. Find time available that is mutually convenient; free period, lunch time, or before school are possibilities.

<u>After the Season Closes:</u>

1. Check in all equipment and gear and carefully process it for use next season. Make out inventories. Send to repair and cleaning. Make final storage.
2. Assist with record-keeping finale and filling out season reports.

SWIMMING

See Also: MEET

schedule ...

Relay Meet Events and Order

1. 7th grade 100 Medley Relay
2. 8th grade 100 Medley Relay
3. 9th grade 100 Medley Relay
4. 7th grade 100 Breast-Fly-Breast-Fly Relay
5. 8th grade 100 Breast-Fly-Breast-Fly Relay
6. 9th grade 100 Breast-Fly-Breast-Fly Relay
7. 7th grade 200 Free (25-25-50-100)
8. 8th grade 200 Free (25-25-50-100)
9. 9th grade 200 Free (25-25-50-100)
10. 7th grade 200 Backstroke Relay
11. 8th grade 200 Backstroke Relay
12. 9th grade 200 Backstroke Relay
13. 7th grade 200 Free Relay
14. 8th grade 200 Free Relay
15. 9th grade 200 Free Relay

Team scores will not be kept. Entry cards should be given to each relay team before reporting to the ready area. Ribbons will be awarded to the first six places at each meet. Each swimmer will be allowed to participate in as many as 3 relays. Each school can enter up to two teams in each event.

season record form ...

See: SEASON RECORD FORM UNDER **SOCCER**

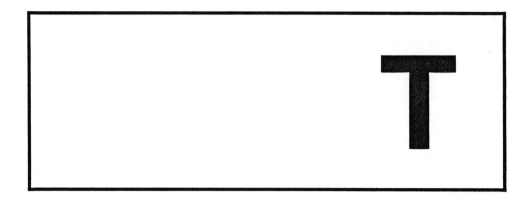

TELEPHONE

See Also: EXPENSES

telephone call record slip...

One of these slips must be filled in for every long distance call made.

Date _____ 19 _____

Person called: _____

City called: _____

No. _____

Amount of toll

Purpose of call: _____

_____

_____   _____
Principal's approval   Signature of person making call

THEFT

See Also: KEYS

memo on...

To: All Coaches Who Use the MHS Gym
From: J. R. Johnson, Assistant Principal, Athletics
Date: February 10, 1982
Subject: The Never-Ending Saga of Theft in the Boys' Locker Room.

Coaches, we must remind you of the responsibility you have as a key holder to the locker rooms, concession stand, etc.

The policy is, and has to continue to be, without fail, that keys are not to be given to students for opening and/or closing the above named places. You, as coach, are to take that responsibility, and by so doing stop the theft that is going on there. Coaches, this is necessary, important, and must be done. We further admonish you to check these areas before and after each use. A coach must be in the dressing room whenever it is being used by students.

TICKETS

See Also: CASH FUND; EXPENSES; HOME GAME ACTIVITY; VISITING SCHOOLS

inventory sheet...

TICKET SELLER	COLOR	START#	#ENDED	#SOLD	PRICE	AMT.	TOTAL

report sheet ...

Parkersburg High School
REPORT OF TICKET SALES

TEAMS: _____

_____ CONTEST HELD AT _____ DATE _____, 19XX

TICKET COLOR	STARTING NO.	ENDING NO.	NO. SOLD	PRICE	AMOUNT
				TOTAL SALES	
TICKET SELLER _____				STARTING CASH	

TOURNAMENT

See Also: MEET; SPECIFIC SPORT

announcement of ...

Dear Coaches:

Once again it is time for the annual Warner Grade School Basketball Tournament sponsored by the Warner Athletic Booster Club scheduled for March 7th.–12th.

Grades for this tournament include 5th.–8th. A player can move up one grade but not down a grade. Games will start at 10:00 a.m. with the final game starting at 8:00 p.m.

If you are interested in participating in this tournament, please complete the entry form below and return as soon as possible.

Thanks,

basketball (sample)...

GIRLS' NINTH GRADE BASKETBALL TOURNAMENT

1. The top eight ninth-grade teams will be seeded by their win/loss percentage through the regular season. In the event of a tie for a seeded position, the higher place will go to the winner of the game between the two during the season. If these teams did not play each other, the top seed will be decided by the flip of a coin.
2. The highest teams will be the host for games in all rounds.

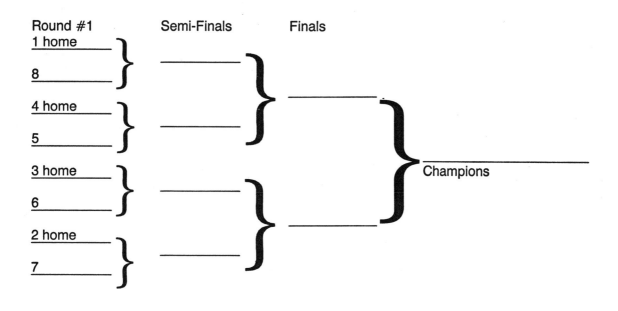

3. Responsibilities for personnel include the following:

    a) Central office will arrange for officials with the Nebraska-Iowa Association at least half way through the season.

    b) Both schools involved in each game must provide ample supervising for the crowd attending.

    c) Host team will collect admissions and pay officials ($16.00 per game). Admission prices will be the same as the regular season—$1.00 for adults, .50 for students, Metro passes honored.

    d) For the championship game the designated visiting team will provide the official scorer and score book. The designated home team will provide the official timer.

double elimination, round robin, or single elimination ...*

			TOURNAMENT SCHEDULE CALCULATOR		
Teams Entered	Byes		Single Elim. No. Games	Double Elim. No. Games	Round Robin No. Games
	Top	Bottom			
4	0	0	3	6 or 7	6
5	1	2	4	8 or 9	10
6	1	1	5	10 or 11	15
7	0	1	6	12 or 13	21
8	0	0	7	14 or 15	28
9	3	4	8	16 or 17	36
10	3	3	9	18 or 19	45
11	2	3	10	20 or 21	55
12	2	2	11	22 or 23	66
13	1	2	12	24 or 25	78
14	1	1	13	26 or 27	91
15	0	1	14	28 or 29	105
16	0	0	15	30 or 31	
17	7	8	16	32 or 33	
18	7	7	17	34 or 35	
19	6	7	18	36 or 37	
20	6	6	19	38 or 39	
21	5	6	20	40 or 41	
22	5	5	21	42 or 43	
23	4	5	22	44 or 45	
24	4	4	23	46 or 47	
25	3	4	24	48 or 49	
26	3	3	25	50 or 51	
27	2	3	26	52 or 53	
28	2	2	27	54 or 55	
29	1	2	28	56 or 57	
30	1	1	29	58 or 59	
31	0	1	30	60 or 61	
32	0	0	31	62 or 63	

*Courtesy of Wilson Sporting Goods Company

entry form for (sample)...

9TH GRADE ENTRY BLANK

200-Yard Dash	time:	**880-Yard Relay**	time: _____
1. _____ _____		1. _____	
2. _____ _____		2. _____	
		3. _____	
220-Yard Dash		4. _____	
1. _____ _____			
2. _____ _____		**Medley Relay**	time: _____
		1. _____	
440-Yard Dash		2. _____	
1. _____ _____		3. _____	
2. _____ _____		4. _____	

880-Yard Dash
1. _____ _____
2. _____ _____

Mile Relay   time: _____
1. _____
2. _____
3. _____

Mile Run
1. _____ _____
2. _____ _____
4. _____

Shot Put   **Long Jump**
1. _____   1. _____
2. _____   2. _____

70-Yard High Hurdles
1. _____ _____
2. _____ _____

Discus   **Pole Vault**
1. _____   1. _____
2. _____   2. _____

120-Yard Low Hurdles
1. _____ _____
2. _____ _____

High Jump
1. _____   COACH _____
2. _____   SCHOOL _____

440-Yard Relay
1. _____ _____
2. _____ _____
3. _____ _____
4. _____ _____

Information on...

9th ANNUAL PANTHER RELAYS
FRIDAY—APRIL 7, 19XX
STIGLER, OKLAHOMA

Dear Coach:

On behalf of the Stigler School System, we wish to extend to you and your teams a sincere invitation to participate in our 9th Annual Panther Relays. The following will give you vital information concerning this meet.

DIVISIONS: This meet will consist of two divisions, one high school division and one junior high division. Only 2A and A schools will be invited.

TIME: All teams should report to Stigler Football field by 1:30. There will be a short coaches meeting at this time to go over last minute changes. Field events will start at 1:45. The Two Mile Run will be the first event beginning at 1:50. Preliminaries in running events will follow the Two Mile Run. Finals will start at 6:30.

AWARDS: Trophies will be awarded to 1st and 2nd place teams in both junior and senior high divisions. Medals will be given to 1st and 2nd and 3rd place in the high school division. Ribbons will be given to 1st, 2nd, 3rd, 4th and 5th places in the junior high division. A plaque will be given to the coach of the winning team.

SUBSTITUTIONS: May be made at the time of registration. Absolutely no changes at start of race. Boys must report on time or be scratched.

LIMITATIONS: Each boy is limited to four events, including relays. Each school is limited to two boys in each event in the high school division. Each school is limited to three boys in each event in the junior high division. Each school is limited to one team in each relay.

TEAM POINTS: Awarded to 1st, 2nd, 3rd, 4th and 5th places (6-4-3-2-1) in individual events and relays double (12-8-6-4-2).

ENTRY FEE: $20.00 for high school and $10.00 for junior high. Make checks payable to Stigler High School Track.

ENTRY DEADLINE: Return the enclosed post card immediately indicating whether or not you plan to attend. If the post card is not returned by March 19 we will assume you are not coming and more invitations will be sent out. NO LATE ENTRIES WILL BE ACCEPTED AFTER MONDAY, MARCH 27, 19XX. On the enclosed post card please indicate the school phone and your home phone.

EQUIPMENT: Each school will have to furnish their own equipment.

ELIGIBILITY: Oklahoma High School Eligibility Certificate is required and should be sent with entry.

This meet is sanctioned by the Oklahoma Secondary School Activities Association and all National Federation rules will be followed. We hope that you and your team can be with us for this track meet. Please return the enclosed post card immediately and return the entry and check by Monday, March 27, 19XX. Concession stand will be open for the meet. Donuts and coffee are available for coaches in coach's office.

Don Satterfield,
Track Coach

TRACK AND FIELD

announcer's form...

See: ANNOUNCERS' FORMS

equipment checklist...

TRACK MEET EQUIPMENT—CHECKLIST

ADMINISTRATION

_____ Awards
_____ Bottle Pool Balls
_____ Bull Horn
_____ Clip Boards (6 or 8)
_____ Meet Summaries
_____ Numbers and Pins
_____ Officials Badges
_____ Order of Events
_____ P.A. System
_____ Pencils
_____ Rule Book

TRACK EVENTS

_____ Cord–Hurdles
_____ Bell–Distance Runs
_____ Chalk–Relay Runners
_____ Finish Cards
_____ Finish Cord
_____ Inspector's Flag (4 to 6)
_____ Lap Counter
_____ Rubber Mallet
_____ Relay Cards
_____ Starting Blocks
_____ Watches–Minimum 4
_____ Whistle

FIELD EVENTS

_____ Broom–Long Jump
_____ Cross Bars–High Jump
_____ Cross–Pole Vault
_____ Cross Bar Replacer
_____ Distance Markers
_____ Field Event Cards
_____ Flags–Out-of-bounds (6)
_____ Height Indicators–H.J. & P.V.
_____ Long Jump Pit Leveler
_____ Markers–Discus and Javelin
_____ Pole Vault Measuring Device
_____ Scales–Weigh Implements
_____ Tape Measures

STARTER

_____ Blanks–22 cal.
_____ Blanks–32 cal.
_____ Gun–22 cal.
_____ Gun–32 cal.
_____ Sleeve–Colored
_____ Whistle

event card (sample)...

EVENT _____

POLE VAULT & HIGH JUMP

MEET _____

DATE _____

CONTESTANT	SCHOOL	NO.	HEIGHT	HEIGHT	HEIGHT	HEIGHT	HEIGHT	HEIGHT	HEIGHT	HEIGHT	HEIGHT	HEIGHT	HEIGHT	HEIGHT	HEIGHT	HEIGHT	HEIGHT

WINNERS

1ST _____ HEIGHT _____

2ND _____ HEIGHT _____

3RD _____ HEIGHT _____

4TH _____ HEIGHT _____

5TH _____ HEIGHT _____

_____ FIELD JUDGES

_____ OFFICIAL SCORER

TRANSPORTATION, TRAVEL, AND TRIPS

advance itinerary guidelines...

<u>ATHLETIC AND ACTIVITY TRAVEL ITINERARY</u>

All athletic and activity groups that travel out of district for competition must complete a Student Activity Authorization Form (CCF–460) to include the following information:

1. School requesting trip
2. Name of organization taking trip
3. Purpose of trip
4. Destination
5. Place of lodging
6. Phone number at place of lodging
7. Method of transportation and name of carrier
8. Departure place
9. Departure time and arrival time
10. Departure place and return trip
11. Departure time and estimated time of return
12. Number of students (boys and girls)
13. Name of certified employee in charge
14. Names of other school employees assigned as chaperons
15. Signature of certified employee in charge
16. Signature of principal

A signed statement from the hotel manager or hotel owner certifying rooms were in good condition and no damages were incurred during the group's stay should be submitted to the principal upon return from the scheduled trip.

expense claim...

CLARK COUNTY SCHOOL DISTRICT
ATHLETIC TRIP EXPENSE

SCHOOL _____ SPORT _____
OPPONENT _____ DATE OF GAME _____
The following number of people went on the trip:
    Coaches _____ Managers _____
    Players _____ Others (specify) _____
Meals (all receipts must be attached)—Total .... $ _____
Lodging (all receipts must be attached)—Total .... $ _____

Other Expenses (all receipts must be attached with an explanation below)

DATE	WHERE AND WHAT MONEY WAS SPENT FOR	AMOUNT

Other Expenses—Total .... $ _____
Total Meals, Lodging, and Other Expenses .... $ _____

I certify that the above information is correct.

_____ _____
ADMINISTRATIVE ATHLETIC DIRECTORY   DATE

financial report on...

PARKERSBURG HIGH SCHOOL
TRIP FINANCIAL REPORT

CHECK # _____   DATE _____
TRIP TO _____
SPORT _____
CASH ADVANCE $ _____
NUMBER OF CARS _____
    TOTAL MILEAGE ALLOWANCE $ _____
  *MEALS $ _____
 * *PARKING $ _____
 * *HOTEL $ _____

Miscellaneous _____

_____

_____

_____

TOTAL EXPENSES $ _____

REFUND $ _____

Signature _____

*Mileage allowance per—20¢ (mileage based on State Rd. Comm. chart).

*Attach receipts to this report.

out-of-district, checklist for ...

ANCHORAGE SCHOOL DISTRICT
OUT-OF-DISTRICT STUDENT TRAVEL

STUDENT TRAVEL

Any out-of-district travel by students under the auspices of the School District, with the exception of travel to contiguous Boroughs or ASAA State Tournaments and Meets, must receive approval of the Principal and the Student Travel Committee as outlined in Section 460 of the School Board Policy Manual.

The "Request For Out-Of-District Travel" form must be completed and include recommendations plus have the approval of the Student Travel Committee prior to any fund raising activity.

CRITERIA FOR OUT-OF-DISTRICT STUDENT TRAVEL

All decisions relative to approval of out-of-district student travel shall be determined using the following criteria:

A. The educational value of the trip.

B. The ability to provide similar activities within the district (including the possibility of bringing in resources from elsewhere to provide the activity locally).

C. The number of students to be involved in the trip.

D. The cost of the trip.

E. Priority of the activity in relationship to other district activities (including competing requests for student travel).

F. The proposed method of raising funds and the perceived impact of fund raising activities upon the students, the school, and the community.

G. The amount of time away from school and the effect of such student absences on other obligations or responsibilities of those students.

H. The amount of school support involved (i.e., teacher release time, use of school equipment, etc.) and the impact of that support on other on-going programs.

I. The degree to which the proposed travel can be supervised and adequate security be provided.

J. The extent to which a proposal anticipates possible contingencies (potential liability, emergency or disciplinary situations, etc.)

permit for (two examples)...

CHAPARRAL HIGH SCHOOL
Field Trip Permit

PART I

Inasmuch as the Administration and teaching staff at Chaparral High School will be assuming the supervisory responsibilities of your son/daughter on a trip away from school, we feel it is important that the student and the parents fully understand the rules which govern such trips. It is our feeling that a trip is a continuation of the school day and, as such, students participating on these trips are subject to the rules and regulations which govern our school while they are on campus. Because the students will be representing Chaparral High School, and because their conduct, behavior, and safety is our responsibility, we have established the following guidelines which must be adhered to while they are away from home.

1. The luggage and personal effects of the students will be inspected prior to departing and at anytime during the trip.
2. Any student found to be in possession of, or under the influence of alcohol or controlled substances will be left home if this determination is made prior to departure. Students found in the possession of controlled substances or alcohol or under their influence after departure are subject to immediate arrest and being sent home at their parents' expense.
3. Students must observe all civil laws and regulations. Apprehension by law enforcement agencies leading to a substantiated charge will not be the responsibility of Chaparral High School.
4. If the trip requires overnight lodging, students will not disturb other guests at the lodging and will abide by all rules and directives issued by the group advisor and chaperones.
5. In the event you are injured or become ill while on the trip, the chaperone will immediately seek medical attention and contact your parents as soon as possible.
6. Students will be expected to know and observe the time and location of all departures. The group will not be delayed by the tardiness of individuals.
7. The establishment and enforcement of any guidelines not covered in items one to six, guidelines that are necessary to insure the success of the trip, will be left to the discretion of the Administrator or his representative in charge.

Any student caught in an infraction of the above listed rules may be sent home at the parents' expense and will be subject to further disciplinary action by the school.

Participation in a field trip is an extracurricular activity. It is a privilege that will be denied hereafter for a period of time to be specified by the group advisor and administration if, in their opinion, the group has misrepresented Chaparral High School through inappropriate behavior.

PART II—CONSENT TO OPERATION, ANESTHETICS AND OTHER MEDICAL SERVICES

This is to certify that I, the parent of _____
age _____, birthdate _____, consent to the performance of any emergency surgical operations and other medical procedures which may be considered necessary

by the medical doctors as a result of injury or other emergency during the school year of
_____ to _____. In the event of an emergency involving my
child during this period, I may be reached at:

NAME IN FULL _____

ADDRESS _____

PHONE NUMBER _____ EMERGENCY PHONE NUMBER _____

_____   _____   _____
Student's Signature   Parent's Signature   Date

* * * * *

CLARK COUNTY SCHOOL DISTRICT
FIELD TRIP PERMIT

Last Name of Pupil _____ First Name _____

   I understand that during the school year my child may take part in field trips and
educational excursions, either in a bus, by private car, or on foot. I further understand that my
child will be chaperoned by a responsible adult at all times while away from school and that the
adult will take all necessary precautions to protect my child from harm and injury.

   In the event my child is injured or becomes ill while away from school on any of the
aforementioned trips. I understand that the chaperon will immediately seek medical attention
for my child and contact me as soon as possible. I further hereby agree to hold the Clark County
School District, its employees, and agents harmless of any injury or sickness directly caused by
the negligence of persons other than employees or agents of the Clark County School District
when such injury or sickness occurs during any of the aforementioned trips.

   I understand that I may revoke this permit at any time and either refuse to allow my child
to take a field trip or to request that my child take certain field trips which I feel would be to his
advantage. If I desire to take either of these actions, I will notify the principal of the school in
writing stating these requests.

_____   _____
DATE   SIGNATURE OF PARENT OR GUARDIAN

I do not wish my child to take part in the aforementioned field trips.

_____   _____
DATE   SIGNATURE OF PARENT OR GUARIAN

requests for (two examples)...

CARLSBAD MUNICIPAL SCHOOLS
TRANSPORTATION REQUISITION

(ALL TRIPS, INCLUDING LOCAL, REQUIRE A REQUISITION)

Note: Place on separate requisitions;
Activity and Operational accounts also Individual Contractors.

NAME OF GROUP TRAVELING _____

A. TO BE COMPLETED BY THE SPONSOR

Date Of Trip	Time Leaving	Place To Pick Up Students	Approx. Return Time	Destination	No. Of People Traveling	Type Of Bus Needed	No. Of Buses Needed	¢ Per Mile Rate

Approved By: _____

SIGNATURE OF SPONSOR   DATE

B. TO BE COMPLETED BY THE PRINCIPAL

Pro-jected Cost	Actual Cost	Account Charged	Contractor Used	Comment

SIGNATURE OF PRINCIPAL   DATE

TRANSPORTATION REQUEST
19 _____ –19 _____

DATE _____

THIS SECTION TO BE COMPLETED BY SPONSORING GROUP

School _____ Date of Trip _____

Instructor name _____ Home Phone _____

Name of group or club _____

Destination _____ Number of Students _____

Number of Buses _____ OR—MINI BUS _____

Departing from _____ Departure Time _____

Return time _____ Return Date _____

SPECIAL INSTRUCTIONS OR REQUEST _____

_____

Trip to be paid by: _____

Principal's Approval _____

Director's Approval _____

NOTE: ALL REQUESTS MUT BE RECEIVED THREE (3) DAYS PRIOR TO TRIP. CAN-
CELLATIONS MUST BE MADE NOT LATER THAN 24 HOURS PRIOR TO TRIP,
EXCEPT FOR EMERGENCIES, i.e., snow, rain, illnesses.

TO BE COMPLETED BY DRIVER

Starting Mileage _____ Ending Mileage _____ Total Miles _____

Bus No _____ Departure Time _____ Return Time _____ Total Time _____

Were there any accidents, or problems with equipment? _____

ATTACH ALL GASOLINE TICKETS, TOLL TICKETS, MEAL TICKETS.

Date report filed _____ Driver's Signature _____

DIRECTOR OF TRANSPORTATION   APPROVAL DATE
(PLEASE READ THE OTHER SIDE BEFORE COMPLETING)

PLEASE READ THESE INSTRUCTIONS BEFORE COMPLETING THE REQUEST
FORM

(Request form is on the reverse side of this page)

Two copies of this request are to be submitted to the transportation office three (3) days prior to need. Sponsoring school or group agrees to reimburse the Board of Education for out-of-town trips at $ .50 (fifty cents) per mile and $5.22 per hour for the driver. Overnight trips require that the driver be furnished meals and lodging comparable to those furnished students and sponsor of activity. Overnight trips require the driver to be paid for ten (10) hours per day (which will include the driving time). Driving time for all other trips shall be computed from the time the bus leaves the bus lot, until the return to the bus lot, PLUS an additional thirty (30) minutes for the driver to clean and park bus.

If a driver is out past the lunch hour, and the sponsor and students are provided lunches, then the sponsor is also responsible for the driver's lunch. Lunch meals should be comparable to those furnished students of the activity.

If driver is paid for extra class activity, there will be no charge for driver driving for that activity. All coaches and activity drivers, are not paid for driving the bus for that activity. Any group using a MINI BUS, agrees to reimburse the Board of Education at the rate of $ .30 (thirty cents) per mile. THE MAXIMUM LIMIT LOAD FOR THE MINI BUS IS 12 PEOPLE. DO NOT ASK IF WE WOULD ALLOW "JUST ONE MORE" PERSON ON THE BUS. These are state laws, and we must comply.

Bills for transportation are due at the end of the month in which the trip was made. Failure to pay transportation bill when due may affect future requests for transportation.

FOR OFFICE USE ONLY:

Trip Number _____

Approved _____ Reschedule _____ Other _____

Drivers: a. _____ Bus # _____

     b. _____ Bus # _____

_____ miles @ $ .50 p/m   Total Mileage Chg. _____

_____ hours @ $5.22 p/h   Total Driver Chg. _____

_____ Misc. Expense   Total Misc. Chgs. _____

_____ Misc. Expense   TOTAL CHARGES _____

Date Billed _____ Date Paid _____ Ck# _____ PO# _____

Dist. Pays   School Pays   Sponsor Pays

    1. MAKE ALL CHECKS PAYABLE TO THE "BOARD OF EDUCATION"

    2. REMIT ALL PAYMENTS TO THE "TRANSPORTATION OFFICE".

UNIFORMS

See Also: EQUIPMENT; ORDERING; SPECIFIC SPORT

care of*...

The care of garments can be covered in four phases: prior to their being used; during the season; the care of garments on a trip; and the care of garments after the season is over and between seasons.

New Garments

The care of new garments should begin as soon as they are received. To prevent mildew, garments should be stored in a cool, dry area, away from the humidity of swimming pool or shower room. Mold will attack garments containing wool, cotton or durene very quickly, but is not apt to affect the synthetic fabrics, such as those made of nylon.

Another important item on the pre-season check list is to familiarize your cleaner with the materials in your garments. Needless to say, it is important to work with a cleaner who has had experience in cleaning athletic garments and who is willing to take the time and effort necessary to do a good job for you.

Athletic garments are about as difficult to clean as any item of clothing. Most are subjected to more dirt, more perspiration, more wear and more strain in one game than is a suit of clothes or dress in a lifetime. Add to this the fact that most garments are made of two or more fabrics and/or knit materials, and the cleaner of athletic garments is confronted with a complex problem.

To help your cleaner do the best job possible it is well to furnish him a complete set of garments well in advance of your first game. Give him complete information on the materials used in inserts and trim. This pre-season conference will enable your cleaner to determine which cleaning methods to use and will give him the opportunity to test the various materials for color-fastness.

During the Season

The period immediately following a game is most important to the care of the garments used in the game.

Before turning the garments over to the cleaner, each garment should be inspected for possible tears, rips or pulled seams. Garments needing repair should be separated so the cleaner can make necessary repairs as quickly as possible. Lettering and numbering should be checked to see if any have pulled loose.

Follow the basic cleaning principles as they apply to your own athletic laundry or commercial cleaners.

On a Trip

Trips always present a problem because it is impossible to follow the prescribed rules for garments care. Pack the garments after the away-game, and then hang them up in your equipment room as soon as you arrive home.

If the team is going on to another game, the time schedule will dictate just when and where it will be possible to dry the garments. If the team spends the night in the town in which the game was played, it may be possible to make arrangements with the hotel to hang the garments somewhere overnight and then pack them in the morning for the next phase of the trip.

Repairs to garments are difficult to make while on a trip. But, regardless of difficulty, repairs should be made as quickly as possible, in order to minimize further damage to the garments. It is especially important that snags and tears in knit garments be repaired promptly to avoid further damage.

While the proper caring for garments is extremely difficult on a trip, it is very important to the life of the garments to give them as much care as possible.

Between Seasons

After the last game has been played, a very important phase of equipment care begins—the final cleaning, repair and storage of garments. Careful attention to this important task immediately after the close of the season will result in savings of both time and money when you prepare for the start of the following season.

Before washing, each garment should be inspected very thoroughly for snags, tears, loose lettering, frayed edges, stains, etc. Complete notes should be made so that each spot needing special work may be called to the attention of the cleaner or renovator.

The final cleaning of the garments should be a thorough and careful process. All repairs should be made with care and, should certain garments need to go through the cleaning process a second time, this should be done now. When the garments are returned to you they should be ready for the next season.

The garments should then be packed in heavy corrugated cartons after first treating the inside of the cartons with a moth repellent. After packing, the seams of the cartons should be sealed with a heavy sealing tape and the carton should then be stored in a cool, dry area where the humidity remains relatively constant.

While the storing away of the garments is taking place, notes should be made concerning replacement garments for next year. If new garments are to be ordered, or even if just a few fill-ins are needed, it is good practice to order them at this time while your needs are fresh in your mind.

<u>Some Basic Principles</u>

1. Buy Quality. Coaches who insist upon high quality athletic garments find it pays dividends. Rawlings' Quality garments look better, fit better, are more comfortable, last longer, and are more economical in the long run.

2. Provide Adequate Storage Space. Garments should be stored in a cool, dry area.

3. Avoid Mildew. Materials, especially cottons, can be seriously weakened by mildew which under certain conditions, can occur in as little as 12 hours. Moist, warm conditions promote mildew. Nylon materials offer excellent resistance to this type of deterioration.

4. Make Repairs Promptly. Snags and tears and small holes that sometimes develop in knit materials should be repaired promptly to prevent further damage.

Football garments will be soaked with perspiration, covered with dirt or mud, grass stains, lime, etc. Football garments should be washed or put to soak immediately. Jerseys should be washed separately from pants—never together. Basketball and baseball garments, of course, may not be as dirty as football garments, but will be wet with perspiration. The first thing to do with baseball and basketball garments is to hang the garments on individual rust-proof wire or wooden hangers with plenty of air space between each garment. Garments should be hung in a room where the humidity is low so that they will dry quickly.

Courtesy of Rawlings Sporting Goods Company

cleaning of ...*

1. Removal of dirt, stains and perspiration, color retention, and sustained legibility of numbers and other distinguishing marks are the ultimate goals of proper laundering and cleaning of athletic garments.

2. Use of specialized all-automatic athletic laundry in your school that gives insured protection against shrinkage, fading, bleeding, fabric and yarn snags, etc., has many advantages. Operated properly, such a machine can wash all types of athletic clothing and bring about a substantial saving of money in a brief period of time. The same machine can be used to wash towels and all types of gym and physical education uniforms. Because automatic temperature controls for water and heat are found in machines specifically designed for use in cleaning athletic garments, guess-work of this important phase of washing is eliminated.

3. Prior to the first cleaning of a set of garments emphasize to your cleaner the need for special care and handling of the garments. Furnish him with sample garments and complete information as to the materials and washing instructions for a test. Follow these approved directions if your school has its own athletic laundry.

4. Dry cleaning will generally remove dirt, stains, etc., from athletic garments but it will not remove perspiration. Garments that are dry cleaned, therefore, must also be wet-cleaned before they are ready for use. This combination of dry cleaning and wet cleaning will pay off in both appearance and durability. With certain exceptions, proper washing and drying is all that is required. Do not dry clean football pants containing spandex, or any athletic garment with heat-applied or screened plastisol lettering.

5. For maximum wear, garments should be cleaned immediately after each game.

6. After a game, garments should be inspected for snags, tears, stains, etc. Extremely soiled garments should be separated from those not so severely soiled. Badly soiled areas should be brushed and/or soaked before laundering, or run through an all-automatic athletic washer with a special "Soak Cycle." Washers should always be loaded lightly to allow for maximum circulation of water through garments to carry off soil in both washing and drain cycles.

7. GARMENTS OF DIFFERENT COLORS SHOULD NOT BE LAUNDERED TOGETHER. Remove colored laces from garments and wash them separately.

8. Use of strong chemicals and/or alkalis (sometimes used for quick removal of spots or stains) will fade colors and weaken materials. Use a neutral (synthetic) detergent.

9. DO NOT USE A CHLORINE BLEACH. Bleaching also fades colors and weakens materials. If bleaching becomes necessary, an oxygen bleach should be used.

10. The water level in your washing equipment should be kept high to hold down mechanical action. Rinse water temperature should not vary more than a few degrees from wash water temperature.

11. All knit materials have a tendency to shrink slightly. This shrinkage can be minimized with the exercise of proper care.

12. Stretching (back to original size) and steam pressing garments is recommended when a commercial steam press is used. The direct heat of a regular household steam iron can cause scorching, fabric abrasion, and shrinkage.

13. Garments should be completely dry before being stored.

DO NOT WASH KNIT FABRICS IN WATER
TEMPERATURES ABOVE 100° FAHRENHEIT.

Extreme hot water will fade color and cause excessive
shrinkage. A mild, no-bleach detergent should be used.

Courtesy of Rawlings Sporting Goods Company

material composition sheet* ...

MATERIAL	GENERAL CHARACTERISTICS	USES IN UNIFORMS
Stretch Nylon, Double Knit Heavyweight	A Double Knit Fabric with approximately 25% to 30% stretch in both directions. Fits well in most sports. Very good color characteristics with excellent fit.	Football pants, basketball pants, baseball uniforms and warm-up clothing.
Stretch Nylon, Double Knit Mediumweight	A Double Knit Fabric with approximately 50% stretch in both directions. Drapes well for an attractive and well-fitting garment. Available in most standard athletic colors.	Basketball shirts and pants, baseball shirts, women's clothing and coaches' clothing.
Stretch Nylon, Double Knit Lightweight	A lightweight Double Knit Fabric with approximately 50% stretch in both directions. A very excellent fabric for women's clothing and other garments where the feel of a lightweight garment is desired. Available in most standard athletic colors.	Women's clothing, softball shirts, basketball shirts and pants and streetwear jerseys.
Stretch Nylon Pro-Mesh	A mediumweight Knit Fabric. Good wearing qualities. Cotton-backed for absorbency. Cleans well. Available in most standard athletic colors.	Football jerseys, hockey sweaters, coaches, shirts, basketball shirts and pants, girdle shells.
Stretch Nylon and Cotton Dura-Knit	A well-balanced mediumweight Knit Fabric with excellent wearing qualities. Stretch Nylon on the front for wear and backed with Cotton for absorbency. Cleans well. Available in most standard athletic colors.	Football jerseys, baseball shirts and pants, softball shirts and pants.
Stretch Nylon and Cotton Heavyweight	A Knit Fabric featuring same characteristics as Dura-Knit except heavyweight.	Football pants, baseball shirts and pants, warm-up clothing.
Stretch Nylon Heavyweight	A Jersey Knit Fabric with good stretch characteristics. Drapes and wears well. Available in most standard athletic colors.	Football and basketball pants.
Stretch Nylon Mediumweight	A new mediumweight Stretch Knit Fabric with excellent fit and comfort, yet light enough to give the player that extra lift. Available in most standard athletic colors.	Football jerseys, basketball pants.
Stretch Nylon Lightweight	A Jersey Knit Fabric with excellent stretch and shape retention. Available in most standard athletic colors.	Main use in basketball shirts. Also offered in ladies' clothing and football girdle shells.
Stretch Nylon—Durene	A Jersey Knit plaited Fabric offering the wear of Nylon on the face and the absorbency of Durene Cotton on the back. Wears and fits well. Available in most standard athletic colors.	Football jerseys, basketball shirts and warm-up clothing.
Stretch Nylon— Spandex	A Knit Fabric with extreme stretch characteristics. Provides good fit and wear. Available in most standard athletic colors.	Football pants.
100% Nylon Pedro Cloth	A very durable Nylon Woven cloth suitable for hockey pants as it has a very high resistance to board burns.	Hockey pants.

*Courtesy of Rawlings Sporting Goods Company

measurement chart*...

HOW TO MEASURE

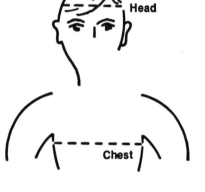

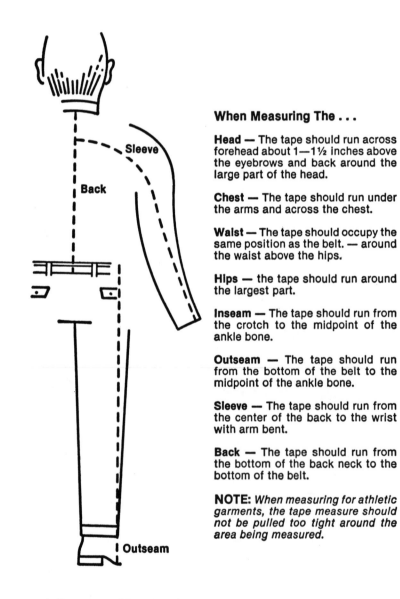

When Measuring The ...

Head — The tape should run across forehead about 1—1½ inches above the eyebrows and back around the large part of the head.

Chest — The tape should run under the arms and across the chest.

Waist — The tape should occupy the same position as the belt. — around the waist above the hips.

Hips — the tape should run around the largest part.

Inseam — The tape should run from the crotch to the midpoint of the ankle bone.

Outseam — The tape should run from the bottom of the belt to the midpoint of the ankle bone.

Sleeve — The tape should run from the center of the back to the wrist with arm bent.

Back — The tape should run from the bottom of the back neck to the bottom of the belt.

NOTE: *When measuring for athletic garments, the tape measure should not be pulled too tight around the area being measured.*

* Courtesy of Rawling Sporting Goods Company

ordering and fitting...*

FOOTBALL

How to Fit the Jersey

1. *Shoulders:* The jersey must be large enough at the shoulders to fit over the shoulder pads.

2. *Armholes:* The openings for the arms should be sufficiently large to allow the player complete freedom of movement.

3. *Chest and Waist:* The jersey should be tapered down from the large shoulders so that it fits the chest and waist snugly, but not so tightly that it will be uncomfortable or tear easily under the normal strains of the game.

4. *Length:* The jersey should be long enough to fit past the hips and into the football pants. Extra long jerseys should be ordered for players 6'1" or taller...Special consideration should be given in the case of extremely large or small players.

5. *Numbering:* The size of the numerals, when they are sewn-on or vinyl-type, is a major importance to the fit of a jersey in that the larger the numeral, the more "stretch" that is taken out of the jersey. This would not only affect the fit of the jersey but also its wear, as it would tear more easily. Where 10- and 12- inch combination numerals are used, therefore, the base jersey sizes ought to be increased. Both high school and college rules require 8-inch numbers on the front and 10-inch numbers on the back. Screened numerals are also available and do allow more expansion than the sewn-on or vinyl-type numerals.

Suggested Sizing Guide (High School)

Jersey		Small		Medium		Large		X-Large	
Size		34	36	38	40	42	44	46	48
Squad	33	0	0	2	7	10	9	5	0
Size	44	0	0	4	10	12	10	8	0

Stock Jerseys should be ordered by Small, Medium, Large and Extra Large; order special order jerseys by numerical sizes.

How to Fit Pants

1. *Waist:* Football pants are sized to fit a corresponding waist measurement. For example, most size 32 pants will fit a player with a waist from 31 to 32½ inches; most size 34 pants will fit a waist from 33 to 34½ inches. Be sure that measurements and sizes correspond.

2. *Thigh:* Proper placement of thigh guard pockets is very important for protection against injury. To accomplish this purpose, the bottom of the thigh guard pocket should be six to seven inches above the center of the knee.

3. *Knee:* Good fit at the knee is necessary so that the knee pad will stay in position. To this extent, the arc in back of the knee is the controlling factor. If the arc is too high, the front of the pant at the knee will not be held snugly against the leg. If the pant is cut straight across at the bottom, it will be held tightly over the knee but will wrinkle in back of the knee and become very uncomfortable after the leg is flexed a few times.

4. *Inseam:* Standard inseam should fit the players from 5'9" to 6'1" tall. Long pants should be ordered for athletes 6'2" to 6'4". Extra-longs should be ordered for players 6'5" or taller.

Shorter inseams should be specified for players less than 5′9″ tall. Long pants are approximately 2″ longer than standard length, while extra-long is approximately 3″ longer than standard length.

How to Fit—Use Actual Chest and Waist Measurements (High School)

Height	Weight Classification	Shirt & Chest Size	Tights Waist–Inseam
Up to 5′3″	98 lbs.	30	24″-26″
5′5″	105 lbs.	32	26″-27″
5′7″	112 lbs.	34	28″-28″
5′8″	119 lbs.	34	28″-28″
5′9″	126 lbs.	36	30″-29″
5′9″	132 lbs.	36	30″-29″
5′10″	138 lbs.	38	32″-30″
5′10″	145 lbs.	38	32″-30″
5′10″	155 lbs.	40	32″-30″
5′11″			
6′	167 lbs.	40	34″–31″
6′1″			
6′2″	185 lbs.	42	36″–31″
6′3″	Unlimited	44	36″–31″

SOCCER

How to Fit

1. *Shirts:* Soccer Shirts are made to actual size—38″ chest wears a size 38. Make allowances for the taller-than-average player, ordering extra-length shirts for players who are 6′2″ or taller. If a player's chest measures an odd number, order the next size shirt.

2. *Pants:* Soccer pants are made to actual size—34″ waist wears a size 34. Odd size waist take the next higher size. Allowance must be made for taller-than-average players; therefore, it is imperative that the player's height be specified when ordering soccer pants.

3. *Warm-Ups:* For the average size player, warm-up jackets and shirts should be ordered according to actual chest measurement. Extra-length warm-ups should be ordered for unusually tall players.

   Warm-up pants are made to actual waist measurement and should be ordered accordingly.

WOMEN IN SPORTS

How to Fit the Uniform—(Measurement Chart from Rawlings)

Size	X-Small (5-7)	Small (8-10)	Medium (12-14)	Large (16-18)	X-Large (20-22)
			SHIRTS		
Bust	28-30	30-32	34-36	38-40	42-44

	SHORTS				
Hips	30-32	32-34	36-38	40-42	44-46
Waist	21-23	24-26	28-30	32-34	36-38

	WARM-UP JACKET				
Bust	28-30	30-32	34-36	38-40	42-44

	WARM-UP PANTS				
Hips	30-32	32-34	36-38	40-42	44-46
Waist	21-22	24-26	28-30	32-34	36-38
Inseam	27"	28"	29"	30"	31"
If height is	5'2"	5'4"	5'6"	5'8"	6'

*Courtesy of Rawlings Sporting Goods Company

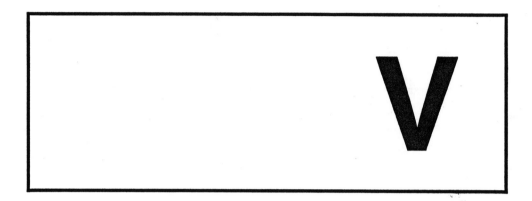

VISITING SCHOOLS

See Also: ANNOUNCERS' FORMS; BOOSTER/PEP CLUBS; CHEERLEADERS; FACILITY; HOME GAME ACTIVITY; OFFICIALS; TICKETS

information for ...

PARKERSBURG HIGH SCHOOL
(HOME FOOTBALL)

Visiting Administrator _____ Date _____

Game Time _____ Parkersburg vs. _____

Location: 2101 Dudley Avenue, Parkersburg, West Virginia

Ticket Information: Advance Student Sale: $1.50   Gate Student Sale: $2.00
Advance Adult Sale: $2.50   Gate Adult Sale: $3.00

Advance tickets will be sent at least 10 days prior to the game. If you do not want advance tickets, please notify us as soon as possible.

Jersey: Big Reds will wear _____.

Dressing Room: Visiting team will dress in Memorial Field House. The locker Room is located on the side next to the main building.

Parking: An area beside the Field House will be reserved for the team bus. All band buses and booster buses will be parked in the Annex Parking lot located at the north end of the Stadium.

Passes: You are to take 25 adult tickets to use as complimentary passes.

Press Box: Accommodations in the press box will be provided for your spotters. Phones will also be provided. Your photographer will be provided space inside the press box or on the roof.

Pre Game Schedule: 6:00 Gates open   7:40 pre game for band
                   7:40 Teams leave field   8:00 kick off

Half-Time: Twenty (20) minutes will be put on the field clock. The referee will start the clock when both teams have cleared the field. Each band is allowed 7½ minutes (including entering and leaving field).

Security: Please collect all valuables and remove them from the locker room. You may wish to secure them with a manager, etc.

OFFICIALS: _____

_____

welcome to ...

Dear Mr. Matthews:

I would like to take this opportunity to welcome the Hilldale High School football team, band, cheerleaders, pep club and fans to Wilburton, the home of the Diggers. We realize and consider Hilldale as being one of the better high school teams and are anxious to have a fine relationship with your high school. If we can be of service, please feel free to call us.

We have a visitor's parking lot and entry gate for your fans. Please notify your fans to turn north at the second stop light (Texaco Station) on Main Street, go to Blair Street and turn west to Centerpoint Road and then turn north and follow the signs. This lot and gate are located at the northeast end of the football field.

Our prices for admission are: Adults—$2.50, Students—$1.50, Cheerleaders—free, Band—free, Pep Club (in uniform—with sponsors),—$ .50, and Bus Drivers—free. Football buses will park in the northeast corner of the parking lot. Band and pep club buses will park in the southeast corner. An attendant will be there to help your drivers park. No cars or buses are permitted inside the stadium.

Your football team will dress on the east end of our new football facility. This facility will be locked; however, I suggest that no valuables be left in players' clothing. Coach Butler and the assistant coaches will be available to assist you in any way possible. Your players' bench will be on the north side and your players will warm up on the west end.

Would you please send me a copy of your line-up for the program? I need this as soon as possible so that I can get it printed.

Sincerely,

Charles E. Adams
Principal

VOUCHER

See Also: BUDGET; CASH FUND; EXPENSES; ORDERING; PURCHASE ORDER; TRANSPORTATION, TRAVEL, AND TRIPS

for an athletic event...

MIDDLETOWN ATHLETIC ASSOCIATION
VOUCHER FOR ATHLETIC EVENTS

Date _____   Please print full name and mailing address:

_____ vs _____   _____

Faculty Rep. or Coach _____   _____

Director of Ath. _____   _____

    I do solemnly declare and certify under the penalties of the law that the within bill is correct in all its particulars; that the articles have been furnished or services rendered as stated herein; that no bonus has been given or received by any person or persons within the knowledge of this claimant in connection with the above claim; that the amount stated is justly due and owing; and that the amount charged is a reasonable one.

Sign Here _____   Date _____

Cross Country	____	Varsity	____	Official	____
Football	____	Jr. Varsity	____	Entry Fee	____
Soccer	____	Freshman	____	Tickets	____
Field Hockey	____	Girls	____	Dues	____
Gymnastics	____	Boys	____	Timer	____
Basketball	____	7 + 8 Official	____	Clinic	____
Wrestling	____	North	____	Crowd Control	____
Baseball	____	South	____	Banquet	____
Tennis	____	Others	____	Police	____
Track	____			Custodian	____
Softball	____			Ticket Mgr.	____
Bowling	____			Others	____
Swimming	____				
Others	____			Fee _____	

WAIVER

See Also: ELIGIBILITY

transfer of eligibility waiver...

CLARK COUNTY SCHOOL DISTRICT
STUDENT ELIGIBILITY TRANSFER WAIVER

_____ _____ _____
Student's Name   Grade   Date of Application

Please give reason for residence change _____
_____

This part to be completed by parent/legal guardian:	DO NOT WRITE HERE —FOR CCSD VERIFICATION—
	Date Enrolled _____
Address of previous residence _____	
Telephone number of previous address _____	
Name of previous school attended _____	
Address of new residence _____	
Date moved into new residence _____	
Telephone number of new residence _____	
Name of school now attending _____	

I signify that by my signature the above information provided by me is correct. I have no knowledge of any recruitment of this student by any person and duly state that this transfer is for educational reasons only. I request immediate reinstatement of eligibility in interscholastic athletics.

STATEMENT OF PENALTY: Falsification of any part of this transfer waiver request may result in the permanent loss of eligibility to the student.

_____   _____
Signature of parent or legal guardian   Date

Please check appropriate box: ☐ Father   ☐ Mother   ☐ Stepfather   ☐ Stepmother
                                                  ☐ Court-appointed guardian
                                                          (If court-appointed guardian, attach a copy of court document.)

_____
Director of Student Activities, CCSD

☐ Approval   ☐ Disapproval

_____
Date

WRESTLING

See Also: AWARDS; MEET

match record form...

School _____ Coach _____
Please print or type first and last name.

9th Grade

	Name	Record	Fall	S.D.	M.D.	D.	F.	Draw
Sample:	John Davis	3-0-1	2	1				1
89								
98								
105								
112								
119								
126								
132								
138								
145								
155								
167								
180								
HWT								

Any changes in the above can be made on December 6, 19

KEY: Fall—Fall = 6 points
    Superior Decision—S.D. = 5 points
    Major Decision—M.D. = 4 points
    Decision—D = 3 points
    Forfeit, Default, Disqualification—F = 3 points
    Draw—Draw = 2 points